Colonize This!

young women of color on today's feminism

Edited by Daisy Hernández
and Bushra Rehman

Seal Press

COLONIZETHIS!:
Young Women of Color on Today's Feminism
© 2002 by Daisy Hernández and Bushra Rehman

Published by Seal Press
A member of the Perseus Books Group
1700 Fourth Street
Berkeley, CA 94710

Library of Congress Cataloging-in-Publication Data

Hernandez, Daisy and Rehman, Bushra.
  Colonize this! : young women of color on today's feminism / by Daisy
Hernanandez and Bushra Rehman.
    p. cm.
  Includes bibliographical references.
 ISBN-10: 1-58005-067-0
 ISBN-13: 978-1-58005-067-8
 1. Minority women—Social conditions 2. Feminism. I. Title.

HQ1161.C65 2002
305.42--dc21
                                                        20020305

      14 16 18 20 22 24 23 21 19 17 15

Designed by Susan Canavan
Printed in the United States of America by LSC Communications
Distributed by Publishers Group West

contents

Our Mothers, Refugees from a World on Fire

Going Through Customs

Talking Back, Taking Back

Acknowledgments

Thank you to our families, both chosen and of origin, who taught us how to be radical women; to the women in this book and those who sent submissions, you've made us think in new ways about this world, our lives and writing; to Cherríe Moraga, gracias, for your faith in this project and for making time to share your words; to our friends who gave so much positive energy and yelled Push! Push! as we were in the final stages of the book: Andrea Dobrich, Tazeen Khan, Keely Savoie, Stacey Holt, Stas Gibbs, Diedra Barber, Chitra Ganesh, Judy Yu, Rekha Malhotra, Mohan Krishna, Rebecca Hurdis; to Rebecca Walker and Gloria Anzaldúa for reading the manuscript and providing such inspiring words; to SAWCC (South Asian Women's Creative Collective) and all the women who've made it what it is; to the women of WILL (Women in Literature and Letters), Marta Lucia, Adelina Anthony, Angie Cruz, Keila Cordova, Kam Chang, Alba Hernández and Teachers & Writers Collaborative; to Anantha Sudhakar and the Asian American Writers' Workshop; to Barbara Rice, Katie Riley and Gracie; and to our literary mothers and sisters.

Gracias Leslie Miller for pursuing this idea with us and Angie Cruz for suggesting that we work together; Christina Henry de Tessan and the staff at Seal Press and Avalon Publishing Group.

Bushra Rehman for sharing this project with me, teaching me your hippie ways, and changing the world with your poetry! Gracias a mi mami, Alicia Sosa Hernández, por ser mi angelito de la guarda y ayudarme en todo; a mi papi, Ignacio Hernández, por su apoyo y sonrisas; y también quiero agradecerles a mis tías: María de Jesus Sosa, Rosa Sosa, y Dora Sosa Capunay; Liliana Hernández, my sister, for giving me the reasons to write; Geralen Silberg for sharing your love and laughter, Leslie Maryon-LaRose and Eugene LaRose for giving so much of yourselves; Diego Hernando Sosa, mi primo, for the conversaciones; my girlfriend, your love and support have been so important to this project; Kristina Kathryn Hermann, for sharing your sensitivity and passion. Thank you Marcia Gillespie for inviting me to *Ms.*, Ann Marie Dobosz, and the staff especially Cheryl Rogers; Gail Collins whose own project gave me the chance to learn so much about women's history; the mujeres at New York University's CLACS program; Jacob Gershoni and the Monday night group.

Residencies at Hedgebrook and MacDowell were critical for this book, as was a grant from the Barbara Deming Memorial Fund.

DAISY HERNÁNDEZ

Daisy Hernández for teaching me your light-hearted ways and sharing this project with me; my family who taught me how to care for others: Amma who always speaks her mind, Amey who is the strongest woman I know, Deddy who taught me generosity and kindness, my sisters who always inspire me and give meaning to my life: Aisha, Tahira, Sa'dia, Iffat, Aliya; my brothers: Atta, Saleem, Naser Bhai; my nieces and nephews: Kulsoom, Sarah, Zakariya, and those to come; Amber's family; the Ciacci Family: Marino, Paul, Julie; Kristina Kathryn Hermann for putting up with us and being such a gentle, peaceful, fun-loving spirit; Norcroft and the women of the lake: Cedar Marie, Patricia Fox, Mi Ok Song Bruining, Joan Drury, Kay Grindland and Willie; my Alaskan family: Hava, Saba, Dubba; the good-hearted artists and organizers of South Asian art and activism festivals, especially Desh Pardesh and Diasporadics; Mohan Krishna; Jon Savant who helped me write again; all my teachers at The College of New Rochelle; the kindness of all the strangers I've met, all the vagabonds and guardian angels on my path.

BUSHRA REHMAN

Foreword

"The War Path of Greater Empowerment"
Cherríe Moraga

Colonize This! is a collection of writings by young women of color that testifies to the movement—political and physical—of a new generation of global citizens, activists and artists. It is a portrait of the changing landscape of U.S. women of color identity, one that guarantees no loyalties to the borders that attempt to contain it. As immigrant, native-born, and survivor-of-slavery daughters, these women are the female children of those "refugees from a world on fire," described in the 1983 edition of *This Bridge Called My Back*[1]. They are women who have come of age with the living memory of disappearance in Colombia and Argentina and the daily reality of war "always a phone call away." They are young sisters (our daughters) who didn't "grow up to be statistics" (Taigi Smith), who have read and been schooled by the feminist writings and works of the women of color who preceded them, and as such are free to ask questions of feminism more deeply than we could have imagined twenty years ago.

The feminism portrayed in *Colonize This!* reflects what in the 1980s we understood as "theory in the flesh," a strategy for women's liberation, which is wrought from the living example of female labor and woman acts of loving. These narratives reflect consciousness born out of what their (our) mothers "knew first-hand: the interlocking system of racism, poverty and sexism" (Siobhan Brooks). In *Colonize This!* mothers serve as mirrors of choices made and unmade. They are the reflection of sacrifice, survival and sabiduría.

They are Cecilia Ballí's mother who each evening wiped off the dining room table after dinner to "double as a desk" for her two daughters; they are she who had no more than seven years of school buying encyclopedias from the grocery store on the installment plan.

They are Ena from British Guiana, who used her sexiness to "get things like kerosene to light lamps and food for her children" (Paula Austin).

They are Tanmeet Sethi's mother who advised, "you have to make home wherever you are. (And) this is what she did . . . coming to the U.S. with a stranger who was her new husband."

They are Siobhan Brooks' mother, once placed in a mental hospital for infanticide, who "in spite of her mental state paid the bills on time, shopped for food and refused the free bread and butter services offered . . . by the government."

They are models of resistance from whom their daughters, through fierce loyalty to them, wield weapons of theory and practice.

In *Colonize This!*, editors Bushra Rehman and Daisy Hernández have created an expanded vocabulary to describe an expanded feminism profoundly altered by massive immigration to the United States from North Africa, South and West Asia and Central and South

America. An echoing theme in this collection is the impact of the U.S. experience in introducing the critical questions of inequalities in relation to gender. Similarly echoed is the profound disappointment in white feminist theory to truly respond to the specific cultural and class-constructed conditions of women of color lives. As Ijeoma A. describes it, consciousness about sexism assumed language and impetus in the United States, but it was born in the "kitchens" of her native Nigeria. *Colonize This!* draws a complex map of feminism, one that fights sexism and colonialism at once and recognizes genocide as a present and daily threat to our blood-nations. The feminism articulated in this collection requires cultural tradition and invention, negotiating multiple worlds; it is a theory and freedom practice, which "allows women to retain their culture, to have pride in their traditions, and to still vocalize gender issues of their community" (Susan Darraj). As Tanmeet Sethi writes, "I am happy to wear the weight of my culture." She speaks of the gold jewelry inherited from family, but more so, she speaks of the profound preciousness of culture. "It is heavy, but not a burden."

As a new generation of women of color, these writers carry a new language to describe their passions, their política, their prayers and their problems. In these narratives, Black feminism finds resonance in hip hop. Racism is now called "driving while black," and "walking while brown" (Pandora Leong) in the middle class neighborhoods of Oregon. White male entitlement assumes a twenty-first century look in blond dread-locked Indophiles, studying Buddhism and "getting down with the people" (Bhavana Mody). Here, sexuality and pleasure are unabashedly integrated in a feminist of color analysis of survival and liberation, and "queer familia" is neither a question nor the subject of debate.

Still some things haven't changed. Stereotyping does not change, as Alaskan-born Asian-American Pandora Leong reminds us. "I do not read Chinese or know anything about acupuncture."

Women of color still suffer the same assaults against our bodies, the artillery of misogyny ever inventive. Patricia Justine Tumang testifies to the "living nightmare" of RU-486 abortion pill; and, Stella Luna recounts her own struggle for self-reclamation as a mother with HIV. She writes:

"I began to realize that I was being imprisoned not only by a disease, but also by a culture that trained me to believe my sexuality was only deemed worthy based on the condition of my physical being. If I chose to live my life according to this structure, then maybe I should just give up and die."

This is the real work of woman of color feminism: to resist acquiescence to fatality and guilt, to become warriors of conscience and action who resist death in all its myriad manifestations: poverty, cultural assimilation, child abuse, motherless mothering, gentrification, mental illness, welfare cuts, the prison system, racial profiling, immigrant and queer bashing, invasion and imperialism at home and at war.

To fight any kind of war, Kahente Horn-Miller writes, "The biggest single requirement is fighting spirit." I thought much of this as I read *Colonize This!* since this collection appears in print at a time of escalating world-wide war—in Colombia, Afghanistan, Palestine. But is there ever a time of no-war for women of color? Is there ever a time when our home (our body, our land of origin) is not subject to violent occupation, violent invasion? If I retain any image to hold the heart-intention of this book, it is found in what Horn-Miller calls "the necessity of the war dance." This book is one rite of passage, one ceremony of preparedness on the road to consciousness, on the "the war path of greater empowerment."

May 14, 2002
Oakland, California

Introduction

Bushra Rehman
Daisy Hernández

December 7, 2001

This morning I woke up to the news radio. Women were throwing off their veils in Afghanistan and I thought about how for years the women I have known have wanted this to happen. But now what a hollow victory it all is. I am disgusted by the us-and-them mentality. "We" the liberated Americans must save "them" the oppressed women. What kind of feminist victory is it when we liberate women by killing their men and any woman or child who happens to be where a bomb hits? I feel myself as a Muslim-American woman, as a woman of color fearing walking down the street, feeling the pain that my friends felt as they were beaten down in the weeks after September 11th. Solemnly, we counted as the numbers rose: two, five, seven . . . My friend telling me: They told me I smelled—they touched me everywhere—and when I talked back, they made fun of me, grabbed me, held my arms back, told me to go back to my country, took my money and ran. My other friend telling me: they punched me, kicked me, called me queer—they had found the pamphlets in my bag, and I'm here on asylum, for being a queer activist—my papers were just going through—I'm not safe in this country as a gay man. My other friends telling me: We didn't want to report it to the police, why just start another case of racial profiling? They're not going to find the guys who did it. They're just going to use our pain as an excuse for more violence. Use our pain as an excuse for more violence. It's what I hear again and again in a city that is grieving, that is beginning to see what other countries live every day.

But where does women of color feminism fit into all of this? Everywhere. As women of color feminists, this is what we have to think about.

—Bushra Rehman

February 12, 2002

At first I think the teacups have fallen. Broken, they sit on a shelf in the attic apartment Bushra and her sister Sa'dia share. The teacups look antique, etched with thin lines that loop like the penmanship from old textbooks. I imagine they have been in the family for years, but then I find out they were created by Sa'dia for her art exhibit. She made the cups and inscribed each one with the name of a woman from her family. Each cup represents that woman and is broken to the degree of her rebellions. Some are cracked a little, others shattered. They are piled on top of each other, as if someone needs to do the dishes.

The teacups broken and the women broken. That's how it feels sitting on this thin carpet, editing these essays on feminism while Washington wages war against terrorism. Life feels like something broken on purpose.

During the Spanish evening news, a man in Afghanistan says, "It was an enemy plane and a woman cried." His words stay with me as if they were a poem. It was an enemy plane and a woman cried. I think of that woman and TV cameras in Colombia, my mother's country. The footage shows bloodied streets and women crying. My mother refuses to look. I can't look away. Her eyes are sad and grateful: my American daughter who can just watch this on TV. My aunt gives us cups of tea and tells me to watch what I say on the phone. Rumors are spreading that the FBI is making people disappear. My aunt with the wide smile. She tapes an American flag to my window, determined to keep us safe.

—Daisy Hernández

When we began editing this book, we knew only a little about each other. We were two dark-haired women who moved in overlapping circles of writers, queers, artists and feminists. We had met in New York City through the collective Women in Literature and Letters (WILL), which organized affordable writing programs that were women of color-centered. It was while editing this book, however, that we realized how much a Pakistani-Muslim girl from Queens could have in common with a Catholic, Cuban-Colombian girl from New Jersey.

We both grew up bilingual in working-class immigrant neighborhoods. Our childhoods had been steeped in the religions and traditions of our parents' homelands, and at an early age, we were well acquainted with going through customs, both at home and at the airports. We followed our parents' faith like good daughters until we became women: At fifteen, Daisy left obligatory Sunday mass and Catholicism when a nun said the Bible didn't have to be interpreted literally and no, Noah's ark had never existed. At sixteen, Bushra discovered her body—and stopped praying five times a day.

Of course, there were also differences. Bushra had been raised knowing that violence was as common as friendship between people of color. Her family had moved from Pakistan to New York City to Saudi Arabia to Pakistan and then back to New York City. Daisy, on the other hand, had grown up with white European immigrants who were becoming white Americans, and her familia had only moved from one side of town to the other. We also broke with our families in different ways: Bushra left home without getting married; Daisy stayed home and began dating women.

Our personal rebellions led to a loss of family that took us on another path, where we met other not-so-perfect South-Asian and Latina women also working for social change. It felt like it had taken us a lifetime to find these spaces with women who gave us a feeling of familiarity and of belonging, something that had never been a given in our lives. With these women we could talk about our families and find the understanding that would help us go back home. We began to realize, however, that working with our own was only the groundwork. To make change happen we needed to partner up with other women of color. To work on this book we had to venture out of our safe zones.

And then 9/11 happened. People from our communities turned on each other in new ways. Girls wearing the hijab to elementary school were being slapped by other colored girls. Any mujer dating an Arab man was now suspect in her own community. People we considered friends were now suspicious of Middle Eastern men, Muslims and Arab immigrants, even if they were immigrants themselves. Living near Ground Zero, we watched people respond to their grief and fear with violence that escalated in both action and conversation, and we felt our own fear close to home: Daisy was afraid that, with the surge of pro-American sentiments, her mother would be mistreated for not speaking English, and Bushra feared for her mother and sisters who veil, and for her father and brothers with beards who fit the look of "terrorists."

In response to the war, we wanted to do "traditional" activist work, to organize rallies and protest on the street, but abandoning this book project didn't feel right. Darice Jones, one of our contributors, reminded us of Angela Davis's words: We are living in a world for which old forms of activism are not enough and today's activism is about creating coalitions between communities. This is exactly our hope for this book. Despite differences of language, skin color and class, we have a long, shared history of oppression and resistance. For us, this book is activism, a way to continue the conversations among young women of color found in earlier books like *This Bridge Called My Back* and *Making Face, Making Soul*.

After many late night talks, we chose the title of Cristina Tzintzún's essay for this book in order to acknowledge how the stories of women and colonization are intimately tied. But when we first sat down to write this introduction and looked in the dictionary, we found that colonize means "to create a settlement." It sounds so simple and peaceful. We rewrote the definition. To colonize is "to strip a people of their culture, language, land, family structure, who they are as a person and as a people." Ironically, the dictionary helped us better articulate the meaning of this book. It reminded us that it's important for women of color to write. We can't have someone else defining our lives or our feminism.

Like many other women of color, the two of us first learned the language of feminism in college through a white, middle-class perspective, one form of colonization. Feminism should have brought us closer to our mothers and sisters and to our aunties in the Third World. Instead it took us further away. The academic feminism didn't teach us how to talk with the women in our families about why they stayed with alcoholic husbands or chose to veil. In rejecting their life choices as women, we lost a part of ourselves and our own history.

This is difficult to write because, initially, white feminism felt so liberating. It gave us a framework for understanding the silences and tempers of our fathers and the religious piety of our mothers. It gave us Ani Di Franco's music to sing to and professors telling us that no, patriarchy isn't only in our colored homes, it is everywhere. There is actually a system in place that we can analyze and even change.

But our experience with white feminism was bittersweet at best. Daisy felt uncomfortable talking about her parents' factory work in the middle-class living rooms where feminists met to talk about sweatshops. Bushra realized how different she was from her feminist sisters whenever there was a flare-up in the Middle East and she was asked to choose between her identity as a Muslim and an American. There was always a dualism at play between our "enlightened" feminist friends at college and the "unenlightened" nonfeminist women in our families. We wondered how it could be that, according to feminist thought, our mothers were considered passive when they raised six children; worked night and day at stores, in factories and at home; and when they were feared and respected even by the bully on the block.

It was only after college, through word of mouth from other women of color, that we learned about another kind of feminism. These groups practiced women of color feminism, sometimes naming it as such and sometimes not saying it at all. Daisy joined WILL, a collective founded by three Latinas to use writing as a political weapon, and that's how she first read Cherríe Moraga's writings on homosexuality and began publishing her own work. Bushra joined SAWCC (South Asian Women's Creative Collective), where she found a desi audience and began performing her poetry first in New York City and eventually around the country. It was among these women that we both began developing a feminist way of looking at la vida that linked the shit we got as women to the color of our skin, the languages we spoke and the zip codes we knew as home.

Our feminism lies where other people don't expect it to. As we write this introduction, the cop who (allegedly) took part in sodomizing Abner Louima has just been released from jail. We see pictures of the cop kissing his wife splattered across the newspapers. This sanctioning of sexual violence and police brutality against a black Haitian immigrant feels like a slap in the face. As women of color, this is where our feminism lies. When the media vilifies a whole race, when a woman breaks the image of a model minority, when she leaves her entire community behind only to recreate it continually in her art and her writing, or when our neighborhoods are being gentrified, this is also where our feminism lies.

As young women of color, we have both a different and similar relationship to feminism as the women in our mothers' generation. We've grown up with legalized abortion, the legacy of the Civil Rights movement and gay liberation, but we still deal with sexual harassment, racist remarks from feminists and the homophobia within our communities. The difference is that now we talk about these issues in women's studies classes, in classrooms that are multicultural but xenophobic and in a society that pretends to be racially integrated but remains racially profiled.

We have also grown up with a body of literature created by women of color in the last thirty years—Alice Walker's words about womanism, Gloria Anzaldúa's theories about living in the borderlands and Audre Lorde's writings about silences and survival. In reading the submissions for this anthology, we found that it was the books that kept young women of color sane through college, abortions and first romances with women. Many of us just needed the books: We needed another woman of color writing about her fear of loving a dark woman's body or about being black and pregnant and feeling the scarcity of her choices.

In working with the writers in this book, we often thought of Audre Lorde's words from her poem, "A Litany for Survival": *We were never meant to survive.* Who would think that we would survive—we, young girls prey to the hands of men, the insults of teachers, the restrictive laws of holy texts and a world that tells us "this is not your world." For the young women in this book, creating lives on their own terms is an act of survival and resistance. It's also a part of a larger liberation struggle for women and people of color.

With these ideas and essays in hand, we locked ourselves up for weeks at a time until the book took form. We chose to focus on the four major themes of family and community, mothers, cultural customs and talking back. Our first section, "Family and Community: A Litany for Survival," describes how we band closer to our birth or chosen families because of the hostility in the world, of someone calling us "spic," "nigger," "fag," "terrorist" or because political and economic wars are only a phone call away to aunties living in Nicaragua or the Philippines. But family is only a safe zone until you kiss another woman, question the faith or go to the movies with a white boy. With our communities we're expected to suppress our individual selves and our dissent in order to look strong in the face of racism. In this section, mixed-race women write to those of us who question their belonging to a women of color community. Women search for chosen families, act like the "man of the house" because there isn't any man and choose different lives after being diagnosed with HIV. Their feminism and community activism are based on the model of family.

"Our Mothers, Refugees from a World on Fire" is about our inclination as young women of color to see our mothers as the "real" feminists, the ones who practice rather than preach. While college may have given us the theories, many of us return home for a working definition of what it means to be a feminist—whether that means learning lesbian femme tactics from a mom who did sex work or taking after a fearless auntie who owned a brothel in Colombia. The mothers in this section are strong women who told us to get married, go to school, pray and avoid sex. They depended on each other, on sisters, neighbors and best friends to watch over us while they themselves were coping with mental illness, poverty or raising too many kids. They are the women Cherríe Moraga wrote about twenty years ago when she said our parents were "refugees from a world on fire." We were just kids then, playing on the streets and translating for our mothers in supermarkets and at the doctor's office.

"Going Through Customs," our third section, is about when every part of us is vulnerable at the checkpoint, when we're asked to check our language, our clothing, our food at the door. Many of us have been negotiating identities from the time we first step out of our parents' homes. When our parents came here with stars in their eyes and fear in their guts, they didn't realize all they would have to give up. When they hoped for a better future for us, they didn't realize they were giving up a chance to have good Hindu, good Nigerian, good Mexican daughters. "Going through customs" is our own way of picking and choosing what we will keep from our traditions and what we will bring into our lives now. It is a young black woman with guitar in hand, playing with the cultures of black and white America.

Our last section, "Talking Back, Taking Back," borrows from the title of bell hooks's book and shows women talking back to white feminists, white Americans, men on the streets, their mothers and liberals. For young women of color, so much of feminism has meant talking back and taking back the world that we live in. It is a taking back of our image, and a breaking down of roles imposed on us, whether it's that of the model minority or the affirmative action kid. These women talk back when someone tells us that racism is over because there are a handful of African Americans in the honors class, when we can't walk down the street wearing what we want because we'll be sexually harassed, when they tell us that Black women have no problem with body image just because all the women in the magazines are white. Here are women talking back to stereotypes and taking back a history that has been denied to us.

We hope that this book will introduce some of the ideas of woman of color feminism to women who have thought that feminism is just a philosophy about white men and women and has nothing to do with our communities. We also want this book to deepen conversations between young women of color. We believe that hearing each other out about our differences and similarities is an important step toward figuring out how to work with whatever divides us.

We have learned so much from the process and from each

contributor. Our own work as writers has taken on more urgency because of this book and we hope other young women will also be moved to action. We know that one book can't do it all, and our lack of money and time made it difficult to reach women who also lacked those resources. But we hope that this anthology will inspire other women to fill in our gaps and move the work forward and deeper. As shani jamila writes at the end of her essay in this book: "The most important thing we can do as a generation is to see our new positions of power as weapons to be used strategically in the struggle rather than as spoils of war. Because this shit is far from finished."

BUSHRA REHMAN AND DAISY HERNÁNDEZ
New York and New Jersey, 2002

Family and Community: A Litany for Survival

browngirlworld:
queergirlofcolor organizing, sistahood, heartbreak

Leah Lakshmi Piepzna-Samarasinha

These are the histories ever present in every young queer/feminist scene, just undocumented—all the ones that weren't in Michelle Tea's or Sarah Schulman's capturing of white queergirl life. We dark funny girls kick ass, change and make history, but the ass-kicking we do doesn't end up in the official records no matter how crucial we are. We don't kick ass the way the white girls do, whether it's in NOW or riot grrrl. For us, it's all about family. And I want to know: When your politics are all about building family—revolutionary queercoloredgirl fam—what happens?

browngirlworld is home and heartbreak, the place where my heart meets my cunt and they cum and rip open at the same moment. I have been an activist, been the one who keeps screaming the chants out in front of the U.S. embassy when everybody else wants to light up, the one cooking chili out of donations for three hundred folks on a broken stove. I did that, but I really went to revolution and feminism cuz I wanted a family that would love me, decolonize me, heal me. The feminism I walked into as a bi-queer brown breed girl was all about the women I wanted to fuck, love and make home with. More than any meeting, I wanted to make places where my girls, my queer dark sistren, could survive. Do more than: Stop self-destructing. Save each other. Not have a nervous breakdown or six by twenty-five. Decolonize our minds, our hair, our hearts. Transform into the phoenixes we were all meant to be.

I'm a loser in that department, though, one who came to this world with a lot of hope and walked away four years later with a string of heart and cherry busts behind me. Pathetic. Growing up, I dreamed of that chosen political fam that would last my whole life, with some departures of years or decades. There's this trope that repeats itself in the books you and I read to save our lives: that if where you grew up is killing you, you can leave and make a chosen, identity-based fam that takes up where your bio-fam left off. That's usually the straight-up white lefty/queer thang. The coloredgirl one I read about in Chrystos, Gloria Anzaldúa and Cherríe Moraga said somethin' more: that if the reason my bio-fam was killing me was because they were trying to destroy the brown, the poor in me, bleach out to American, I could run to the girls who were not trying to forget. I wanted that. I grew up surviving because I believed in that. It's hard to let go.

Makes perfect sense why. I'm a mixed brown girl, Sri Lankan and New England mill-town white trash, who grew up alone and starving hungry for a sane home. I grew up with my dad being the only Sri Lankan in Worcester, Massachusetts, only he'd clear his throat uncomfortably and say he was from "The British Commonwealth." I grew up with my white mama who called him, laughing,

4

her "houseboy," and told me to not repeat her mistake and marry anyone dumber than me, while she ripped my hair straight and bloody scalped. I was a brown kinky-headed full-lipped girl in apartheid Massachusetts, white boys chasing me down the street to try and fuck the hot Latina they saw, with browning colonial family photos locked up in trunks, simmering electric heat lightning silences exploding whenever I asked the obvious questions. I wanted to run away. Revolutionary change happens through laws and guns, tear gas and tablas, but it also comes through the families and communities we build to replace the dead life we want to flee.

I grew up in the Reagan eighties dreaming of apocalypse and revolution, knowing we would fight and win it all or die. I fled to many activist scenes, looking for that place. Anarcho-punk as a kid, riot grrrl, anti-Giuliani, anti-cop, anti-Contract on America ass-kicking in general. When I moved to Toronto for queer-women-of-color-only community in the mid-nineties, along with many others, I thought, *I don't want to waste any more time on white folks.* Or on white queers, on white girls breaking down weeping in women's studies classes. No more Queer Nation, those whips and chains are a white thing. How could I have wasted all this time on fuckin' Susie Bright when my people are in the real shackles of the International Monetary Fund, the colonial mind and the Indian Peace Keeping Forces raping a third of the women in the Northern Provinces of Sri Lanka.

Later on, I said goodbye to the straight-of-color scene when my ex went het, joined the Nation, got addicted to using the back of his hand, when the good sistas and brothers all forgot why he and I

couldn't go on the same bus to Philly for Millions for Mumia—
'cause all that woman and queer stuff was seen as a personal issue,
something embarrassing like menstrual pads. So I went to my girls,
the one place I could trust, the place Angela Davis said I should find,
where my gifts could make the most difference.

whirlwind girls

The Black, brown, red and yellow girls I went home with are found on
the edges of women's studies classes, silent or keepin' on raising her
hand, a financial-aid baby or fresh from dark middle-class private
school. Eating a free meal at the women's drop-in; the sista outsidahs
sitting on the steps, bitch-bonding after the mandatory antiracism
training about which white girl said the most stupid thing, getting
scholarships to fly to conferences we live on for years afterward. For
all our everyday fucked-up-trauma, we need to carry around a video
camera to document our lives, cuz things happen so fast and ain't
nobody gonna believe it otherwise.

When I moved to Toronto, I threw myself in the middle of prison
abolition, antipsychiatry and anticolonial women's activism. Staying
up all night fucking to the changing cayso/jungle/hiphopmetal/dub
beats, then throwing my clothes on and rushing to do the radical
women's radio show. Marching with thousands of other broke, dark
faces, we stormed up Spadina Ave. to the copshop each time another
man of color branded as crazy was shot. Me and one brown and Black
girl, we went for $5 jerk chicken dinner from the restaurant we all
went to next to the radio station before they tore it down to make

another glitzy mall. She and I sat on the back porch of that tiny two-bedroom, smoking weed and getting ready for the club, debriefing after every meeting, plotting, trying to fix each other up, watching the call display glow with her girlfriend's name and not picking up, finally walking down the street at 2 A.M. to the Caribbean Kitchen to get yet another $6.99 curry goat with green mango special. Me, her, her white girlfriend, her Trini brown fag roommate, our little sis and co-worker at the only all-Black dyke-run women's center on any campus, our half-desi femme queerboyfavorite auntie; we waz girls together. No place was safe for all of us; the South Asian queer art show thought we were too light or too Black, too broke or too crazy. We were too queer for Mumia, too political for the bar.

I said I loved her. That was when all the problems started.

Flowchart: You meet, someplace. Each other seems somethin'. Sanity, similar faces, seeming nice in a sea of inanity/assholishness. You go for coffee. You do e-mail. You see each other on the same fringes of the same meetings. You go drink after. You go out in a big pack. You go to her house. Then there's the first big revelation of something intense, close and personal. Usually with much apology for being that way. You say you love each other. Sometimes you fall on the bed, grab ass on the dance floor. You check in, be each other's therapists about all the bullshit every week. And then the first time she opens her mouth while lying back with a blunt/a drink/a piece of western sponge cake in her hand, she lets out something that stops you cold: *Bring me back some of that weird Asian stuff when you go to Japan, girl. You know, she was one of those fuckin' Latinas who don't speak Spanish. Yeah, I got this BIG*

BLACK DICK *from Good Vibrations! I don't want any Muslims in my house anymore—not after what happened.*

You freeze in that moment. Fucked up: *Not safe no more.* This is what you always feared, what you knew was gonna happen, what you were stupid for thinking you could avoid. Do you say anything? Maybe you can say something and she can hear it. Or do you say something diplomatic and carefully worded, and afterward do you bitch on the phone to other fam all you couldn't say to her? More often though, you go away. I went away. Froze and threw a look to some other place in the room and tried to pretend it didn't happen and sat on my anger like sitting on plutonium flames. Just like surviving my mama's house: Be quiet until you can leave for real.

Then does it all finally comes out after months of you telling yourself that you would say something, and she says, *What the fuck, what, how the fuck could you say this? Have you been thinking about this all along?*

Maybe she gets married, maybe she goes out with a white boy, maybe she goes back to grad school, maybe she goes back on rock, maybe she transitions, maybe she gets all the good gigs, maybe she gets evicted, maybe she goes back to the psych ward, maybe she fucks your lover at the play party and she likes her better than you.

You're her sistagal, until the wrong word, the wrong tone, the wrong polyamory meltdown, the fight about classism in your relationships, melts you both down. And then you can't work together anymore. You can't put on gigs with each other anymore. You can't borrow money or knock on her door at 3 A.M., she can't call you when she's freakin'. Your margin of survival is cut down, but you don't know the way back.

And do you eventually have a circle of fractured half-friends and go home alone?

We're sistas. We treat each other like sistas. That's the blessin'. That's the problem. We come together cause we're both bein' fucked over by the same people. We get close. And then we fall in love with each other 'cause us third-world diva gals are beautiful and blessed like none other. We fly with each other, there is nothin' like us staggering home at 2 A.M. down the sidewalk, nothin' like our brilliance, shrieking, lifesaving giggles, orgasms. Oh, how we fly.

Nothing hurts as much as another brown woman saying the words you least want to hear. Nothing has ripped my heart open as much as seeing her turn and think, *I'll use all the holes you showed to me—all the fucked-up shit I learned to survive everywhere from the seventh grade schoolyard to the white queer dance floor—to burn your ass.*

All those years a blur of meetings and dance nights and collapsed on the couch after. In building this radical fam, we wanted to build a circle that would be safe, would be a place where the pressure of trauma would not be there. In an attempt to protect each other, we compiled lists of who was good and safe and who was fucked-up. A glance, a word dropped, a phrase that was just *wrong*. Survivors are trained from birth to be exquisitely sensitive, for our own survival's sake. At the first sign of a thrown water glass, the first whisper of footsteps coming down the hall at 3 A.M. behind a smiling face, we're gone. We do not forget these lessons—we still need them every day. We still go, go, gone. Those girls and me, they left town, they left city, we left, let each other disappear. We were raised colonized and confused, to trust the enemy, not our own hair. But we would make hard choices to live, leave each other by the side of the road, for now we deserved the best, didn't we?

What's with all these half-smiles? What does it mean when I do my own in self-defense so nobody wrong gets under my skin? Is it just here or is it everywhere? Can we not be dykes without drama? Is drama gonna be what stops us from saving the world?

The mid-nineties witnessed many of us, including the queer girls, moving away from coalition work with white folks to working in our own communities. Although my examples are fully personal and local, these patterns of creating chosen fam and queergal-of-color organizing have affected every place we have tried to do exclusive organizing, in the particular wave of politicization that has happened since the mid-nineties. The early nineties saw a revitalization of organizing against the Gulf War, Bush, cop brutality and the prison industrial complex. There was no *Blu* magazine, few of the kickass of-color millions organizing we sometimes take for granted now. By 1995 many brown and Black folks had gotten sick of working in coalitions dominated by old- and new-school white leftists who were arrogant about their intellect and profoundly ignorant about the histories, experiences and politics of POC communities. Many of us felt we were already dying, and doing change like this wasn't helping us die any less.

Coming together under broad identities like "people of color" or "queergirlofcolor" brought together folks who'd been at war with each other for centuries and didn't necessarily want to just stop. We thought everything would be all chill and problem-free, because we'd all been on the edges of the same meetings bitching about the same dumb white folks and SWGs (silly white girls).

But when your strongest point of unity is that you all hate the same people, you've got problems.

In moving to all POC politics, I found strength, power, found and made authenticity purity tests (yeah, my Punjabi sucks, but *you're* a half-breed) and the brutal mix of gossip with politics. Broad assumptions of "safe space" that left communities shattered by confusion when rapists, abusers and provocateurs make their presence known.

Dynamics of family building, trust, histories of abuse and trauma factor into every political movement's organization. When we do not understand them, we fall apart, never speak to each other again and are not able to see what is at stake beyond our own personal survival. We are not able to keep surviving with each other, to build institutions that will save each other on a mass scale, and last.

The day after

I wake up in one of my lovers' arms four days after my twenty-sixth birthday, my mouth filled with thick yellow water, and a voicemail picked up at midnight pounding in my head. Another message from another of my queer of color fam, telling me for various reasons s/he is now going to be one more person I will pretend not to see when we pass each other on the sidewalk. Thanking me for my freaked-out call worried s/he might've been hit in the skull with a tear gas canister like the many fired point blank at the anti-free trade protests in Quebec City, but continuing, "I don't hate you, but I just think our lives are going on such different paths that I can't be in contact with you right now." I can picture the futon s/he sat on, the one we sat on so many times, that s/he probably smoked a big joint before picking up the phone to call me, silent dial, that s/he worked hard to sound as composed as possible, because the voice started to break only once. My heart closes her church doors as the message comes on, *press 7 to erase this message, press 9 to save.*

I am leaving you, you are leaving me. We fucked each other over. To give the details would violate confidentiality. Would violate us. S/he needed to leave friends behind, me included, to be who s/he needed to be. But we needed each other to survive.

"Good sleep?" my lover asks.

"One nightmare," I say.

One more person who I cannot work with, be in the same room, get gigs from each other, borrow cash or bathtubs, go shopping and cook food together, $2 fish in green curry and jasmine rice for both of us. One more of many people who kept leaving and leaving my crew that year, who changed cities, changed jobs, politics, genders, lives but most of all friendship/organizing circles.

Now on the far side of twenty-five, no longer precocious, semi-established, I hold my lover and think, no, I don't think this all means that "identity politics are bullshit." I do think of Gloria Anzaldúa's essay in *Making Face, Making Soul,* where she says of queer women of color, "We just can't fucking get along." My lover serves as a kind of

Switzerland in the middle of our community, being Black and queer but male and often not leaving his house. He listens to my grief-filled ranting, walking up to the Hong Kong noodle restaurant where she and I ate so many dinners. When I stop, he says, "I find that, in general, alliances that are based on friendship are the only things that last. Not alliances based on words and letters."

Were we, are we utopian? Not in the way it's used to curse our longings as if food, respect and justice are luxury, but in thinking that in this concept, *queer women of color*, surely there wouldn't be any problems. That this category formed on the edges of meetings, in dreams of all of us sitting down together, would erase all the blood that is also between us. How do we learn that sistahood does not mean no more struggles between us?

I have let go of that utopian dream. Especially when I finally started asking folks point blank if they had chosen family, they mostly said no. Now I look at heart at the same time as I look at identity. I don't know any other way to say it, though it sounds cheesy.

We know how scary this world can be. Physical, emotional, spiritual survival: none of them are givens for us. We need each other. But we also change fast. We make the world change, and we change as fast and slow as it does. When I was a child and when I was a raw, ripped-open eighteen-year-old, I needed a perfect chosen political fam with the desperate need for forever of a fucked-open three-year-old girl. Perfectly valid. But healing my childhood means replacing that jump-off-the-cliff desperate need with a different kind of faith.

When I was younger, in early abuse healing, I used to listen to folks talking about having faith in the universe, having "trust in the process," even when shit was crazy and they were losing every friend and bit of security they'd ever known. I'd suck my teeth. *Of course,* if you had money and goodies (like they mostly did, more than me), the universe came through. If you didn't have privilege, shit happened and you had no fucking cushion. Without a hell of a lot of luck, you wound up on lockdown, stuck in prison or poverty or the psych ward. No second chances for us (broke/crazy/nonwhite/nonnormal). And it is true that right now I've rocked all the privileges and dumb luck thrown my way and made it (for now) out of that sea of trapped people who don't matter, and a lot of folks I know didn't. It is also true that there is something that keeps reaching for all of us, no matter how desperate our life is.

If we keep reaching back and fighting like hell to fix what they fucked up in us, the people you desperately need may leave. But they will also keep coming, in new forms. The world is chaotic and uncertain, but not all of it is our parents' house.

Maybe, through the past five years of whirlwind, I have gotten past the initial point of healing and decolonization to be able to get beyond perfection expectations, get beyond exiling the other, get beyond seeing any betrayal or mistake as worse than that of our enemies, and at the same time knowing how to call shit when I see it. I am married to the idea of being awake. Awake like it says in the *Survivor's Guide to Sex:* not being cynical or automatically untrusting, but being awake to the possibilities that are really present in any relationship.[1]

It's been weird and important, this cautious return from separatism. It's more real to say I grew up a punk rock crazy freak girl, rather than making myself out as a warrior in brown who never listened to anything but Asian Dub Foundation.

Over two crackling fucked-up phones, Brooklyn to Toronto, my friend Marian Yalini says, "It's the places where we hurt each other when we're close, girl, that our most important work lies in. It's where the big changes happen. Where the world blows open or it doesn't." Between us, lying so close, there, as we screw up, make mistakes, as the big doors open or close.

What it comes down to is that there is no fixed safe or sane place for any of us, as much as we desperately need it. The same shit we said to the white girls about how "safe space" didn't mean "never uncomfortable" space applies to us, too. We have to stay in the icky places, master the art of moving one step past what we know, listen to each other instead of shouting and do that tricky two-step of both trusting we know when we're being fucked over and knowing the difference between the truly evil and abusive and someone who screws up but is not evil. This is the difference between purity and practicality.

Strive to be kind to each other's whirlwind girl. Strive to remember that each one of us is precious and necessary, that drama and wars put out our light. Strive to remember this is our one, short life, and the choices we make will determine what comes of it. To know that when we need to cocoon to be clear about that, but not to insist that everybody make the same choices that we need to. Politics and passion are lovely, but not enough. Damn. Sounds like a perfect prescription for that sane family I never had, the one whose longing has shaped my life. Not perfect. But good enough. Just good enough.

I dream of making a child and making a family to raise her in. It is just a dream, but it's a potent one that symbolizes much. When I picture the family I want for her, it's different than before. It includes folks who aren't there everyday, but who are there when they can be, when they are in town—mentally or physically. This fam involves the lovers and friends I had this past year. Despite everything, I imagine my brown daughter growing up with a white mama like I did. But instead of my racist, crazy one, I see my Newfie trannybutchchick sweetheart cracking jokes and being gentle with her. She ran away from her bio-family seven years ago to become the girl she is, doesn't pretend to be what she's not, apologizes, listens with eyes more open than anyone I've ever seen.

I dream of making this child with my other lover, a man who's the son of Maroons from Jamaica and Black folks who ran like hell past the Mason-Dixon to Detroit to Windsor, Ontario, intermarried with Nishnawbe and Cree. I see this queer, mostly dark family that is part of the changing of the world, living in houses with wrist restraints and Saul Williams on the minisystem, organic mangoes in bulk from the co-op, my fam that lets each other disappear down the paths that are what they need, and lets them come back, that flows in and out, not promising perfection, valuing each other enough not to implode. We are all runawayfreakshow children. Who love each other, who fuck up, but who will not abandon this. This, which is still all we have.

For the fam during the whirlwind years: Adrineh, Darcy, Hana, Bo-Yih, Sam and for David Findlay and Ga Ching Kong for helping with the redefinitions.

Colonize This!

Cristina Tzintzún

I worry about dating whites, especially white men. I worry that even though my skin is white like theirs, they will try and colonize me. I see what a white man did to my beautiful, brown, Mexican mother. He colonized her. It is not love that drew my father to my mother, as I used to think; rather, it was the color of her skin, her impoverished background, her lack of education, her nationality, her low self-esteem, her submissiveness. In his mind these qualities reinforced his superiority. Instead of recognizing the differences between him and her as beauty, my father saw them as a means for exploitation.

My father met my mother in Morelos, Mexico. She was working at a store when he came and asked her for change. He told her that he was from the States and that he would be back for her. She just thought he was a crazy, gringo hippie, and she paid no attention to him. Later that day he came back for her. He told my mother that he and his friend Zauza, named after the Tequila brand, were going to take her to their place. My mother naïvely thought that they were kidnapping her—she had never seen gringos dressed so oddly. So she went

17

with them fearing for her life. They took her to their house where the rest of their roommates were tripping on acid. My mother was doubly frightened by this, not only were they kidnapping her, but they were going to turn her into a drug addict. After a few hours they took my mother home, and after that they came to visit her regularly.

Two years later my parents got married. They raised my older sister in Mexico for her first year. Then they came to the States to "visit" but never returned to Mexico to live. If my mother could have returned to Mexico safely with us, her children, she would have. She feared that my father would kidnap us—not an unrealistic fear considering my uncle did the same thing to my aunt when she left him for the first time. Also, the economic possibility of raising three children in Mexico as a single parent was unrealistic. My mother was no longer in her early twenties and therefore considered undesirable for employment in machista Mexican culture. Her only choice was to raise us in the United States.

Both my father and my mother raised us to be proud of who we were. Shame was not part of my vocabulary. As a child I was proud to identify myself with brown, with poor, with Indian, with "other." I specifically remember my father teaching me the avenues to fight my oppressors. He was the one who taught me feminist theory. He taught me about systemic racism. I listened to my father's advice. I was not like most girls. I always spoke my mind. I had no reservations about acting "unfeminine." I was raised with such fire. I was aggressive. I spoke like the boys did and never gave it a second thought. I was not worried about it if they would like it or disagree, or if they would like me.

I worry about dating white men because of my father. He is a "progressive" man, or so people think. Only those close to him realize his hypocrisy. Most consider him to be a liberal, a feminist, an antiracist, an anticlassist, but I know he is not. He is the wolf in sheep's clothing. He disguises himself as a humanitarian, but this deception makes him the worst offender of them all.

I was told never to submit to any man, but I was only demonstrated submission by my mother and domination by my father. I was raised with eyes closed but ears open. I heard my father tell me that as a womon, a Mexican, I should not let anyone degrade me because of my race or gender, yet this is exactly what he did to my mother. When he made fun of her accent, when he forced her to have sex with him, when he beat her, when he cheated on her, when he told her that she was stupid, when he told her that without him she was nothing.

I saw the contradictions between my father's actions and words, but I had trouble processing it all. I did not realize what it meant that my father only cheated on my mother with African-American, Asian and Latina womyn. But the flashing lights became harder to ignore when I would hear my father tell other white American men that they should go to Mexico and marry a nice Mexican girl. So that she could take care of him, that they are such good cooks and so submissive that they would make anyone the perfect wife. I heard him only encourage my brother to date Mexican girls. They would be so grateful to go out with a gringo. To my father it did not matter whether my brother liked them or not.

When I would hear these comments I'd tell my father that he is a racist. That just because he is white and American does not mean that every brown womon wants him. I'd tell him that just because they are poor and Mexican, he thinks he is better than they are. That they are people too, people with emotions not to be toyed with, that they are not his brown dolls! My father rolls his eyes. I'm too damned PC, he says.

I remember the first time I saw sex. It wasn't on TV, or catching my parents. It was my father with another womon, and I was three. My parents used to sell jewelry door to door. Sometimes there would be deliveries to be made, and on such an occasion I accompanied my father while my brother, sister and mother waited in the car. I remember a petite African-American womon answering the apartment door and my father locking me in the bathroom, telling me to stay in there. I was frightened but also curious why I was not supposed to open the door. When I did, I saw the answer: my father naked having sex with another womon. I quickly shut the door, my stomach churning, knowing that something was wrong. When I went back to the car and told my mother what I had seen, my father called me a liar and my mother chose to believe him, too hurt to admit the truth to herself.

My father never did try hard to hide the other womyn. My mother, however, did try hard to deny and forgive. It was difficult for her to accept the truth. In the beginning, she not only became angry with my father but with the other womyn. She blamed them for "making" my father cheat. My mother felt worthless. She, like many other Mexican womyn, fell into the trap of thinking that without her man, she could not do or be anything. Not until my mother was able to see the value in herself was she able to face reality. She finally saw the truth behind the other womyn's situations: that these womyn were the same as her.

When I think of colonization, I think of my father's "conquests." I think back to all the faces that he has colonized. I think back to Dow, the womon from Thailand; Denise, the long-time girlfriend; Guadalupe, his soon-to-be new wife in Mexico. And I think back to all the faces which I never saw. The girls in the whore houses from here to Mexico to Thailand. I see faces as young as mine. I remember the note I left my father with a package of condoms, before his business trip to Thailand, begging him to think of his actions, begging him for once to think of the lives of these girls. I noticed it, he did not; this was rape. Sex with a thirteen-year-old girl. My father is a rapist. She was forced to work in the brothel; she is not a prostitute—she is a slave. And I want to hold her hand and beg a million apologies. I want to cry with her. I want to look into her eyes, for I can only imagine her pain; she is my sister. We are both human, both equal, but my father does not acknowledge this. For my father even has the audacity to claim that he knows what it is to be a womon of color, because he used to have long hair in the sixties.

As long as I can remember, my father has always been fascinated with womyn of color. He likes to flaunt money and power in front of these womyn. He thinks this makes him superior, more powerful, and more intelligent. So he chooses to date only womyn of color—these are the womyn he feels he can exploit. Black, brown or yellow, my father loves them all—he is so multicultural.

When I think of all the womyn my father has used, I feel sick. My father exploits their poverty, their desperation, their need to eat. And for me it is not some far-off image of who these womyn are, or of their economic situations. No, these womyn are my close relatives—my mother, my aunts, my grandmother. You see, my father is not the only person I know who "colonizes" womyn of color. No, it runs in the family. My grandfather is also married to a Mexican womon (my father's stepmother). She married my grandfather so that her daughter would have economic stability, so she would have a father, but what kind of father calls his daughter "his little spic"? My uncle has been married to three different Costa Rican womyn. He smugly says to me, "Any womon can be bought." I just smile and nod. While he thinks he is fucking these womyn, they fuck him. Like Raquel, his second wife, who left him black-eyed and bruised when he raised his hand to her, or Guiselle, who stole $10,000 dollars from him. I admire these womyn—they could never be colonized.

I know that my brother is going to help me stop the circle of colonization. He refuses to partake in my father's racist, sexist, exploitative games. And for him like me, it is an internal struggle. One that requires me to question what I feel and most of all my memory. I must make sure again and again, that my father's superiority complex has not seeped into me subconsciously. I have met other mutt/colonized children like myself, but instead of overcoming their colonization they succumb to it. They become internally conquered. They shame themselves into believing that half of them is inferior. They choose to deny their culture and heritage. They make such claims, that their brown skin originated from their French background. And sometimes they become the worst type of colonized people, those who try and hide their feelings of inferiority by persecuting those like them.

It took me till the age of eighteen to connect the dots of why I exist, of why my family was and no longer is. I saw something amiss, something foul in my father's actions and words. I knew there was a lie. I knew the truth was deep and painful. When I found it, I was left confused. I did not know what to do with it. My whole existence is based on things I cannot tolerate. I was raised with eyes closed because I did not see my family for what it was. It was based on the ideals of "isms." It was there to soothe my father's ego. I often wonder if my father even sees anyone as his equal. I wonder if he knows that when he demeans other womyn of color that he demeans me. His actions and words pierce me to the core. This is not just any man who is saying these things, this is my father. This is half of me. This is where I come from.

I am careful to learn from other people's mistakes as well as my own. I know that in the past I have let comments slide. My first boyfriend (white) found it funny to tell me to go get him a Coke so that he could pretend I was his Mexican maid. His friends called me spic and told me I smelled of tacos. Back then I didn't know how to challenge their discrimination. I kicked the boy who called me spic, but I had no words. For the first time I could not speak. My "friends" then thought such words were not racist, that the only hate word that existed was "nigger." Their definition of racism was so rigid, pseudo-liberal and white. I knew I was faced with racism, yet my peers could not see this through my brown eyes.

It was my mother's mistake not to challenge my father; it was my mistake not to do the same to the people I dated. I know I will not make these same mistakes twice. I know I cannot be colonized. I realize now that I can't be with anyone who wants to pat me on the head and tell me how neat it is that I am Mexican but never actually wants to hear me talk about it. Far too many times I have tried to speak of my struggles or those of my people to be met with bored or un-understanding eyes. It leaves me frustrated and isolated. When one friend learned what I was writing this piece about, she replied, "Blah, blah. Heard it all before. Nothing new." My body goes numb when she says these things. I want to punch her, slap her. Instead I just call her an asshole. When I am done with this essay, I will make her read it. Her lack of emotion and understanding makes it next to impossible to speak to her. She is as sensitive and caring as an electroshock. I see her words as self-absorbed ignorance, resentful and dismissive of a culture she does not even try to understand. I struggle to make my voice heard so that she and people like her will learn that there is more than just a white experience.

In my parents' relationship my mother constantly struggled for equality. She fought to be seen as my father's equal. In many aspects she succeeded; in my eyes and my siblings' eyes she was equal if not *more* than my father. Her unconditional love and support gave us the strength and independence we needed. When my mother became tired of my father controlling the family money, she became self-employed. With the small amount she earned working, selling jewelry at local festivals, she would buy us the fast food my father wouldn't let us eat. She would take us to dollar movies and bus trips downtown to the children's science museum. Around my mother I could always be myself. I never had to live up to any false expectations, unlike with my father.

My mother is the strongest womon I know, she stayed with my father so that my siblings and I could have an education, so that my sister and I would have the means to take care of ourselves, so we would not need to depend on any man as she had. She felt she had no escape from my father, she was not from this country, she did not speak the language, nor did she have anyone to turn to. So my mother did the best she could. My mother hid her tears, cried in her pillow, and I slept soundly. This was her sacrifice. She did not want us to feel her inferiority. She put her feelings of inadequacy aside and raised us to be proud. And for this I am absolutely grateful to my mother. In fact, I feel fortunate that I was raised with such true contrasts. It helped me find balance. My mother now tells me that her biggest fear when my sister and I were growing up was that we would be submissive. We laugh about her worries now. My mother says that she could not have hoped for more feisty, self-assured daughters.

I do not hate my father. I love my father. I respect him as a father but not as a person. If it were not for him, I would not be as proud and outspoken as I am today. If it were not for him, I would not be passionate about womyn's issues. I look at my father and I see the best example of what not to be. He preached one thing but did another. This taught me to question not only him but the world around me. This helped me see through the lies society fed me. It also made me take action. My father always spoke of the injustice in the world, the racist war on drugs, factory farms, homophobia, free trade. He taught me so much, but he left so much out. He spoke and spoke but never did a damn thing about these injustices. He saved his activism for reading books and preaching to those he could feel more intelligent than. It is because of my father that I am a vegan, even though he eats meat. It is because of my father that I don't tolerate homophobia, even though he says "dyke." It is because of my father that I teach English classes to undocumented immigrants, even though my father calls them "wetbacks" and tells me I should charge them for my services. If it were not for him, I would not be committed to a life of activism. I see his true colors, and I am glad he is my father. I do not wish to change what I cannot, my father or the past. Yet, I choose not to speak to him. He is too sad and pathetic to know how to love. To him love is something to manipulate. And my love is far too precious to be treated in such a manner. I know that to continue speaking with him only hurts me. So I must keep severed ties with this man that I still call daddy. I have hope for my mother. After twenty-one years she has signed divorce papers. She was ready—her three children out of high school, her sacrifice complete. I, like her, have been waiting for her freedom for some time now. And at last it will soon be here.

It was my father who instilled the basic principles of feminism in me, but it was feminism that taught me who I was as a womon. During my high-school years I felt isolated from my peers. They seemed shallow, spoiled and sheltered. I was uninterested in their idea of weekend fun, of football games, and catering to the needs of rich white boys. I found no relief in the alternateen scene; skipping school to do drugs and secretly wishing to be "popular" bored me. Instead, I opted to be the outcast. I wanted to analyze the culture that maintained my middle-class white neighborhood. I wanted to know why their system seemed to be so afraid of me. Of why when I questioned something, my new name became dyke or bitch. I made the decision to confront every homophobic, racist or sexist word I heard. Sometimes it seemed like I never got a chance to shut up. When I wasn't challenging my peers and teachers, I spent my time reading. I read all the feminist literature I could get my hands on. They gave me the support I needed. They made me feel less alone. They made me proud to call myself a feminist and queer. Those books taught me more than my school ever could.

I appreciate the outlet those books created for me. Although they gave me something to identify with, they never gave me anything to identify with as a Latina. I remember reading *Listen Up: Voices from the Next Feminist Generation* and being angry that the book contained only one Latina contributor, who I was only able to tell was Latina, not by what she had written but by her Spanish surname. I felt the book had represented many other minority groups well, but I felt invisible. I find it frustrating that when most books mention womyn of color, that "color" and "gender" are presented as something separate. I am not just a woman or just a person of color—I am a womon of color.

In the past year a new part of myself has awoken, my history. And I don't know how to say it or what to do with it. I have lived my whole life until now away from reality. I am based on my father's superiority complex. I stand here before you because of racism. I look into the mirror and wonder, who am I? What does being based on white superiority make me? This is a question that I will have to answer, and I know there is no easy answer. I am mixed. I am the colonizer and the colonized, the exploiter and the exploited. I am confused yet sure. I am a contradiction.

This is for my beautiful mother

Organizing 101
A Mixed-Race Feminist in Movements for Social Justice

Lisa Weiner-Mahfuz

I have vivid memories of celebrating the holidays with my maternal grandparents. My Jido and Sito ("grandfather" and "grandmother," respectively in Arabic), who were raised as Muslim Arabs, celebrated Christmas rather than Ramadan. Every year, my Sito set up her Christmas tree in front of a huge bay window in their living room. It was important to her that the neighbors could see the tree from the street. Yet on Christmas day Arabic was spoken in the house, Arabic music was played, Arabic food was served and a hot and heavy poker game was always the main activity. Early on, I learned that what is publicly communicated can be very different from what is privately experienced.

Because of the racism, harassment and ostracism that my Arab grandparents faced, they developed ways to assimilate (or appear to assimilate) into their predominantly white New Hampshire community. When my mother married my Jewish father and raised me with his religion, they hoped that by presenting me to the world as a white Jewish girl, I would escape the hate they had experienced. But it did not happen that way. Instead, it took me years to untangle and understand the public/private dichotomy that had been such a part of my childhood.

My parents' mixed-class, mixed-race and mixed-religion relationship held its own set of complex contradictions and tensions. My father comes from a working-class, Ashkenazi Jewish family. My mother comes from an upper-middle-class Lebanese family, in which—similar to other Arab families of her generation—women were not encouraged and only sometimes permitted to get an education. My mother has a high-school degree and no "marketable" job skills. When my father married her, he considered it an opportunity to marry into a higher class status. Her background as a Muslim Arab was something he essentially ignored except when it came to deciding what religious traditions my sister and I were going to be raised with. From my father's perspective, regardless of my mother's religious and cultural background, my sister and I were Jews—and only Jews.

My mother, who to this day carries an intense mix of pride and shame about being Arab, was eager to "marry out" of her Arabness. She thought that by marrying a white Jew, particularly in a predominantly white New Hampshire town, that she would somehow be able to escape or minimize the ongoing racism her family faced. She converted to Judaism for this reason and also because she felt that "eliminating" Arabness and Islam from the equation would make my life and my sister's life less complex. We could all say—her included—that we were Jews. Sexism and racism (and their internalized versions) played a significant part in shaping my parents' relationship. My father was never made to feel uncomfortable or unwelcome because he had married a Muslim Arab woman. He used his white male privilege and his Zionistic point of view to solidify his legitimacy. He created the perception that he did my mother a favor by "marrying her out" of her Arabness and the strictness of her upbringing.

My mother, however, bore the brunt of other people's prejudices. Her struggle for acceptance and refuge was especially evident in her relationship with my father's family, who never fully accepted her. It did not matter that she converted to Judaism, was active in Hadassah or knew all of the rituals involved in preparing a Passover meal. She was frequently made to feel that she was never quite Jewish enough. My Jewish grandmother was particularly critical of my mother and communicated in subtle and not so subtle ways that she tolerated my mother's presence because she loved her son. In turn, I felt as if there was something wrong with me and that the love that I received from my father's family was conditional. Many years later this was proven to be true: when my parents divorced, every member of my father's family cut off communication from my mother, my sister and me. Racism and Zionism played a significant (but not exclusive) role in their choice. My father's family (with the exception of my Jewish grandfather, who died in the early seventies) had always been uncomfortable that my father had married an Arab woman. The divorce gave them a way out of examining their own racism and Zionism.

Today my mother realizes that her notions about marrying into whiteness and into a community that would somehow gain her greater acceptance was, to say the least, misguided. She romanticized her relationship with my father as a "symbol of peace" between Jews and Arabs, and she underestimated the impact of two very real issues: racism within the white Jewish community and the strength of anti-Semitism toward the Jewish community. At the time she did not understand that her own struggle against racism and anti-Arab sentiment was both linked to and different than anti-Semitism.

For me the process of grieving the loss of the Jewish side of my family after the divorce led me to realize that their choice was a painful recognition and rejection of my mother and ultimately our Arabness. I needed to figure out how to not reject my Jewishness, while at the same time learning how to embrace my Arabness on my own terms rather than on those of the adults around me. Today I do not consider myself to be "less" of an Arab because I did not grow up with a direct and explicit understanding of myself as one. I also do not consider myself to be "less" of a Jew because I am half Arab. I consider myself a woman who is working to understand how spoken and unspoken messages have shaped my experiences and political perspective.

Making the Connections

My understanding of injustice started with a series of visceral reactions. As a child I remember feeling a pit in my stomach when I sat in temple listening to stories about the Holocaust or when my mother and her siblings used to talk about being beat up in school because of their "funny" names and hair. I later experienced that same reaction in high school when I learned about slavery in the United States and then again in college, when I took my first women's studies class and began to understand the impact of heterosexism on my life and the lives of all women. Despite these reactions, however, I did not have the language to articulate why these feelings were so personal to me until I started exploring feminism. Feminism awakened my commitment to fighting injustice. Feminism challenged me to see how deeply I had internalized my own assimilation. Feminism taught me that one can experience privilege and oppression simultaneously and that using my white privilege to try and hide my Arabness was not an honest way to live in the world, nor did it guarantee me safety—after all, being Jewish provides no refuge in an anti-Semitic culture.

Audre Lorde's book *Sister Outsider* provided me with a feminist framework for understanding the interconnectedness of oppression and my own identity as a Jewish/Arab-American, mixed-race, mixed-class, lesbian feminist. This book made a particular impact on me because Lorde was making visible and political her perspective as a woman with multiple identities. Before reading this book, I did not understand that my power and my commitment to fighting oppression lay in finding those places where my experiences of privilege and oppression seem to be at odds with one another. Lorde's work and life taught me that I must not be afraid to go to those complex and "messy" places to understand myself, the history of my people, and to learn how to use my identities in a clear and subversive way. Reading *Sister Outsider* was just the first step in helping me to see that this was possible. Figuring out the strategies and politics involved in *how* to do this at the intersections of my own identities has been and will continue to be a lifelong process.

Although feminism has shaped my personal and political

perspective, it has also been a sharp double-edged sword in my work as an organizer. Time and again I have experienced being in a "feminist space" where I have been asked or forced to check my full self at the door—my Arabic words, my lesbian ideas or my Jewish experience. This, to me, is not feminism. I now focus on understanding the interconnectedness of my own identities and the role that oppression and privilege play in my life and work as an antiracism activist. This has been particularly difficult because many on the "left" uphold the mythology that since we work against "the evils of the world," we are somehow free of racism, sexism, classism, anti-Semitism, ableism, and adultism (the institutional power adults have to oppress and silence young people). After years of antioppression training and organizing work, however, I now know that many "progressive" people and organizations are just as invested in either/or dichotomous thinking and in perpetuating oppression in the world.

Six years ago I attended a conference in Boston entitled "Race and Racism in the Nineties." I participated in a workshop about women, spirituality and antioppression work. During the workshop the facilitators, a white woman and an African-American woman, divided the group into two caucuses: a white caucus and a woman of color caucus. Before breaking up the group, I raised my hand and asked where mixed-race people were to go. This question opened up a flood of questions and challenges toward me. The white women in the room, including the white facilitator, said they felt I should caucus with them because I could pass for white. Most of the women of color concurred with this. I recall feeling confused and vulnerable because I did not anticipate what I would be opening up by calling attention to the dualism that was at play. I also felt angry and hurt because I felt the women in the room responded to me based on my light skin rather than on my experiences or the politics of what I was trying to raise. The discussion proceeded with the facilitators spending ten minutes talking to the group about the privileges of being able to choose—as if I were not in the room. The level of tension in the room was palpable. Bodies stiffened and voices raised a notch.

I was frustrated with myself because I did not know how to handle the "logistics" of putting complex racial issues out in a group in a way that clearly demonstrated in word and deed that I was taking responsibility for my privilege while simultaneously taking an uncompromising stand against white supremacy. Although I had Audre Lorde's words floating around in my mind, I had not yet learned how to apply her teachings to my own experience. Finally, the group resolved that I could "choose" where to go. The feeling in the room was that the situation had been resolved. But it was not resolved for me. I felt alone. I felt that regardless of where I chose to go, it would be the wrong choice. I felt like the illegitimate bastard child that no one wanted or knew what to do with. Many of the women of color were angry with me. Many of the white women felt as if they had made an "antiracist" intervention by challenging me on my racism. Still as the group broke up into two, I made a choice and walked toward the room that the women of color were to meet in. As I approached the door, it quickly slammed in my face.

On this day "feminism" was extremely painful for all of us in the workshop. Everyone was angry and upset because I did not neatly fit into either the white or the colored framework. No one, including myself, knew how to grapple with the complexity in a constructive way. I struggled to articulate that taking responsibility for my white privilege did not mean I was "admitting" to being white. It meant I was recognizing my privilege and trying to establish my accountability. But in this case this difference and its complexity were not honored; they were not seen as something necessary to explore. It was also a hurtful experience because I had hoped that I could turn to other women, especially activists, to mentor and challenge me around how to bring my whole self to my work as an organizer. I learned that receiving that kind of support depended on two things: getting clarity about how my experiences of oppression and privilege overlap and challenging my own assumption that all women activists were automatically going to approach their work with an antioppression analysis.

Resisting Classic Scripts

In talking with other mixed-race activists about their experiences, I have discovered that this is a classic script. This is how racism and internalized racism are often directed toward mixed people. In many activist circles it has become easier to delegitimize and shut us out, rather than to take on the challenge and opportunity that mixed-race people with antioppression politics can present. Our multiple perspectives and commitment to challenging oppression can deepen the discussions about and sharpen our tools for challenging white supremacy.

Yet the presence and voices of mixed-race people are often deeply feared. We are feared because interracial relationships are still taboo in our culture. We are feared because our mere existence calls into question the status quo and the way that race is constructed in our society. We are feared even by people on the "left" who propose to be working to challenge these deeply rooted beliefs and constructs. We live in a white supremacist culture that banks on dichotomous thinking to keep people divided and fragmented within themselves. Those of us who do not fit into either/or boxes therefore experience an enormous amount of pressure to choose one "side" of ourselves over another. We are not considered whole just as we are. We are taught that these are dualisms: Jewish/Arab, public/private, visible/invisible, Black/white, privilege/oppression, pride/shame. But these are false separations that don't exist. They are imposed. My struggle and that of other mixed-race people is to not internalize these dualisms and become paralyzed by a society that rejects our complexity in the name of keeping things simple and easy to categorize.

I have learned many lessons about how important it is to be accountable to those that experience oppression in ways that I do not. Being accountable does not mean that I allow my legitimacy to be freely debated by individuals or groups. From my perspective the question of who is a legitimate person of color (based on their skin color) is misguided. Rather, what is important to me is how individuals and groups use their privileges to challenge oppression. This means that where I experience oppression, I resist it alongside those who experience that same oppression. Where I experience privilege,

I stand in solidarity with those whose lives are being impacted by challenging others who benefit from that same privilege.

Maintaining my accountability is not a choice, but it is certainly fluid. Each situation that I am in calls me to assess myself in relation to the time, place and company. For example, when I am with a group of darker-skinned people of color, I am very conscious of my privilege and actively take steps to acknowledge it. When I am in the company of white people, I am conscious of my privilege in a different way. I am prepared to challenge the assumption that my light skin makes me an ally in perpetuating racism.

I have come to define accountability in a complex way, one that both takes in account and challenges identity politics. Identity politics have given me the opportunity to define and claim myself as a complex and whole person and to build community with those who share common experiences in the struggle for justice. Yet identity politics, when narrowly defined and used as a tool to divide, have made my ability to maintain accountability a treacherous experience. I often feel pressure to choose one community over another, one part of myself over another. As mixed-race people with multiple identities, this pressure to choose can cut deeply and painfully into our souls. More often than not, I find identity politics to be defined narrowly in progressive circles. This can limit our work to build coalitions and solidarity across communities and movements because this leads us to simply replicate all that we want to eradicate in the world.

For personal and political reasons this essay on feminism covers racism and other forms of oppression. I have had to make sense of

Lisa Weiner-Mahfuz

and to develop the tools for challenging why I, as a mixed-race, mixed-class, Jewish/Arab-American lesbian, have been shut out of so many "feminist" spaces. Developing and practicing antioppression politics is not just about my own survival, it is about creating a feminist movement that speaks to and represents the experiences of all women. I refuse to be shut out and I refuse to allow other women who do not fit into the mainstream feminist movement to be shut out. Being an antiracist activist is the best way that I know how to honor my mother's experience, to honor my own identities and to honor women, such as Audre Lorde, who paved the way before me to work for justice.

Many thanks to Lisbeth Meléndez, Cynthia Newcomer, Randi Kristensen, Ana Lara and Stephanie Morgan for their support, feedback and excellent editing skills.

Man of the House

Juleyka Lantigua

I grew up in a wooden house sunk into the sidewalk of what by Dominican standards was a good neighborhood. That meant our sidewalks were cemented and clean, the aqua paint on our house was not fading like cheap makeup and the families on my street knew each other well enough not to mind our business.

Until I was ten, my first family and I lived in the Dominican Republic. My father was a bit of a local celebrity—a hometown baseball prodigy turned civic leader. He was involved in city hall politics and helped our city secure its first national league baseball team. While my father played minor league politico, my mother morphed herself into a beautician, an arts and crafts instructor, a Mary Kay saleswoman, a hairdresser and even a teacher for the deaf. She was superwoman whizzing through town on a sky-blue moped whose long, curved neck made it look like a motorized ostrich. Off she went to hair salons, neighborhood associations, informal women's clubs and after-school programs.

If her patchwork job history constituted a career, then she was the

ultimate career mom. But not in the (North) American sense of it—
there was no carpooling to soccer practice, no coming home late at
night and fixing TV dinners, no out-of-town conferences that watered-
down bedtime stories into cooing answering machine messages. Her
work did not take away from the elaborate meals she prepared for us,
or from orchestrating magnificent birthday parties with dozens of
cousins. She did it all. And she did it with beauty-pageant grace.

My dad took to the role of father the way he knew best. He
brought home leftovers from his salary after his binges with friends.
He disciplined us when necessary and made sometimes astonishing
but mostly common efforts to keep my mother happy. That usually
translated into taking us out for pizza and making a big to-do about
it, or reminding her that he had returned home early one night in the
past two weeks. It was frustrating watching my mother deal with my
father's unwillingness to be an equal partner in their marriage. Of
course, that perspective came to me years later when I learned what a
partnership really is. But I learned my first lesson in feminism back
then: Always take personal responsibility—as a woman, sister, daughter or partner.

By committing herself to fulfilling her end of the deal—raising my
sister and I, caring for our house, working outside of home—my
mother defied Dominican social standards that make a wife and family dependent on the man of the house. She did not wait for my father
to take action, but instead she stood up for herself and for us. Proud,
independent and determined, Mom worked as many jobs as was necessary, stayed up late into the night mending school uniforms, rose

before dawn had blinked awake, traced the city limits with her moped's exhaust and kept arguments to a whisper. Yet her relationship with my father worsened by the day. The more she found herself able to handle the household and our care, the less she demanded from him.

When I was seven, my father died following a car accident. After the funeral we moved to the campo with my mother's extended family. My mother's scooter excursions became long pilgrimages, because we now lived miles outside the center of town, where her customers/students/clients lived. No matter. She remained as attentive, sharing the rearing duties with my grandmother, who was thrilled to have her granddaughters at home. Aunts and uncles formed a tight circle of mother/father figures who took care of our schooling, trips to the beach, disciplining and caring-after.

A couple of years after my father passed away, my mother began exchanging letters with a Dominican man who lived in New York. They learned about each other from a mutual friend, one of my mother's clients who owned a hair salon. The striped airmail envelopes crisscrossed the Caribbean Sea for two years before the two met. There was constant busy talk from relatives about my mom, sister and I moving to the States when this man married her. Although she paid attention, Mom seemed too busy taking care of us to notice. I now understand her readiness to ignore the mounting pressure for the young widow to remarry.

Like pieces of torn cassette ribbon, snippets of conversations my relatives had about our future mix randomly in my head:

"They'll live much better over there."

"Claro. What's a single woman supposed to do around here?"

"Do you think he'll put the girls in private schools?"

"Sin duda. He's a family man. He knows what's best for them."

"She can open up a hair salon, like she's always wanted."

"Over there, she'll have rich clients. She'll be making money in no time."

"We probably won't see them for years. That's what happens to everyone who goes over there."

"But they'll come back with nice clothes and expensive shoes and gold chains, like all the others."

On his first visit our family welcomed my future stepfather like a crown prince atop a royal elephant. There was a backyard cookout with a whole roasted pig, continuous domino games, bottles and bottles of Brugal rum and enough plátano dishes to fill a cookbook. His first stay sealed our fate; wedding preparations started the afternoon he boarded an American Airlines 747 back to Nueva York. I learned my next lesson in feminism then: Your personal choices as a woman depend entirely on how you define yourself. My mother—like all the women in my family—chose to define herself sometimes as an individual woman, other times as a dedicated mother and often as a supportive wife, never to the absolute exclusion of any part.

But it wasn't easy. My workaholic mother was stretching herself to make ends meet. Her raison d'être was her young daughters, who looked to her for everything. Although our family was generous in every way, the assumption—the expectation, really—was that she would soon remarry. That was her only choice; accept a man into her life so that she could continue charting her daughters' prosperity. The unexpected twist to remarriage came in the form of long lines at the American consulate, travel visas and green cards, making us all permanent residents of our future.

By any measure my mother is a modern woman; she is fearless, self-reliant, a hard worker and an independent thinker. We would have been just fine, perhaps even great, without a man in her life. But every social nuance and every familiar whisper confirmed the inevitable; she had to choose, and she had to choose to have a man in her life. I often think that by remarrying she chose against herself.

As we prepared to move, I was distracted by daydreams about living in the States. Firmly grounded in her own reality, however, my younger sister was deathly against us moving. She tried everything: brokering secret deals with my grandmother so she could stay with her, bargaining with my mother with promises of good behavior, threatening to run away if she was forced to move. She even tried convincing Mom that she did not need to remarry because we had everything at my grandmother's. But even last-minute antics at the airport yielded no response from Mom. She had chosen, and she had done so for all of us.

Crammed into a one-bedroom on Montgomery Avenue in the South Bronx, my new taped-together family quickly fell into a routine. My stepfather continued his job of ten years at a frame factory. My sister and I were enrolled in public school. Mom stayed home in the beginning, because she didn't know her way around and didn't speak enough English to look for a job. For a while our synchronicity worked. Everyone was up at the crack of dawn. Mom made breakfast, dressed us and we were off to school. Stepdad went off to work. Mom cooked and cleaned and dealt with our schooling. We'd come home and there would be the same elaborate meals we were used to. My sister and I would do our homework, eat dinner, watch some TV and go to bed. Stepdad would come home in the early evening, shower, eat, read his Bible and go to bed. Repeat. Repeat. Repeat.

Soon my stepfather's salary was not enough for the bloated household, and Mom found work in a factory in a faraway place called New Jersey. I knew it was far because she had to meet a van every morning to get there. The house had to adapt to a new routine and now I was responsible for getting my sister and me to school and back. Mom would lock the door from the outside as early as 5 A.M. My stepdad started missing his morning coffee. Mom would leave semicooked meals that I would finish preparing when I returned from school. Most of the time, my stepdad came back earlier than she did. He'd spend the evening in their room watching TV or be off to church for the círculo de oración. For a while that worked too. Repeat. Repeat. Repeat.

The one person daring enough to point out the change from the Dominican Republic was my sister. She started getting restless and with every discomfort of our new life she demanded to go back "home." Because both adults were now working and there was no money for a sitter, my sister and I spent endless afternoons and weekends locked inside the tiny apartment, whose living room had been split in two with wood paneling to create our bedroom. I was blinded by the newness of it all. Born a wanderer, I wanted more than anything else to walk around my new city, see all the places I'd seen in postcards, ride every subway train to its last stop. I was looking ahead, not backward, as if my neck had been locked in place with a medical brace. On another level, I also knew that it would be a while before we would go back "home," because we were struggling to make ends meet.

My stepfather and I lived under the same roof for more than twelve years, and it would be a gross lie to say we spoke more than a thousand words to each other the whole time. He was quiet around the house. Except for the occasional argument with my younger sister (usually over control of the remote or her predilection to turn the radio up full blast), he rarely addressed us directly. I suppose my sister and I were not his children to discipline. After a while—especially after my mother gave him two wonderful children of his own—my sister and I were not his to acknowledge: "Go ask your mother." Sometimes it felt like we were unwanted dowry my mother had brought to the altar. She, in turn, was a secondhand dress prized for its ornate beauty and nostalgic value, purchased with glee despite its flaws. This was explicit in the codified language of absolute silence.

Years passed and everyone became accustomed to my stepdad's continuous hush. We often forgot to include him in major decisions. He would come home and there would be a new overstuffed couch in the living room or the television would be pumping cable programming into the house. Sometimes he would come home and we wouldn't even be there; off to the park or to play in the snow or down the block at Mom's friends. For as long as I can remember, it was him and us.

At this point, whatever notion of family had been ingrained in me by my first family back in the Dominican Republic was slowly eroding. I started to understand that family means everyone involved doing their part to push forward, to get over the common hurdles and help each other overcome personal obstacles. Mom had exemplified that virtue for so long that it was easy for me to model it; doing much more than I thought was required of a young girl. At age twelve that meant I bagged groceries at the local supermarket. The couple of dollars I earned each day were lunch and snack money for my sister and me.

Because of my stepfather's lack of involvement with the family, socially prescribed roles didn't fit in my house. The sisters were the mother. The mother was the man. Back then, my mother, sister and I didn't philosophize about the meaning of our shifting roles. We never called it feminist or felt liberated or patted ourselves on the back for being self-sufficient. Each of us did what had to be done, from babysitting every weekend so Mom could work a double shift to lying about our age to get an after-school job at thirteen. My stepfather held steadfastly to what he understood as his place in our home: he would hand over a portion of his weekly earnings to my mother and spend his free time in church or playing dominoes with friends. He never really opined or questioned what we were doing to make it work, satisfied that he had done enough.

Little by little his silence painted him invisible.

We didn't quite take him for granted. That would have required first recognizing his presence. We simply went about our lives, bumping into him like an old rocking chair left around for its evocative significance. My mother wasn't much help either. She was so consumed by threading together the delicate coexistence of two families—she, my sister and I, and she, her husband and two new children—that his eventual erasure went unnoticed. At times it seemed she was still making sense of the big-city marriage meant to rescue her from the provincial life her first husband's death had led to.

In the beginning, my stepfather accepted his role as breadwinner with the grace and discipline of a mule conditioned to toil the earth. He went to work, went to church and played husband and father with the dignity his rural upbringing and elementary education had endowed. That suited everyone fine until I became a teenager full of ideas and opinions. Why didn't my stepfather help around the house more? Why did I have to sacrifice my after-school activities to babysit his children? Church became his sanctuary, a place to run to when the demands of a full-time family became too great. He joined the choir, became a deacon's assistant and rose to leader of the circle of prayer. My mother accepted his divine therapy, but I failed to understand why he was allowed to hide in church on weeknights while my mother, sister and I raised his kids.

Soon my questions evolved into confrontations laced with spite and resentment. I started feeling trapped, but luckily college was around the corner. Like a soldier off to basic training, I came back from my first year with more ideas, questions and artillery. Even after just one semester of college I was armed with the arrogance and ignorance of an intellectual ashamed of her beginnings. Why was my family so incapable of getting it together? Why were we not as progressive as the families who dotted my college campus on Family Weekend?

At this point in my college education I had been around well-off students long enough to envy their carefree attitude toward money and their families. Parents were striving to be friends with their kids, while their children worked hard to portray the idyllic campus setting advertised in college brochures. On the rare occasion of a visit, my family tried hard to imitate that sense of artificial familial and financial bliss. But simultaneous English-to-Spanish translations, brunches of sneaked cafeteria bagels and roundtrip tickets on Greyhound gave us away. I was ashamed that we weren't like my classmates' families—apparently middle class and happy—so I lashed out at the easiest target, my stepfather. Much of my anger was misdirected toward him partly because during college I had learned that men are the source of all problems that afflict women, a notion reinforced by the liberal women on campus. And I swallowed it whole, like a potion that numbs you from the inside. This was my next lesson in feminism, and the first one I unlearned.

My stepfather was not at fault. We had expected him to fill a role that had never been defined for him. He had simply modeled himself on generations of Dominican men who abuse the privilege of being male in a country that suffocates women so men can take deep breaths. Our family existed in a different place now, somewhere between the social values of the Dominican Republic and the economic realities of Immigrant, U.S.A. As a budding woman of conscience raised by a woman of great will, I refused to believe that we depended on him, on men at all. Had the women in my family accepted that, we would have gotten nowhere, accomplished nothing. We never expected that my stepfather would build this new world for us with his bare hands. His two stepdaughters, Americanized by our education, grew more intolerant each day, however. My sister was now a teenager and had accepted the sitcom realities TV offered. She wanted to live the Dominican version of *Family Ties*. She wanted a world of pesky (and comedic) family quarrels, all magically resolved before dinnertime or the next commercial break. Instead, she had to make do with a rebellious college-age sister, two all-consuming younger siblings and a mother too tired to blink.

It was hard to know what my mother was feeling during those hard years. Sometimes she would break down and cry out of frustration from the piling bills or lash out at a minor disobedience. She was quick to punish and often held grudges for weeks, leaving my sister and I to tiptoe around her. Up to then, her universal will and dominion of her home had gotten us through most of my young adulthood and my sister's adolescence. But these virtues failed at keeping our uneasy cohesiveness from collapsing. It continued to be him and us, although now "us" also included his children. If asked, my stepfather would probably say we turned his children against him during a couple of years of continuous struggles. What was he to do? Fight or flee? He decided to stop fighting. He left the house and his children. He went to live with his sister and her family upstate.

As the oldest, in college, and assumed to be the most know-ledgeable about all things American (from the VCR to the tax system), I became the partial decision-maker in the house. Should the little one enroll in an after-school program? What curfew should my adolescent sister have? When should my brother's friends be allowed over? My new status brought on more responsibility than I was ready for, but there was a need to make everything work. My sister, Mom and I together became a type of mom/dad/sister Transformer, like the 1980s animated series I learned English watching. We were interchangeable parts of a working whole. In many ways my sister understood and accepted her new roles with more tact and willingness than I did. She took jobs during high school to help with expenses; she sacrificed going away to college for her first year, while I focused solely on getting out of the house and finishing college—and finally becoming my own person.

My mother and sister taught me my next lesson in feminism: Your life as a woman is an extension of the lives of your family members. They sacrificed for me, knowing that my success would help our whole family. They nursed me through college, study-abroad ventures and summer internships. For my mother there was the expectation that if she sent me off to college, I would come back home. I would become a professional, get a well-paying job, move back to the house and be the other breadwinner. That's how the immigrant dream played out in her mind.

After college I returned home ready to launch my independence. During my absence my stepdad had moved back, and the family was living under a new, tacit but unsteady cohesiveness. I knew enough not to meddle. Caught up in the monumentality of adulthood, I saw their marriage for what it was. He had rescued her—a young widow with two young daughters—in exchange for a dutiful wife who would give him the children he had always wanted but had not been prepared to raise. Neither of them had anticipated the power immigration would exert over their lives. Their wedding vows had not included fine-print stipulating what to do about the demands of their immigrant life in New York. I doubt that my mother knew she was teaching me to be a feminist along the way, as she struggled to make sense of her marriage and her family.

That was my most recent lesson: Feminism is comprised of values that are important to you as a woman, not ideals arrived at by forced consensus to which you should adjust your own life. To me, that is the core failure of (North) American feminism—the alienation of women like my mother who don't have the leisure to fantasize about a life free of the influence of men, who have the demands of an extended family and the rigors of defining themselves in a place between two real and often contradictory worlds.

As I entertain adult notions of parenthood and let my imagination float into a distant future—children, husband, who knows?—I know my role as mother/wife/companion will depend on how I choose to define myself in the moving now that will be my present. I also know that our own roles and family itself shift and change depending on many factors. Culture, class, gender, tradition, womanhood, immigrant life, growing up Dominicana in Nueva York—they will all influence and shape my life as I go.

What Happens When Your Hood Is the Last Stop on the White Flight Express?

Taigi Smith

When I think of home, I envision a place where memories and wounds run deep like murky rivers, a place where dreams sing like unfinished songs, the soil where we lay our roots and our heads. San Francisco's Mission District was the place I called home, a close-knit community where poor and working-class folks lived side by side while struggling to obtain a piece of Americana. After two years of living in New York City, I am ready to return home. It is almost Thanksgiving and between trips on the D train and fifteen-hour work days, I barely feel the autumn leaves beneath my feet in Brooklyn. My body shivers from the November chill, while my nose, red from wind-burn, runs uncontrollably. I find myself wishing for the comforts of home and smile: In a few days I will be in San Francisco, sitting at my mother's table, full of sweet potatoes, pasta and, if I'm lucky, turkey. At forty-five years old, my mother is still unconventional and has yet to cook a traditional Thanksgiving dinner. She faithfully replaces the turkey with a simpler bird: Cornish hen.

Will my mother, who like me, spent several years in New York, recognize that at twenty-four years old, I have found myself on the brink of insanity, unsure of where the next year, let alone my entire life, will lead me? Will she be able to see that working at a TV station has made me aggressive, competitive and edgy, or will she be deceived by my nice clothes, make-believe smile and pleasant demeanor? I am heading home, to the streets of the Mission, in search of my comfort zone, Shotwell Street, where the memories are good and the streets familiar.

In the summer of 1980, I was a tall, skinny, eight-year-old, with big feet and wild braids. My friends and I gathered at our usual spot on Twentieth and Shotwell to amuse ourselves. There wasn't much to do during the long days of summer. We were the children of bus drivers, housekeepers, migrant workers, the unemployed and the mentally ill. Most of our mothers were raising us alone and struggled, like single moms do, to provide us with the basics. The mothers of the Mission worked long days to afford simple things for us, like Top Ramen, notebooks for school and shoes that fit. They weren't afraid to scream our names from their windows or yell at us in public.

We lived together on this block surrounded by automotive shops and single-family homes in the heart of the Mission, America's Latino pit stop for high hopes and big dreams. Some families had come seeking refuge from the bloody wars that had ravaged El Salvador and Nicaragua during the 1980s, while others had immigrated toward *el Norte* to escape the desperation of Mexico's barrios. My mother, then a twenty-four-year-old single-parent, found the Mission through a friend, and although she'd never admit it, Moms was a hippie seeking solace from the craziness of the Haight-Ashbury, the legendary stomping ground of the Grateful Dead and reefer-toking flower children. She acted like a womanist even then and didn't know it. I consider her a womanist because of her strength. She has run more than twenty-five marathons in her lifetime, and she still logs about fifty miles a week. She raised me with a loud voice and a burning passion, as if her life depended on my failure or success. She raised me on her own, without welfare and with an intensity that I've never been able to replicate. She was gutsy enough to hitch a ride across country to forge a better life for herself and me, and for this, she remains my hero.

Moms convinced the owner of our building to rent her a one-bedroom apartment for less than $200 dollars a month. We were one of a handful of black families in the Mission then, so it was almost impossible not to notice us. I learned how to make quesadillas on an open flame at my friend Marcy's house while her mother spoke to me in Spanish. Most mornings, I would wake up to the sounds of Mexican ballads blasting soothingly from the building next door. Even today, I can still hear the sounds of wailing mariachis playing guitar and singing songs *de amor.* I always knew I was different than many of my Mexican friends and neighbors; we spoke different languages and ate different foods. But I never felt out of place in the Mission. As children of the Mission, we were raised to love and accept each other. Even today, as adults, we remain friends.

The Mission of the 1980s was a place filled with music and dance. On the far corner of Twentieth and Shotwell was an old garage that had been transformed into a dance studio. For months you could hear the sounds of Brazilian drums resonating from the walls of a once vacant garage. At night women and men would emerge from the building salty with sweat, glistening and seemingly exhausted. You could hear them chattering incessantly, in Spanish and English about Carnaval, the Mission's answer to the legendary Rio de Janeiro annual event. For months dancers packed the studios that laced the Mission to practice for the twenty-four-hour festival of samba, salsa and steel drumming.

During Carnaval the neighborhood women transformed themselves with fifty-foot feathered headpieces and barely-there thong bikinis to parade down Mission Street twisting, gyrating, shimmying and singing. A woman could take off her bikini top and flaunt her breasts without embarrassment or inhibition during this raw celebration of femininity and womanhood. It was not until I, at twelve, put on my own bikini and feathers and danced with the Brazilian troupe Batucaje' that I truly felt the electricity generated when women of color come together to celebrate themselves as beautiful, cultural and creative beings. Here we could dance, sing, sweat and flaunt ourselves and our bodies like no other time. This was Carnaval.

I also remember the rallies on Twenty-Fourth and Mission during the eighties and the sounds of political activists demanding freedom, shouting, "No More, No More, U.S. out of El Salvador!" They were white, Latino, young and old—most of all, they were loud and unrelenting. Many were women, unafraid of showing civil disobedience and unfazed by the threat of arrest. Who would have thought that almost twenty years later, these same women would be fighting against land developers to keep the neighborhood they called home?

. . .

I finally made it home for Thanksgiving, but something strange had happened to the Mission. I had only been away for two years, but it had been transformed into a place I found hard to navigate or recognize. Many of my childhood friends had already disappeared, and some Latino families I grew up with were nowhere to be found. The brown faces had diminished, and I was trapped in an unfamiliar scene filled with Caucasoids and trendy bars. It was gentrification.

Gentrification: The displacement of poor women and people of color. The raising of rents and the eradification of single, poor and working-class women from neighborhoods once considered unsavory by people who didn't live there. The demolition of housing projects. A money-driven process in which landowners and developers push people (in this case, many of them single mothers) out of their homes without thinking about where they will go. Gentrification is a premeditated process in which an imaginary bleach is poured on a community and the only remaining color left in that community is white . . . only the strongest coloreds survived.

The word on the street was that the neighborhood was being taken over by white people—yuppies and new media professionals who would pay exorbitant rents to reside in what the *Utne Reader* had called "One of the Trendiest Places to Live in America"—and there was nothing people of color could do. Some were going to housing court in hopes of saving lost leases, but most attempts to fight greedy landlords were unsuccessful. The neighborhood folks, many of whom had protested in the 1980s against the contras in Nicaragua, were now feeling helpless. They were tired of fighting or simply unsure of how to protect themselves. They had seen their neighbors wage unsuccessful battles against landlords, and they were just hoping they wouldn't be next. The streets were now lined with Land Rovers and BMW's, and once seedy neighborhood bars now employed bouncers and served $10 raspberry martinis. Abandoned warehouses had not been converted into affordable housing but instead into fancy lofts going for $300,000 to $1 million. The Army Street projects had been demolished, leaving hundreds of people, many of them women with children, displaced and homeless. The message was clear: It was time for the blacks and the browns to get out—the whites were moving in and that was it.

For poor single mothers, gentrification is a tactic "the system" uses to keep them down; it falls into the same category as "workfare" and "minimum wage." Gentrification is a woman's issue, an economic issue and, most of all, a race issue. At my roots I am a womanist, as I believe in economic and social equality for all women. When I watch what has happened to my old neighborhood, I get angry because Gentrification like this is a personal attack on any woman of color who is poor, working class and trying to find an apartment in a real estate market that doesn't give a damn about single mothers, grand-mommas raising crack babies or women who speak English as a second language.

The shameful thing is that the yuppies have changed the fabric of a neighborhood that was by all accounts an affordable, great place to live. The Mission wasn't one of those neighborhoods destroyed by the

1980s crack epidemic. It wasn't a destitute community with burned-out buildings and shuttered-up storefronts, where gunshots rang out in the night. It was a cultural mecca where working-class people of color took pride in the community. The colorful murals that decorated the walls of local buildings were a testament to the rich culture of local Latino artistry, the numerous thriving *marquetas* and restaurants were living proof of a small yet growing business district. We had nightclubs, supermarkets, auto body shops, meat markets, florists, delis and clothing stores owned and operated by first- and second-generation Mexican Americans. For many of the immigrants, the Mission was a break from the poverty that had surrounded them in Mexico and El Salvador. Although the work days were long and hard, most of my neighbors were grateful for the job opportunities that came their way. At least in the United States, there was a way to support one's family.

Many of us existed in a microcosm where working for white people as cooks, housekeepers and migrant workers was a way of life. Many years later I realized this type of work was actually part of a larger system in which poor people (many of them women) did the low-level, low-paid work that no one else wanted to do. As a result of this system, most of us remained poor. Today I see that we were probably making the best out of a difficult situation. Even now, we (me and the women I grew up with) insist that we would purchase homes and raise our children in the Mission if we had the financial means—our memories of the community are that good.

The infiltration of our neighborhood by the wealthy and the

privileged is heartbreaking. To act as if our neighborhood is something that they needed to "clean up" or "take back" is insulting. It is as if our new neighbors deny that our businesses, familial relationships and community ever really existed in the first place. Many of the white people who have moved into the Mission see us in stereotypical terms—as immigrants, as people with thick accents and brown skin, as people who play loud music and collect welfare. In essence, they ignore who we really are. Our new neighbors can't see that our homes are impeccably clean and that many of the Latino families here are headed by both a mother *and* a father. And although we barely scrape by at times, we go to work and pay our bills. They want to believe we are all on welfare, destined to become single mothers and crack addicts. The truth is, however, that most of us have proven them wrong. We learned well on Shotwell Street from our single mothers and other women: Teena is now a sheriff, Maricela a police officer, Sonia a journalist at the *San Francisco Chronicle* and I am a writer and a producer. None of us grew up to be statistics.

I started calling myself a womanist while attending Mills College in Oakland, California. Mills, a liberal arts women's college, catered to families who could pay $22,000 a year. I was able to afford it thanks to a tremendous financial aid package. Many of the white women at Mills who called themselves feminists didn't understand my experiences as a black woman. In women's studies classes, for example, the individual histories and struggles of black women were often ignored.

It was in an African-American women's studies class that I learned the word "womanist." Dr. Dorothy Tsuruta was at the time the most progressive (and only!) full-time African-American professor at the Mills. She was regularly criticized because many of the white women who attended her classes felt alienated. They became upset and felt excluded when Dorothy told them that the term womanism, as defined by Alice Walker, was meant specifically for women of color. Dorothy was eventually fired from Mills for shaking up a system that really wasn't in the business of liberating young, black minds.

For the black girls at Mills, Dorothy was like manna for our culturally starved souls. She spoke to us in ways we understood, and most important, she recognized it was tortuous for us to attend a college where we were so widely misunderstood. I remember when a white female English professor who called herself a feminist declared that slaves had a special bond with their masters that many of us couldn't understand. I was the only African American in the class, and I was stunned by this statement. I declared myself a womanist when I realized that white women's feminism really didn't speak to my needs as the daughter of a black, single, domestic worker. I felt that, historically, white women were working hard to liberate themselves from housework and childcare, while women of color got stuck cleaning their kitchens and raising their babies. When I realized that feminism largely liberated white women at the economic and social expense of women of color, I knew I was fundamentally unable to call myself a feminist.

I really don't need another white feminist to tell me that poverty, teen pregnancy, infant mortality, AIDS, unemployment and gentrification are class issues. I was once on the board of a progressive, young women's reproductive rights organization, and the other board members were very wealthy white women who viewed many of the problems of women of color as "class issues." We would spend hours talking about how white and black women had a hard time getting along because of our class differences. As a black woman, however, my problems have always been directly connected to race; for me, class is secondary. Most white feminists I've encountered seem to think class is the source of all problems. While the roots of gentrification have as much to do with class as with race, it is hard to ignore that most of the people being driven out of neighborhoods are not poor whites in Appalachia; rather, they are the poor blacks and browns in the inner city melting pots. Some would argue that gentrification only occurs in major cities, but as a news producer, I've traveled around the country. I can say firsthand that gentrification is kicking people of color out of communities everywhere. From Saint Paul, Minnesota, to the outskirts of Louisiana, to the South Side of Chicago, to the flatlands of East Oakland, we're being evicted from our communities.

When I returned home to the Mission, I attended the open house of a new loft building opening up on Shotwell Street. I was the only black person there. Because I've had access to higher education, I am now able to support myself and live a middle-class lifestyle, but even if I had the money to live in the Mission, I wonder how many landlords wouldn't rent to me as a young, single, black woman. The other people who had come to the opening were white, and they looked at me as if I didn't belong there. I felt as if they wouldn't want me as a neighbor even if I had the money to live among them. While I represented everything they wanted to get away from, it was ironic that they were trying to move into a neighborhood that was historically black and brown.

I've tried hard to intellectualize gentrification, but the harder I try, the more complicated it becomes. When I was looking for an apartment in Park Slope, Brooklyn, I was making enough to rent a studio off Seventh Avenue, yet all of the real estate agents I spoke with blatantly refused to show me apartments in the pristine, lily-white neighborhood. They kept taking me to Prospect Heights and Fort Greene, which at the time were mostly black neighborhoods. Gentrification is more about the color of my skin than the money in my pocket.

Although my building in San Francisco had been spared from the claws of wealthy land bandits, it was a cultural war zone, spurred on by economic and racial disparities. In fact, the entire community had become a war zone, where guerrilla tactics were the weapons of choice. Someone had posted signs all over the neighborhood urging people to deface the live/work lofts, scrape up the fancy, high-priced vehicles that now lined their streets and flatten yuppie tires. This vigilante had become a sort of folk hero, and the signs were part of an underground movement called the Urban Yuppie Eradication Project. The posters urged fellow Missionites to burn down the million-dollar lofts and make life hell for the new pioneers. In their own defense the yuppies held a rally, ironically, on the corner of Twenty-Fourth and Mission—the home of the infamous political protests of the 1980s. Although the local media came out for the event, only a few yuppies were brave enough to show up.

My mother had formed a sort of guerrilla coalition in her building. Along with other people of color, she had vowed to fill vacant apartments with friends and family when they heard that their new neighbors wanted to rent to filmmakers, writers and other artist types. The new renters were communicating via e-mail with the building manager to secure any vacancies, and although the plan almost worked, they failed to fully homogenize the building. It was these people who viewed me with suspicion when I returned to Shotwell Street. Their icy glares easily translated into "What are *you* doing here?" They were suspicious of the black girl "loitering" around the building. It really didn't matter that I had spent almost twenty years of my life there. They didn't care that I was a published writer, a successful TV producer or a graduate of Mills College. To them I was another black woman they were trying to get out of the neighborhood. I needed so badly to say, "This is my neighborhood. I grew up here," but my anger silenced me.

More than the air of wealth that now permeates the neighborhood, it is the attitude of superiority that angers me. It is the look of hate that aggravates me, the icy glare that says, "We are willing to take over this neighborhood at all costs." It leaves me wondering about the future of my friends and neighbors. I realize that women of color may never have a place to truly call our own. At times I think about returning home to the old neighborhood to organize my former neighbors, but doing that would mean giving up the life I've worked so hard to create in New York.

As my mother's only child, it is my responsibility to make sure she will always have a place to live, whether that be in San Francisco or elsewhere. It angers me that someone's greed could take away the apartment she has called home for almost thirty years. Countless women are grappling with having their rented apartments put on the auction block without regard for where they will go next. And the chances are that the person who buys that building/apartment/ duplex will probably be a white person with more power and a lot more money. What is to become of all the other mothers and grand- mothers in the Mission whose children have neither the income nor the knowledge to help?

I pay more than a thousand dollars a month to live in a Brooklyn neighborhood where the amenities include a round-the-clock liquor store, a marijuana delivery service, illegal all-night gambling and numerous buildings for Section 8 families and people on welfare. My building is earmarked for upwardly mobile professionals and white people. Throughout the neighborhood, signs of "revitalization" are cropping up. White kids walk smugly down the street, sometimes riding rickety bikes or skateboards. Internet businesses are opening up alongside yoga studios, and I have a fully renovated apartment with superfast T-1 Internet access. I am on the cusp of the revitalization, and although I have an amazing apartment in the midst of the hood,

I am more than conscious of the fact that the low-income women around me may not be here for long.

I am sure they look at me and the other professionals moving in and wonder "What are they doing here?" Do my low-income neighbors realize that the new buildings being put up like wildfire are not for people like them but for people like me, who can afford to pay inflated rents for renovated apartments in the hood? I am keenly aware of exactly what is happening, and I realize that neighborhoods don't have to be financially rich to be culturally vibrant, and that white people moving into poor neighborhoods do little good for the people that already live there. When white people move into black neighborhoods, the police presence increases, cafés pop up and neighborhood bodegas start ordering the *Wall Street Journal* and the *New York Times*. You rarely see low-income housing built alongside million-dollar lofts or social service centers built next to yoga studios. When I think about this, I am caught somewhere in the middle, because although I have the money to live in a neighborhood that is being gentrified, I still hear the words my black real estate agent whispered to me: "Just think of this as your own little castle in the hood."

I don't want them to take over my San Francisco neighborhood, but five thousand miles away, in another state and another community, I "am on the front lines of gentrification," as a neighbor so politely put it. When I come home at night and see the crackheads loitering in front of the building next door, I realize I may have switched sides in this fight. When I dodge cracked glass and litter when walking my dog, I realize that this neighborhood really could use a facelift and that the yoga center that just opened up on the corner is a welcome change from the abandoned building it used to be.

Parts of my Brooklyn neighborhood are symbolic of what the media and sociologists say is wrong with "the inner city." I live on a block where the police don't arrest drug dealers who peddle crack in broad daylight, where young black men drive around in huge SUVs but barely speak grammatically correct English, where I see the same brothas every day standing on the street corners, doing absolutely nothing. They don't hustle or harass me but instead politely say "hello," as if they've accepted me. I feel strained by my situation. While I am intimately aware of what is happening to my new neighborhood, I feel powerless. I've been in Brooklyn long enough to know that although it is not the most savory neighborhood, it is a community where people feel connected, where the old folks know each other, where neighbors still chat. But sometimes I feel like telling the young men on the corner, " Get the hell off the street! Don't you see that life is passing you by? Don't you see this is what *they* expect *you* to do? Don't you see they're moving *in* and in a few years, you're gonna have to get *out?*"

In my neighborhood men shoot each other, the sidewalks are cracked and many of the buildings are abandoned, and I've witnessed two drug raids from my bedroom window. When I come home at night, I put on my sweatpants and walk my tiny dog on littered sidewalks, past tomboys in goosedown coats doing each other's hair on stoops of aging brownstones. When I see these girls, I remember my own childhood and think that they deserve more than this. They deserve a neighborhood that is clean and safe and provides some hope, a place where they can learn that some dreams do come true and that Prince Charming doesn't drive an Expedition and sell weed to his friends.

Walking the streets, I realize my neighbors and I are alike in many ways. We like the same foods, the same music, and most important, we are a group of African-American people living together in a neighborhood that is on the verge of change. But in the end we are also very different. If the rents go up, I will have options and they may not. They may have to move and I will get to stay. Although we look the same, we are different. We are connected by race but remain separated by a slip of paper called a college degree. Our block, our hood, our neighborhood has become the next stop on the White Flight Express.

Fast forward. It is 1998. I sip chocolate martinis in what was once an immigrant's watering hole. Ironically, the bar is now called Sacrifice. A jukebox replaces the mariachis and top-shelf liquor takes the place of Night Train. An old flame, Ron is trying to convince me to marry him. I'm thinking I haven't seen this guy in years, but I thank him for his compliment. And then I see a short man, a few inches over five feet and wearing dirty gray pants and a button-down shirt. His eyes are glazed over and he is barely able to stand. He is singing a song and I recognize the accent, from Juarez or Tijuana. He mumbles something profane in Spanish and appears to be confused by the sea of white faces (and me!).

He searches the room for his *compadres*, and it becomes evident that this place he had once known so well is now as foreign as it is to me. He blinks his eyes a few times and tries to shake himself from this drunken haze but soon realizes that what he is seeing is no illusion. He stares at the blond woman with the multiple tattoos and pierced lip and wonders where his friends might be. He has never seen white people in this bar and as he looks at her, I stare at him and relate to his longing for days gone by. And then he turns from her and looks at me as if to say "What are you, *una negrita,* doing here?"

We lock eyes and I allow him to see my shame while I share his sadness. I too am lost in a place I knew so well. Like the old man looking for a drink, I am saddened, disillusioned and disgusted by the changes. Like him, I also feel powerless. He glances around a bit more, struggles to his feet, curses a few words in *Español,* throws down his tequila, closes his eyes and stumbles out of the door.

HIV and Me
The Chicana Version

Stella Luna

When I was a little girl, I dreamed of being an actress. I enjoyed making up silly dances and putting on shows for my friends and family. Being the youngest of five children and arriving six years after my sister, I had the privilege of being the center of attention throughout my childhood. Our family lived in a suburb of Los Angeles that was generally classified as Mexican middle class. My father was a second-generation Mexican American who believed in strong family values and a religious foundation. As in many Mexican-American households, our family always came first. My mother wasn't allowed to work because my father believed her place was in the home taking care of our family. I never saw my mom question this arrangement, but I noticed actions that discreetly displayed her desire. For example, my sister and I weren't allowed to do any of the household chores or cooking. She would say, "One day you are going to be forced to do this stuff to keep your husband happy, so I'm not going to force you to do it now." I happily obliged, but in the back of my mind, I began to visualize marriage as the beginning of a lifelong service to others.

As I grew into my teens, it became quite apparent that dating was a privilege and not a right. Under the watchful eyes of my father and my three brothers, I was given strict rules to obey. I didn't mind these rules, but what bothered me was my mother's constant fear of my getting pregnant. I found this confusing because my parents never had a sex talk with me and it hurt to think they had such little trust in me. Years later, my mom would brag to her friends how her girls "didn't have to get married because they were pregnant." She considered this a personal achievement.

After high-school graduation I began working full-time as a secretary, and I loved having my own paycheck. I began dating one of my coworkers, an Anglo man, and my family was furious. Brett wasn't like the *machista* guys I had grown up with. Instead, he encouraged me to explore my own ideas and become more independent. My dad disliked him and didn't appreciate that "this white guy" was placing all kinds of crazy ideas in my head. My dad's anger heightened when I decided to start spending the weekends over at Brett's house. My mom accused me of "ruining myself." I grew tired of the bad blood between my boyfriend and my family, so Brett and I decided to get married. Deep down inside, I honestly knew I wasn't ready to get married, but I just didn't want to see my family hurt and upset anymore. My father was happy with our decision, and my mother insisted that I could still be married in a white dress. I angrily thought to myself, "Why wouldn't I be married in white?"

Soon after we were married, Brett was offered an engineering position in Arizona and we moved. I really didn't want to leave my family, but my dad convinced me that I had to support my husband's career. Soon after our arrival in Arizona, I became very homesick and felt like we had made a terrible mistake. I discovered that Brett and I were very different people, and I couldn't imagine spending the rest of my life with him. I also found that I couldn't be an adequate partner to him, because I was still figuring out who I wanted to be. Brett was also unhappy and accused me of being a "daddy's girl" who still needed to grow up. Sadly, I had to agree with him.

We got a divorce a year later. My family was devastated and insisted I immediately move back home. But I had just started a job that I really enjoyed, and a friend had asked if I wanted to room with her. I had never lived on my own before, and I was anxious to see if I could succeed without my family's assistance. I still wasn't sure what I wanted to do with my life, but I knew I had to find out on my own. I wanted to prove to my family that I wasn't a helpless little girl.

I loved my newfound freedom. I began dating again and became involved in a short-lived relationship. Even though it didn't last, the relationship would come back to haunt me in years to come. I had saved up enough money to move into my own apartment, where I became acquainted with a sweet guy living across the hall from me. Within six months of dating we were married. Despite the fact that Jay was Anglo, my family absolutely adored him. I think it was because he had a gentle spirit and an enormous respect for our family. My father trusted Jay because he was a hard worker and held strong values. I felt like I had met my soul mate.

Unlike my first marriage, my life with Jay was so easy and non-confrontational. I remember looking forward to coming home each night and just being together. The early years of our marriage were an incredibly happy time in our lives. Two years later in 1993 I discovered that I was pregnant, and we were overjoyed when the doctor confirmed through an ultrasound that the baby was firmly nestled in my tummy. He informed us that as a routine procedure, he asked his patients to have blood tests performed to check for anemia, hepatitis, diabetes and HIV. My husband asked why I needed to be tested for HIV, and the doctor told us that it was a test he offered all of his patients. It seemed unnecessary but I agreed to the blood work. We left the appointment and didn't think anymore about it—until two weeks later, when I received a phone call that would change my life forever.

I was one month pregnant when the call came from my doctor. One of my tests had come back with unexpected results. He asked if I had ever been a drug user. Offended, I said no. He asked if I had ever had sex with someone I presumed to be bisexual. Again, I answered no. I began to feel dizzy. The doctor said that although he was confused with the results, I had tested positive for HIV. Just then, Jay walked through the door and I handed him the phone and burst into tears. Through my crying I could hear Jay shouting to the doctor that there must be some kind of mistake. I glanced up to look at him and he had tears streaming down his face. He was asked to come into the office the next day so that they could run an HIV test on him. The doctor was bringing in a specialist to discuss our options.

Jay grabbed my hands and told me that he was the one who was probably infected first. I wasn't sure how to react. I called a couple of our gay friends and told them about the test results. We hoped that maybe they would be able to bring some insight into this whole nightmare. We knew that they had lost a number of friends to this disease, and we felt safe sharing our sad news with them. Our friends came over and spent the evening trying to calm us down. They hugged us as we cried and tried to tell us that it was going to be all right. I would have never made it through that night without them. That evening, we all formed a special bond that has lasted more than eight years.

At the doctor's office the next day the specialist told us that the life span of someone with AIDS was five to ten years. He said if our baby was born infected, his or her chances for survival were close to none. He encouraged us to abort the baby. We went home that night and thought long and hard about our future and our unborn child. We came to the conclusion that even if I died from AIDS, we still had to give the baby a chance at being born HIV negative and living a full life. We believed our baby was created out of love and it wasn't right to destroy it.

A week later Jay's test results came back from the lab negative. My mind went into a tailspin. I instantly recalled the person I had briefly dated between my two marriages, and I assumed he had to be the one who had infected me. I called him and told him, but I never heard from him again. Although it narrowed down only to my relationship with him, he never confirmed it. It amazed me how the disease had been spread around.

My pregnancy progressed normally, except for the blood tests that I was required to take to ensure that my immune system was still strong. The treatment for HIV positive pregnant women in the early 1990s was not very progressive. Clinical trials were still being conducted on the dosing of Azidothymidine (AZT) to pregnant women to lessen the chances of their child being born with the disease. Because this method was still considered experimental, I wasn't offered any type of drug treatment. Instead, I relied only on herbs and vitamins to keep up my immune system and minimize my stress levels.

Jay tried to be supportive, but I noticed that he was slowly distancing himself from the situation. We had decided not to tell anyone about the HIV. The only people who knew were our gay friends, my sister and Jay's best friend at work. This lack of disclosure made it very difficult for me to cope with my feelings. It also began to make me feel resentful toward Jay. I began to think that he was ashamed of me. I recalled my feelings when my parents got upset that I had decided to sleep with my first husband before marriage. Maybe everyone did have a right to be ashamed of me. I had hurt the people I loved because of my intimate decisions. I wondered, Did I actually have the right to bring another human being into this world when my moral behavior had brought on such a horrible disease?

On a cold December morning, my son Alex was born. He seemed to be a very healthy baby. When he was three days old, he was given his first HIV test. The doctor had high hopes, and when the results came back negative, we felt like we were finally out of the woods. I returned to work and we sought out a caregiver for our son. When Alex was six months old, he was given another HIV test to confirm his negative status. We anxiously awaited the results. Sitting at my desk at work, I saw Jay walk in with a stricken look on his face. I immediately told my boss that I had to leave and I followed Jay out the door. We walked hand in hand and he began to weep. Alex's pediatrician had called: our son's test had come back positive.

The pediatrician believed that the disease hadn't manifested itself in Alex's system back when the first test was taken. He had given Jay the name of a pediatric infectious disease specialist at the children's hospital. The piece of paper with the specialist's phone number was crumbled in my husband's hand. We held each other and cried and talked about moving to Seattle. We had always dreamed of living in the Northwest, and we agreed that if we lost Alex to this disease, we would just run away to a place where we wouldn't feel so much pain.

That night we held onto Alex so tightly. I felt like God was yanking him away from us. We couldn't believe that this beautiful baby was going to die. We didn't know how we were going to survive through this nightmare. The following day, we told Alex's caregiver about his condition. We apologized for not telling her before, but we honestly didn't think that it was going to be an issue. We told her that we still wanted her to take care of our son, but after careful consideration, she told us that it would be impossible for her to subject her other parents to the risk. Our hearts were broken, but we really tried hard to understand.

The next day I went into work and put in my two weeks' notice. I told my boss the whole story and although he was shocked, he was very understanding. That night, he called to tell me that his wife had offered to take care of Alex, and it didn't bother her that he was HIV infected. I broke down in tears at his kindness. I thanked him but explained that maybe it was time for me to stay home and spend as much time with my baby as possible. In reality, I thought that it was time for my son and I to stay home and prepare to die.

We took Alex to his first appointment. We were scared and didn't know what to expect, but the doctors were wonderful. They told us there was some new medication being tested for HIV treatment and that they could possibly get Alex on a clinical trial. A few months later he was given AZT and two other antiviral drugs. I poured the liquid directly in his baby formula and tried to get over the ugly feeling I had about giving my son an experimental medicine.

Sitting at home with my son and our diagnosis, I spent a lot of time getting upset about our situation. I even ventured out to an HIV support meeting, but I left the meeting feeling isolated because I was the only female there. I was beginning to feel like I was the only woman in the world with HIV. I really began to wonder what God had against me. One day I spotted an article in the newspaper proclaiming that "the new face of HIV" was a woman who had been diagnosed with the disease and had given birth to a baby. The article concluded by giving information about a women's support group held in the Phoenix area. I immediately called the agency to find out the details and then anxiously waited for the day to arrive.

I was so nervous when I walked into that meeting, but the women immediately put me at ease. I listened to the women's stories and was amazed at the courage they had toward combating HIV. I was also surprised at the diversity of the women. This confirmed my understanding that HIV could infect anyone: All you have to be is human. I became friends with these women. Some had overcome obstacles such as IV drug use, but there were also college students and housewives—women who didn't understand how this had ever happened to them. I began to realize that I wasn't alone in combating the disease. It was such a comfort to know that I had people to talk to who would understand my feelings and not judge me. It is incredible to realize women's strength during times of struggle. I experienced this strength firsthand as I watched the group come together as sisters and empower themselves to fight for their lives and their dignity.

Later, we would use this empowerment as the foundation to advocate on our behalf in the HIV/AIDS community. In the midst of this local HIV women's movement, renowned HIV/AIDS specialist Dr. David Ho announced to the nation that he and his team of researchers had developed a combination therapy that was proving to slow the progression of HIV in clinical trials. My doctor immediately sent me to a clinical trial site and enrolled me in an experimental program. I began taking a combination therapy (a.k.a. drug cocktail) that was similar to the drugs my son Alex had also began being treated with. Although I was riddled with horrible side effects, I continued my routine and anxiously waited to see if it was going to improve my blood count. In the meantime Alex's blood work was showing incredible improvements. In fact, his CD4 blood count, which indicates the immunity in his body, was within normal range.

With such great strides in research, some of the women in my HIV community decided we were now ready to stand up and have our voices heard regarding the HIV issues that affected the women and children in our community. We laid down the criteria for our mission and presented it to a leading HIV/AIDS agency in town. We wanted to convince the government and nonprofit contributors that there was a lack of funding for services geared toward women and children, such as childcare, transportation and effective treatment programs that specifically focused on the medical and psychological welfare of our families.

The agency believed in our mission and agreed to take us under their umbrella. The HIV Women's Task Force was born. Besides providing our group with a place to hold our meetings, the agency also gave us opportunities to go into the community and talk about our experiences living with HIV. I was honored to be elected to serve on the agency's executive board of directors. In that capacity I spoke to forums across our area about the changing face of HIV/AIDS. Public speaking was important to the community, but it also served as a healing method for all my years of silence. It empowered my spirit and helped me overcome my fear of rejection and shame.

While these wonderful things were happening in the community, my home life had turned into a disaster. Jay had always been a private person, and I felt like he resented my public speaking engagements.

Despite the distance growing between us, I continued my community service work. A number of my engagements took me to the state university and the local community college. I listened to students and encouraged them to practice safe sex and be tested regularly. At about this time I also began to have a strong desire to return to school. In one of my engagements I expressed a wish to someday pursue an education. After my speech a man came up to me and handed me his business card. He told me to give him a call and he would help me pursue my dream. I looked at the card and realized that he was a financial aid officer from the state university.

Jay, however, seemed reluctant to support my idea. He felt we were surviving a major event in our lives, and now it was time to sit back and have a normal lifestyle. Life was crazy enough with my community activism. I was determined not to let his position get me down. I made an appointment with the financial aid officer and we began the process of applying for financial aid for college. A few weeks later I received my acceptance letter from the university.

Jay and I went into marriage counseling, but despite our efforts, we decided to separate three months into my first semester of college. I felt like my world had fallen apart, but I also understood that perhaps we had been through too many trials to ever completely heal our relationship. I really wished that we were able to move past the sad times in our lives and just be happy again. It was hard to imagine what life would be like without the man who I still so desperately loved. Jay, Alex and I were supposed to be a family. This isn't how my life was supposed to turn out, but I couldn't be angry with Jay for blaming me for this whole mess. I made a vow that I wouldn't cause him any more pain. I was determined to keep me and Alex healthy and to try to be the best mother I could.

The following month, Alex and I moved into our own apartment and began an adventure that would prove to be an incredible growing experience. I enrolled Alex in preschool and began working part time as a waitress to help make ends meet. Jay and I decided on joint custody, and he agreed to keep Alex on the weekends so that I could work and still have time to study (and some spare time to sleep!). I was thankful for this arrangement.

When I began my first year, I had personal reasons for wanting a college degree. I believed that I was given a second chance and I wanted to make the most of it. I decided on an English major, with the intent of possibly becoming a teacher someday. In my second semester I enrolled in a class on Chicano/a culture to fulfill a university requirement. At the time I didn't realize that this class would change my way of thinking forever. We explored many aspects of Chicano/a culture and analyzed the reasoning behind many of our traditions. I was introduced to authors like Gloria Anzaldúa and Cherríe Moraga, who broke the silence on Chicana feminism and made a statement about female oppression and colonization. It was incredible to read about redefining my cultural understanding regarding my own sexual and personal identity.

Since my diagnosis, I had been dealing with shame and a lack of self-worth that I felt could only be redeemed by sacrificing myself for my family, community and even my own child. I thought that if I gave everything I had inside to the people I loved, I would perhaps be able to prove I wasn't a bad person. The truth was that I really wasn't a bad person. And I didn't need to dedicate my life to defining the kind of person that I was. I realized that I was imprisoned not only by a disease but also by a culture that had trained me to be as clean and untouched in soul and body as the Virgen de Guadalupe. Because of my HIV positive status, I was considered useless in a culture that reduced women to their bodies. If I chose to live my life according to this structure, maybe I should just give up and die.

Overcoming the guilt of being HIV infected is quite a challenge for Chicanas. If we disclose our status, it very well may destroy the foundation to which we try hard to adhere. And this would bring shame to our families and communities. We stay silent perhaps because we believe we rightfully deserve to die. I could finally understand why so many *mujeres* just give up. Many HIV-infected Chicanas don't seek medical care because they are too scared and ashamed to come forward. Who was going to tell these women that they didn't have to live this way?

I was.

I guess this is when you could say I became politicized. The following semester, I enrolled in more Chicano/a studies classes, looking at Chicana history and theory and thinking about issues directly related to the HIV/AIDS Mexican-American community. I began to understand the reasons why Mexican Americans weren't participating in the HIV community. My heart broke when I realized many of my sisters were going to die because they just couldn't relate to services that weren't culturally and linguistically suited to their specific needs. I changed my major to Chicano/a studies and anxiously look forward to graduation day, after which I plan to help my community by truly making a difference. It is strange to think about how much I have changed. Before college I believed I was a strong person. Now, five years later, I have a new definition of myself. My New Mestiza is strong-willed, empowered, inspired, beautiful and sexy! It is times like these when I don't see this disease as a detriment. Instead, I accept HIV in my life as a special task that was bestowed upon me to help the HIV community, which is closest to my heart.

I think about my beautiful, healthy child and I remember being told he had no chance for survival. I think back to the prognosis that I had only five to ten years to live, yet today I am healthy, happy and managing a disease that almost handed me a death sentence. It is difficult sometimes to realize that my life didn't exactly turn out the way it was supposed to. But in the long run I believe that it turned out to be something more than I ever could have imagined. I remember being asked at a conference, "If you could be cured of HIV today, but when the disease left your body, it took with it all the strength, unconditional love, compassion, endurance and empowerment that you have acquired since being diagnosed, would you still agree to being cured?"

I thought really long and hard about my answer, and with tears in my eyes I proudly held my head up and replied, "No."

Love Feminism but Where's My Hip Hop?
Shaping a Black Feminist Identity

Gwendolyn D. Pough

The very idea that someone can attribute coming into Black feminist consciousness to the masculine spaces of rap music and hip-hop culture must seem outrageous to some people. When you add the abstract concept of love into the mix, it might become a little bit more astonishing. Even though third-wave Black feminists such as Joan Morgan, Eisa Davis, Tara Roberts, dream hampton and Eisa Nefertari Ulen have begun to make a case for a Black feminist identity and agenda tied to hip-hop culture, the linking of hip hop and feminism is still a bit much for some to bear.[1] And although Black feminist diva bell hooks has started the much-needed dialogue on love, feminism and the revolutionary potential such a combination would grant, there are not a whole lot of feminists openly checking for the L-word. Given the history of oppression women have suffered at the hands of patriarchs who no doubt claimed to love them, it is not hard to imagine why love would be thought of as suspect. But, nevertheless, I feel the need to explore the connections between love, hip hop and my coming to voice as a third-wave Black feminist.

My development as a Black woman and a Black feminist is deeply tied to my love of hip hop. LL Cool J's soulful rap ballad "I Need Love" (1987) was the first rap love song I heard, and it would not be the last. Rap and rap artists' never-ending quest to "keep it real" is not limited to real-life struggles on American streets. Some rappers show an interesting dedication to exploring aspects of love and the struggles of building and maintaining intimate relationships between Black men and women. Although this reeks of heterosexism—as do many rap love songs—it also points to the very real nature of the relationship between Black men and women and most men and women of color. When you call someone your sister or brother, or comrade in the struggle against racism, a bond is created. In that bond there is love. Rap music therefore offers space for public dialogues about love, romance and struggle in a variety of combinations.

This kind of public dialogue is found in the answer/dis raps of the 1980s, which gave rise to women rap stars Roxanne Shanté and Salt-N-Pepa. These women paved the way for other women rappers by recording very successful songs, which were responses to the hit records of the men who were their contemporaries. Shanté gave the woman pursued in UTFO's "Roxanne, Roxanne" a voice and ultimately let it be known that women would no longer suffer insults and degradation in silence. Salt-N-Pepa's "The Show Stoppa (Is Stupid Fresh)" was a direct refutation to Doug E. Fresh and Slick Rick's "The Show"—a song in which women are portrayed as objects of conquest.

As a Black woman coming of age during the hip-hop era, I saw the answers that Shanté and Salt-N-Pepa put to wax as more than just temporary jams to get the body moving. They let me know I could have a voice as well. They offered the strong public presence of Black womanhood that I had seen in my mother and her friends but had not witnessed in my generation in such a public forum. Before I ever read bell hooks's *Talking Back: Thinking Feminist, Thinking Black*, I heard Shanté and Salt-N-Pepa rapping and securing a strong public voice for women's issues in general and young Black women's issues specifically. Their talking back and speaking out against unwanted advances that could easily be read as sexual harassment gave me a model for dealing with similar issues as I braved inner-city streets. In addition, their talking back changed the way I looked at romance and courtship as well as the voice I could have in those socially scripted spaces. I no longer thought I had to simply smile and keep walking when brothers made catcalls or lewd comments as I walked down the street. I felt perfectly fine and justified in rolling my eyes and telling them how rude they were or that they would never "get the digits" behaving in such a manner. I began to make up rhymes about these street encounters that sought to disrupt the men's behavior by offering a woman's response. One rhyme in particular was a direct reflection on a street corner encounter with a rude guy who also claimed to be an MC. I rapped:

> I was on my way to the jam, you see.
> Saw a fly guy, you know he was sweatin' me.
> Told him my name was MC Gwenny Dee.
> He looked at me, laughed and asked sarcastically,

Gwenny Dee, hmm, can you rhyme?

I said not only can I rhyme, I'm a one of a kind.

He said, How can this be, you're a girl?

And a female can't make it in an MC's world.

I said, please tell me what you're talking about

when you say females can't turn it out,

when you say that the best MCs are the men

and chances for a female are zero to ten

Well, I'm here to say, whether you like it or you don't.

So, fellas listen up, 'cause I'm sure you won't:

Females make the best MCs, you know.

So just step on back cause we run the show.

Your gear and your gold make you look fly,

but you rap wack enough to make me cry.

And that's true, you know why,

'cause I don't lie, as a matter of fact, I'm really too fly.

Got to the party everyone was chillin'.

Looked on the stand saw dude justa illin'

Trying like a dummy to rock hard, with a rhyme he stole

off a Hallmark card.

My own clearly old-school flow and rapping skills aside, this is how I began to use rap to talk back in ways very similar to the women rappers I listened to on the radio. I wrote this rhyme when I was a fifteen-year-old aspiring rapper. The rhymes I wrote and the developing prominence of female MCs on the radio prompted me to look for a

DJ and a crew so that I could start my rap career. With very few women rappers to serve as role models, the success of these answer/dis songs let me know that women could make it in the rap arena. They also inspired the kinds of raps I wrote—raps that were pro-woman and critiqued the inequities of gender that my young mind saw. I am not arguing that I had a strong and carefully theorized critique of gender as a fifteen-year-old B-girl. However, strong and successful women rappers and the space that hip hop provided gave me a chance to develop a critique that I now know to be the beginnings of my current Black feminist consciousness.

Even though I had no idea what feminism was at the time, I had seen strong Black women all my life. My mother was a single parent and she worked hard to make sure that my sisters and I had the things we needed. She did not call herself a feminist. But she left an abusive husband and told any other Black man who could not act right where the door could hit him. Having this strong female presence in my own home not withstanding, there was something particularly inspiring about seeing that presence personified in my own generation. Hip hop gave me that.

Another way that hip hop helped me to develop a feminist consciousness was the exposure it gave me to sexual harassment and the attitude it gave me to deal with it. The thing that stands out very clearly about that time for me was being the only girl in someone's basement as we took turns on the microphone. At different times I warded off advances from fellow male MCs and even the DJ. It seemed like every one of them wanted to at least try and get me to have sex with him. When none of their advances worked, they eventually stopped. DJ Ronnie Ron, however, took offense to my performance of the rap I've included here. He thought the rhyme was aimed at him, because he too had tried to get with me and failed. So he put on an instrumental cut, grabbed the mike and proceeded to freestyle a dis rap just for me. I stopped working with him, and after a few other failed attempts at finding a DJ, I stopped writing rhymes.

As I reflect back on that time, I realize now that there was something about writing rhymes and saying them on the mike—hearing my voice loud, strong and clear—that made me feel strong. After I gave up the dream of becoming a rapper, the acts of writing and performing still give me a surge of strength. The only difference is that now I'm writing feminist critiques of rap and performing them at academic conferences and other venues. I also use rap to teach other young women of color about feminism.

As a woman born in 1970, who was nine years old when the first rap record hit the airwaves (The Sugarhill Gang's "Rapper's Delight"), I grew up on rap music. Reading Tricia Rose's discussion of the evolution of hip-hop culture through the changes in clothing commodified by rappers and hip-hop audiences reminds me of my own evolution: from a teenage B-girl wearing Lee jeans, Adidas sneakers with fat laces, LeTigre shirts, gold chunk jewelry, and a gold tooth to an "Around the Way Girl" college freshman sporting a leather jacket, baggy jeans, sweat hood and Fendi/Gucci/fake Louis Vuitton.[2]

Once I was in college, however, my relationship with hip hop changed when I stopped consuming the female identities put forth by male rappers as the girl of their dreams. As I had once been willing to be LL Cool J's "Around the Way Girl" (1989), I began taking issue with the very notion of Apache's "Gangsta Bitch" (1992). While I still consumed the music, I began to question the lyrics and constructed identities. Although both of these songs sought to give "props" to the girls in the hood, I found myself struggling with the image that Apache put forth. It was then that I realized it wasn't the "bitch" that bothered me. It was the things he applauded that did. Things like the gangsta bitch fighting other women and helping him to sell drugs to other people in the hood that bothered me. These things did not fit in with the feminist identity that I was developing.

Like many of the academics and Black popular critics now writing about rap, I have a love for hip-hop culture and rap music. This love prompts me to critique and explore rap in more meaningful ways. I am no longer the teenaged girl who spent Friday nights listening to Mr. Magic's "Rap Attack" and writing rhymes, Saturdays reading her mama's Harlequin or Silhouette romance novels and Sundays writing rhymes and short stories. While I have grown up on and consumed hip-hop culture and popular romance, I feel it is important to note I am all grown-up.

Although I still listen to rap music and read a romance novel every time I get a chance, Black feminist/womanist theories and politics inform my listening and reading. Whenever I can, I go back to my undergraduate university to work with the youth participating in the summer Pre-College Academy. These high school students are from the North Jersey area, and I see it as a way to give back. I do it to spread feminist consciousness to new up-and-coming feminists. Young women growing up today are not privy to the same kind of pro-woman rap that I listened to via Salt-N-Pepa, Queen Latifah, Yo-Yo, and MC Lyte. Even though I like Lil' Kim and Foxy Brown, I know that younger women of color need the critical tools to unpack some of the messages they get from these artists.

One student during the summer of 2000 was obsessed with fancy cars. She asked me, "Ay, yo, what you pushing, Miss Pough?" After telling the student that I drove a Ford Escort, she kind of frowned, pushed up her noise and said, "Oh, that's cute." This student's fascination with fancy cars and her desire to one day "push" one was not a problem in and of itself. There is nothing wrong with desiring nice things, especially when those things are out of reach and they give one something to work for. The problem occurs when students like this young lady have these desires absent of a critique of materialism and the harsh realities that go along with it. It is one thing to desire nice things and quite another to put drugs in one's purse because "the police won't check or suspect you" and a drug dealer boyfriend can buy you nice things in return for drug smuggling. It is one thing to want a nice car and quite another to think that the only way you will get one is to use your body sexually.

Parents and educators alike admonish rap because of lyrics that use profanity and glamorize sex and violence. Parents do not want their children listening to it, and educators do not see the educational value in it. I believe that the value resides in the critique. This means that we need to create spaces—both inside and outside of the classroom—for young women especially to make the kinds of connections to larger societal issues that they do not make in the clubs on the dance floors. For me, a critical look at hip hop that is based not only on a love for the music and the culture but on a love of the people that are influenced by it, is what I want to inform my Black feminist consciousness and ultimately my action.

June Jordan's poignant essay "Where Is the Love" haunts me. Jordan discusses the need for a self-love and self-respect that would create and foster the ability to love and respect others. As I think about hip hop and the images of niggas and bitches that inhibit this kind of self-love and self-respect, I am faced with a multitude of questions. I am concerned particularly with rap and the love that hate produced—love that is fostered by a racist and sexist society. This is the kind of love that grows *despite* oppression but holds unique characteristics *because of* oppression. In many ways it is a continuation of the way Black men and women were forced to express love during slavery and segregation, when Black people were not allowed to love one another freely. Family members could be taken away at any moment. The legacy of slavery—it has yet to be dealt with properly—is the legacy that haunts Black people specifically and the rest of the country in general.

This legacy stands behind the war zone in which Morgan attributes Black men and women today living and trying to love. This legacy prompts me to value love as the connecting factor between hip hop and my identity as a Black feminist. Love has been and continues to be a struggle for Black people in the United States. Yet Black people have found ways to love each other and to be together anyway, despite separations and sales of partners during slavery. During the days of segregation and Jim Crow, Black people—especially parents—had to practice tough love to ensure that loved ones would live to see another day and not become the victim of Klan violence.

While the hip-hop generation has the legacy of African-American history to build on and strands of these kinds of still love persist, the hip-hop generation also has its own demons. Life for young Black Americans is different, and the very nature of relationships within hip-hop culture is necessarily going to be expressed differently. What continues to fascinate me is that despite all the historical baggage and contemporary struggles, young Black people are still trying to find ways to love, just as their ancestors did. A recognition of the plight that Black men and women are up against, along with a realization that in spite of it all living and loving go hand in hand, is central to any brand of feminism that is going to work for young Black women.

A new direction for Black feminism would aid in the critique and exploration of the dialogue across the sexes found in rap music and hip-hop culture. Black feminists such as dream hampton, Tara Roberts, Joan Morgan and Eisa Davis have begun to explore the relationship between love and hip hop. Rap music provides a new direction for Black feminist criticism. It is not just about counting the bitches and hoes in each rap song. It is about exploring the nature of Black male and female relationships. These new Black feminists acknowledge that sexism exists in rap music. But they also recognize that sexism exists in America. Rap music and Black popular culture are not produced in a cultural and political vacuum. The systems of oppression that plague the larger society plague subcultures of society as well. Black feminists are looking for ways to speak out against sexism and racism while starting a dialogue with Black men right on the front lines of the battlefield against oppression.

On these front lines I will be fighting and hollering out, "Love feminism but where's my hip hop?"

Our Mothers, Refugees from a World on Fire

Black Feminism in Everyday Life
Race, Mental Illness, Poverty and Motherhood

Siobhan Brooks

In 1948, when my mother was sixteen, she had sex and got pregnant with my sister, Connie. She gave birth to her on Valentine's Day. Teenage pregnancy was seen as deviant behavior (the father had left), so she was removed from the tenth grade in San Francisco and sent back to the South to relearn the proper "traditional values." My aunt, who was eighteen at the time and a firm believer in traditional values, thought my mother was too young to have a child and that she wouldn't be able to give my sister a "good" life. My aunt, who had married a man in the military, went South where my sister was being raised by relatives and unofficially adopted her. They moved to Seattle to live a middle-class lifestyle.

In the 1950s my mother—now a single mom—was placed in a mental hospital for infanticide of her second daughter, Tara. No one in the family knew much about Tara; they had never met her. "During that time it was very hard for single mothers, especially Black women, to make it economically," my aunt told me when I was sixteen and had arrived in Seattle thirsty for family history. My mother had been very poor and my aunt suspected she had had problems getting food for Tara. My mother had taken her to the hospital, claiming that she had fallen, but Tara was already dead when my mother brought her in. The doctors were suspicious of her injuries, suspecting that she had been thrown against the wall. My mother had a nervous breakdown then and was taken to Napa State Mental Hospital. She had schizophrenia.

When I heard this story as an adolescent, I was upset my family had not told me earlier what was "wrong" with my mother. This was the reason why I had never heard from Tara. All this time I had thought she was alive. My mother had told me I had two sisters, but I had only heard from her first daughter, Connie. I didn't hate my mother because of it, but I was enraged that everyone in the family knew but me. Such stories are not unusual within traditional Black communities, even if they often remain family "secrets." Abortion wasn't an option for many poor and working-class Black women like my mom. When I think of the reproductive movement among many white middle-class feminists of the 1960s and 1970s—the black and white television footage of white women holding pro-choice signs, showing hangers with an X through them—I think it was "their" movement. Those feminists seemed to deal with abortion as a choice for middle-class white women. They didn't deal with the issues of poverty and lack of education, the realities of infanticide and racism or making abortion accessible for all women.

I never discussed abortion with the women in my family, but I knew they were against it, as they were very involved in the church.

Abortion and queerness were viewed as sins. My sister Connie had been much more active in the civil rights movement than in the feminist movement, even though she had worked mostly with Black women. She had attended high school in Seattle during the height of 1960s integration and had seen white parents, especially white women, protesting her very presence at a high school their children attended. She did not relate to white feminism because the poverty of women like our mother was never an agenda for them. I think largely the white mainstream feminist movement rarely considered issues of class regarding motherhood. They felt motherhood was imposed on them, and they were fighting to be in the workplace, not recognizing that Black women and other women of color and poor white women were already in the workplace. Some of these women served as nannies for the elite white women, allowing them to attend such "feminist" meetings.

Growing up, I knew better than to get pregnant because of my mother's warnings about how I would end up on welfare, like most of our female neighbors who were single mothers. Many hadn't completed their education. My mother did not hold these views because she claimed to be a feminist; she held these views because she knew firsthand the interlocking systems of racism, poverty and sexism. She wanted me to survive and have opportunities that were denied to her growing up. In fact, she never used the words "feminism" or "racism." We also never talked about my father, whom I have only recently learned was Puerto Rican. Like many kids growing up in the projects to single mothers, I knew that to bring up issues concerning my father might be grounds for punishment.

• • •

In 1972, when Angela Davis was acquitted of murder charges in Marin County, California, I was born in the Sunnydale Housing Projects in San Francisco. We never discussed Angela Davis in our home. In fact, my mother wanted me to stay away from political activism altogether. Although she didn't say it, I think she feared that I would be killed, like our leaders of the day who had been killed and arrested during this time. Growing up in the 1970s, it seemed to me as if neither the civil rights movement nor the feminist movement was happening. Few people around me ever talked about them. I remember watching footage of Malcolm X and Martin Luther King Jr. giving speeches, Angela with her infamous Afro and fist in the air, Black people being hosed down by the police, white women burning bras and scenes of the Vietnam War.

I remember thinking that we were free now. We weren't being hosed down, and we didn't live under the stifling conditions of southern racial segregation with signs that read "Black" and "White." It never occurred to me, however, that our lives in poverty in the projects was testimony that we were *not* free, that racial segregation still existed. None of our neighbors talked much about politics; rather, they just lived life day to day. They were the least economically affected by these movements.

My mother used to live in the hippie neighborhood of Haight-Ashbury, but the rents increased and she had to move. Being a Black single woman without a high-school diploma, the projects were waiting for her. She worked as a maid for hotels, but when I was born she applied for disability because of her disfigured feet from years of wearing high heels. She was thirty-nine years old. When I was young, she would tell me how she had frantically looked for vacancies and there were none. But Sunnydale always had vacancies. These projects were the largest in San Francisco, built post-World War II, and they looked like red and white row houses. Sunnydale's residents were also predominately Black. Even then, it had a bad reputation for violence and would later be known as Swampy Desert. I could tell that she felt defeated having to move into the projects, and she tried her best to make it our home. She was also dealing with reentering mainstream society after her stay at Napa.

As a whole, my family never talked about what their lives had been like in the South, before they migrated to the East and West Coast. There are only a few times that my mother talked about race. In one incident she was thirteen and went on the Ferris wheel at Ocean Beach. It was her first time riding it and she was excited. She hopped in and the operator, a young white guy a few years older, buckled everyone's seat belt but hers. She told me how frightened she was when it reached the top, and she held on for her life as it swayed back and forth. She tried not to look down and felt her sweaty hands loosen with each sway. When it finally reached the end of the ride, she went up to the operator and told him that he had forgotten to fasten her seat belt. When he looked at her with sheer hatred, she realized it had been deliberate.

I remember another time, when I was little. I was sitting on the bus in the front and an old white woman got on and ordered me to move.

I didn't understand why I should get up for her, but my mother instantly swooped me up and placed me in her lap while this white woman sat down. Because we lived in the midst of racial apartheid and gender oppression, we did not need to talk about it—it was our daily reality.

Feminism was not a concept I grew up with. I never thought of myself in a gendered way, even while I was sexually harassed by the neighborhood boys as a teenager and socialized to be a good girl on account of my light skin and hair texture. But I always knew I was Black, largely from the racist media images on television and in the movies—from the maids in Shirley Temple films to the stereotyped characters in *Good Times* to the portrayal of the "apes" in *Planet of the Apes*. We laughed at these shows while knowing the images weren't really us. This is how I learned to be ashamed of being Black. Even after the Black pride movement, no one wanted to be the maid, mammy or the apes.

When I was young, my mother and I would get dressed up on the first and fifteenth of the month and go downtown, so she could cash her welfare check. I would be happy because I knew she would buy me something from Woolworth's. She wore her favorite black and white suit, makeup, wig, dark penciled-in eyebrows, orange lipstick that she never applied to the top of her lips and dark, round sunglasses. I didn't understand that we were on welfare and that was why we stood in long lines with some people who looked "professional" in business suits but most of whom looked homeless and poor, some of whom smelled of urine. These people in the lines were also predominately Black and Latino/a, mainly women.

My mother lived in fear of the welfare agencies that were always trying to locate my abusive father and reincorporate him into our lives. If there were any political discussions in my neighborhood among the women, it was how the welfare agencies kept us all living in a constant state of fear of being cut off. The other discussions were how as Black women we often lived in fear of Black men attacking us, of being homeless and of being "relocated" by the housing authority because of white gentrification. Black women often feared that their sons would be killed by the police, the drug trade or one another; that their daughters would get pregnant, molested in the local preschool or raped. These were the two gendered realities for poor Blacks. I didn't have a language for what our oppression was, but it seemed never-ending and often normalized.

Women in Sunnydale looked after each other and each other's children, even if it could be perceived as nosey. They went food shopping for each other, strategized about how to get more money from the welfare system, drove their neighbors's children to school and looked after the elderly. Such involvement in my well-being helped fill in the gaps due to my mother's schizophrenia, which often made her frightened of the "outside" world. Because of this fear, she wanted to keep me close at all times (it didn't help that we lived in the projects, where danger was always unpredictable). When I was eight, for example, an old Black woman with gray hair and glasses saw me playing outside and inquired as to why I wasn't in school. When I said I didn't know, she contacted a social worker who helped my mother with the process of enrolling me in school. Because of that neighbor, I started school at eight in the second grade. This is just the way things were in Sunnydale.

The term "mental illness" was not used among people in my community or usually within the Black community at large. Only recently we have begun to look at issues of mental illness among Black people, especially Black women, such as depression. Growing up I read little "feminist" literature that dealt with women of color and mental illness, outside of perhaps some fiction. In fact, I never saw my mother as having a mental illness at all because she was functional. I thought all mentally ill people were hospitalized. The books at my high-school library that dealt with mental illness usually talked about white women, as in *I Never Promised You a Rose Garden* or *Sybil*. Neither the feminist movement nor the civil rights movement had dealt with mentally ill women of color. In the mental health field young Black women are often portrayed as pathological for being single mothers, which is pegged as the cause of our poverty.

One of my earliest memories of my mother was of her talking to herself, and this behavior was considered normal in our household. When I was a child, I tried to mimic it and stopped feeling that this was odd behavior. She would often burst into angry, unpredictable spells of screaming and talking to herself. In fact, she spent a majority of her time alone, smoking in the kitchen and watching television. I would wake up to hear her screaming about things I didn't understand. How a "nigger" was keeping her down, how she wasn't going back to Napa, how in the future she would have a better life, that she was really white, how she was supposed to marry a white man and live in a house. Sometimes it sounded as if she was making up words or speaking a language I didn't understand. She would look off into space with darting eyes, a dazed look across her eyes, wearing a torn green turtleneck and a gray skirt, even though she could afford not to, screaming furiously, sometimes to the point of hoarseness and drooling.

In the presence of other people, she could appear "normal" but would sometimes talk to herself in a handkerchief. I suspect the neighbors may have occasionally heard her screaming or beating me with a belt. Sometimes she would scream at me in the third person and say things like, "Get out of Siobhan's room, you little nigger!" and throw me out onto the porch. I'm sure that there must have been times when the neighbors heard her or saw this behavior. My mother was one of the oldest tenants in the community, so there was a place for her. Everyone knew her, including our Greek mailman. In our community we did not use the term "child abuse" but we were aware that it existed. My friends' parents would sometimes suspect that I wasn't getting enough food because I was underweight. They would invite me over for meals and have me take food home. They never said I was being abused and never made me feel as if there was something obviously wrong with the way we lived.

Domestic violence also occurred in Sunnydale but was not called by that name. It was discussed and dealt with among the women, however. I remember a big Black woman who quickly ran in the nude across the lawn from our neighbor's place, where an older Black man lived, to my mother's place. He was beating her and she didn't have time to put on any clothes. Another one of our female neighbors went to jail for stabbing her husband, who used to beat her. When she came out, the women in the community did not judge her. They knew she did what she felt was right. Looking back at these women, I doubt any of them would have used the term "feminism" to describe their actions. I did not link phrases like "child abuse," "domestic violence," "drug addiction" or "mental illness" to my experience.

To my colored eye, the TV shows and billboards about abuse sponsored by white feminists who were trying to raise consciousness, it looked like these issues only affected white people. It was as if issues of abuse had nothing to do with us, that only white people were worthy of naming abuse. Suffering and systematic abuse in communities of color was so normalized. We often didn't even know we were oppressed. Some of us thought suffering was just a part of being Black. To have access to health care, good education, healthy food and safe, affordable housing, to have aspirations and a desire to improve one's mental and physical health was often seen as "white."

Many of us did not have access to such things, and we often died young—where was a feminist movement to help us? The Black women I grew up with prided themselves on being "strong Black women," not "weak" like white women or "crazy" like white people who were in therapy. These women were angry, as they felt they'd been forced into being the backbone of the community. To justify their sexism, some Black men also subscribed to this notion. These women prided themselves on raising children, supporting men and their families on low wages—without health care, let alone mental health care. For a Black woman to be depressed was seen as a type of luxury. Despite my mother's mental state, she paid the bills on time, shopped for food and refused the free bread-and-butter services the government offered us. When she died recently from emphysema and I told some of my friends about her mental illness, they asked if she had been on medication. I didn't know she was supposed to be.

As a college student at San Francisco State University, I started calling myself a feminist when I came into women's studies. Like many young women of color from poor and working-class backgrounds, college was the first environment where I learned a language for racism, sexism and classism. I was also coming into consciousness around being Black and learning Black history. I shaved my head of permed hair.

My first women's studies class was about sexuality and the body, and how our vaginas were never seen as part of our whole body. We read *Our Bodies, Ourselves* (edited by the Boston Women's Health Book Collective) and *Powers and Desires: The Politics of Sexuality* (edited by Ann Snitow, Sharon Thompson and Christine Stansell) and talked about body images of women (mostly white) in magazines and sexuality. I found this class interesting but very Eurocentric, despite the inclusion of some readings by women of color, such as an essay by Cherríe Moraga. I thought of my Mexican childhood friend Lupé, who lived in the projects, smelled of strawberry hair spray and wrote in lipstick on her bedroom wall the names of the boys she had kissed—where was she in this?

We discussed the pornography debates, and I learned many women were doing sex work to pay for school. This led me to work at the Lusty Lady, a peepshow in San Francisco known for its "feminist," "sex-positive" politics and commitment to hiring female managers. I later became a union organizer there and fought to get more women of color hired.

Most of my professors were women of color, but most of the students were white and middle class. These students often spoke with the universal understanding that "woman" meant white like them. When race was discussed, at least one white woman would start crying out of white guilt. We could all exist as "women" in the classroom but not within our differences based on race, class and cultural identity. I felt that these crying spells frequently functioned to mask white women's racism about issues affecting women of color. White middle-class women who had been socialized by the dominant culture to be quiet could speak out in their women's studies classes. But time and again, they could not see that while their participation could be personally liberating, it could be silencing for women of color (and the few men of color), who because of race and gender often did not feel entitled to speak. I began to understand why most women of color were in ethnic studies, not women's studies. I felt the racial isolation of being one of few women of color in the department, since many women of color felt that feminism was a white lesbian thing. Some saw the concept as separating them from the men in their communities. The voices of queer women of color who were active in the fighting for our civil rights were often silenced within ethnic studies departments and tokenized in women's studies.

In a class called "Women and Violence" taught by a Black woman who was a lesbian mother, the white women felt the class should only focus on them. There were few women of color in the class, so the professor made sure we felt empowered to speak by prioritizing our participation. I loved this class because we talked about real issues that affected the lives of poor women and women of color. My mother and I had never talked about feminism or racism, but this class made me feel that at least experiences of poor working-class women of color like us were being studied—we weren't invisible.

Reading works by many poor and working-class women of color gave me a blueprint to write about my own experiences with poverty and mental illness. We read *Bastard out of Carolina* by Dorothy Allison and *Beloved* by Toni Morrison. The class loved Allison's novel—many of the women were from middle-class backgrounds, but they could relate to the reality of sexism and violence within the family. But when we read *Beloved*, suddenly some of the women felt that the class was getting "off track," that we were talking about race, not gender. The other Black female student and I loved it. I felt empowered reading about infanticide, since it was close to home for me.

One white woman raised her hand and protested, "Why are we reading about Black people? I thought this was a women's studies class." The professor lost her temper and told her that in case she didn't know, it was a Black woman teaching the class and that Black people can also be women. The white woman started crying and angrily left the class. I was amazed at this white woman's sense of entitlement and privilege, of being able to protest and cry in the classroom. I can think of only a few times I've ever seen Black women in my community cry, even when tragedy occurs.

In a class called "Feminism and Marxism," taught by lesbian Asian-American socialist feminist Merle Woo, a similar incident happened. There were three wome n of color in the class, including myself—all of us Black. We talked about internalized oppression, the body and race. The subject of nose jobs came up for the Jewish women in the class along with skin color and slavery regarding Black people. The Jewish women tried to equate the "Jewish nose" to body images for Blacks. The Black women silently listened to what the white Jewish women had to say, giving each other that "Can you believe these white people" look. After the Jewish women were finished, a Black woman expressed that she felt the dialogue was racist. Even though Jewish women also felt pressured to conform to European beauty standards, it was nowhere near the extent that Black women and other women of color do, because in this country Jewish women can pass for white while we cannot. The Jewish women got upset and accused us of not understanding them. They dismissed our feelings but wanted theirs validated.

Their words were a symbolic form of violence. That the experiences of women of color are dismissed in the classroom reflects the physical violence that happens to us on the street. What I experienced in the classroom was not so different from what happened to my mother years earlier, when the Ferris wheel's white male conductor would not fasten her seat belt. The mentality is the same: our humanity is not valued.

At the next class a Black woman who had been one of the few to actually major in women's studies besides myself brought in a definition of white privilege, listing all the ways white people are visionally, culturally, racially and economically privileged relative to people of color. This dialogue happened over a period of two days. The second day the Black woman left the class. Although I respected her choice, I remained because I didn't feel a need to leave. The Jewish women then thanked me for "understanding" where they were coming from. I was the token "good" Black. This put me in an awkward position: Even though I didn't leave the class, my staying didn't mean that I agreed with them either. I stayed because I wanted to bear witness to what was going on. So often women of color leave white environments because of fear. They feel like their presence doesn't matter, that if they speak they will not be listened to. Even though I didn't say anything, I wanted to stay and have my presence as a Black woman known. Just because they were getting upset that the Black women in the classroom were bringing issues of racism to their attention did not mean that we had to leave the situation.

My upbringing in the projects and my mother's mental illness prepared me for hostile environments. I always had to navigate between the "normal" world and my mother's world, often hoping those two worlds would never meet. I feared my survival would be at risk if I were ever taken away from her. As I became older, I learned to survive balancing the Black world of my community with the white middle-class world that in many ways showed me my world did not matter. Women's studies was no exception. I learned my skills back home from dealing with racist school teachers who placed me in English as a second language (ESL) classes in fifth grade, even though I had only spoken English at home. I had to fend for myself because my mother did not understand what was going on. The ESL teacher finally realized that I should not have been in her class, and I was placed in regular classes. I had to go through this experience alone, but I knew my people back home thought I was intelligent and that I mattered. This knowledge got me through fifth grade, and it got me through women's studies.

This kind of navigating between two worlds is not new to women of color, to immigrants or to many of us born in the United States. We come from different cultures, speak different languages and have different worldviews, many of which are not respected in white environments. Many white women are often afraid of difference and try to ignore it or silence us when we bring up our race and class differences. They often say they don't see race, only human beings. But this is a lie and we all know it. They do not seem to understand that for women of color, our race is a central part of our humanity, especially in a white-dominated society, such as the United States. It is incidents like these that make women's studies hard for women of color and that keep the classes mostly white, even at a progressive college like San Francisco State, where the ethnic studies program had grown directly out of the civil rights movement. In women's studies we read the work of some women of color, but surprisingly not that of bell hooks or Angela Davis (even though she used to teach at State). Rather, I read them in my Black studies classes.

The white women in my classes often did not understand their racial and class privilege, and they frequently didn't see themselves as being racist. In my friend's class on women and nature, for example, which was mostly white, there were white women appropriating Native American culture: carrying dream catchers or wearing Native American jewelry. They had a blast hiking off into the wilderness, but my friend had to get over her fear of nature, a fear many urban women of color have toward nature since many of us are taught at an early age not to go into parks alone for fear of being raped.

Once a white woman and I were talking about class and education, and she said that I must have had the same education as she because we were attending the same college, learning in the same classroom. She was trying to argue that the problem in this country was really one of class, not race. She was shocked when I told her I didn't start school until I was eight. Another time a white woman asked me to get her a scone as I was heading toward the cafeteria. I had never heard of a scone. I could only hope that the pastry would be clearly labeled. These women just assumed everyone was coming from a similar environment as theirs.

The everyday feminism that I grew up with was missing from my classes; the women had the theory but not the practice. Even though many of these women were involved in some sort of "progressive" organizing, it seemed we spent hours in classes and consciousness-raising groups trying to convince them that people of color were humans. Then there were the women in Sunnydale who organized against welfare cuts and drugs in their neighborhood, for better housing and daycare, who would never call themselves feminists. They were more "feminist" in their actions than many of the white women in my women's studies classes.

I think about my mother who took time to read to me every night before going to bed, bought me school clothes from Macy's, struggled to keep food on the table despite her illness and loved me enough to instill a sense of self-esteem even though we lived in the projects. I honor her strength in raising a Black girl in the midst of oppressive poverty—a challenge for many poor Black mothers. This is the kind of feminism that doesn't make it to the doors of women's studies classes. Despite the racism, majoring in women's studies made me feel empowered as a queer Black woman. I am proud to call myself a feminist. I learned critical thinking skills in women's studies that changed my life forever, and I met great friends. I attended readings of many Black feminists that I admired, such as Alice Walker, who had defined the term "womanist."

But I often think about the harsh life my mother and many Black women like her have lived in this country as a result of slavery, economic exploitation and systematic violence. Women's studies classes do not have to be a struggle for power between white women and women of color, yet that is often what they are because of white women's racism. White women must understand that the anger women of color express in and outside of the classroom toward them is not an issue of "hurt feelings" or "misunderstandings." To reduce our experience of that racism to "misunderstandings" is both racist and reductionist. It is akin to men telling women that we are overreacting to their sexism. The anger of women of color is a rational response to our invisibility. It is a rational response to a racist, sexist, capitalist structure. It is not constructive for white women to tell us that our anger is making it hard for them to relate to us, that our anger makes them feel uncomfortable, that we are not willing to find common alliances with them. This is a classic example of white women's racism. They fail to realize that in telling us there is no place for our rage, they are becoming a part of what is colonizing us—the denial of our reality. They have to accept the fact that they don't understand our experiences and have an opportunity to learn something, maybe even about themselves, as opposed to wanting to shut us up. Only then can any true understanding result among us.

As I write this essay, I am reminded of feminists of color who have come before me, like Cherríe Moraga, Audre Lorde and bell hooks. When I read their writings about the racism of the women's movement in the seventies, much of what they are writing about can be applied to women's studies programs today. This is the sad tragedy of feminism, that despite such writings, today this is still a large part of our interactions with white women. It seems as if many women's studies programs became an institutionalized version of their white privilege. I lament that women like my mother are not usually considered in women's studies. It is for women like my mother and my friends' mothers that I do activist work with women of color: to bring the everyday knowledge of these women back into feminism.

I would like to dedicate this essay to my mother, Aldean Brooks, my deceased sister, Tara, and my friend's parents.

In Praise of Difficult Chicas
Feminism and Femininity

Adriana López

Feminist might not be the proper sobriquet to describe my great aunt, Tía Esthercita, but she sure was fearless. In the late 1950s she flouted the church's social dictums, scoffed at being ladylike and defied los *hombres machista*. She smoked cigars, huffed down whiskey and indulged in numerous international love affairs with very doting, sometimes married, men. She owned a farm on the outskirts of Bogotá, Colombia, and a three-bedroom modern apartment in Las Torres de Fenicia, a high-rise luxury building in the once chic downtown part of the capital. I could never quite figure out how my aunt could afford this lavish lifestyle and why my mother's family always rolled their eyes and spoke furtively when the subject turned to our eccentric aunt—a woman with *cojones*.

The Secret
In my early twenties Tía's secret was divulged to me one night over lots of sake with my mom. As the story goes, Tía married for reasons of convenience at fourteen. She broke up her marriage a year later by

simply walking out on her husband because divorce was not legal in Colombia until the early 1990s. She was a street-smart hustler: charismatic, undereducated but possessed with a prodigious entrepreneurial ambition. She constructed a house on a piece of affordable land she purchased next to a cemetery in downtown Bogotá (in 1932 women were granted property rights) but had trouble finding tenants. So she agreed to convert the house into a high-end brothel and have it administered by outside parties. The brothel catered to an upper-class clientele of businessmen and politicians. With the profits Tía Esther bought herself a white Ford Galaxy and launched her own taxi service along with a *salsamentería*, a deli that her younger brother managed.

As she told the story, my confident, headstrong mother seemed overcome with pangs of guilt, unsure how such information might affect her only child who was on the verge of womanhood. To truly understand Esthercita, whom we had gotten to know during our visits to Colombia, my mother believed that I had to understand how my Tía was able to live the life she lived. This information was also something that my mother hoped I wouldn't tell too many people. I was given a warning that neither my father nor my mother's older sister had ever told their husbands Esthercita's full story. But instead of feeling ashamed, I claimed it for myself, incorporating our family's scandal into my new feminist theory—Esthercita had been involved in a cultural taboo and in my mind that was more inspiring than if she had been a sacrificial good girl. I found nothing wrong with her source of income.

For those new to Latin American culture and all its ironies—

especially the deliciously anarchic attitudes of Colombia's people—it is a bit difficult to explain the acceptability of my great aunt's actions. In Colombia morally loose ladies and sacrilegious attitudes coexist with respect for the family unit. When listening to my mother's story, I, a *gringa* born in the comparatively puritanical United States, had to remember that the norms here weren't the norms in Esthercita's homeland. Although sex work has been demonized by mainstream Western feminists, I still felt that its roots stemmed from women who were out to defy the status quo, as it often gave women a form of self-sufficiency and power, especially in economically stressed countries.

When I spoke to my Tía in 1999, Esthercita admitted that she had to conceal the brothel from our family for a while, as well as the many men in her life who simply wouldn't understand her method of money-making. She was also thankful that our family managed to get over the initial shock rather quickly (Hell, nobody was truly a saint in my family). When I gently questioned her further about this time of her life, Esther didn't flinch. She spoke about it freely and without shame. The prostitutes, she told me, were decent, well-dressed ladies from the city who were managing to make a living during an era when there wasn't much out there for women except marriage. She also claimed she didn't have much involvement—she was only the land-lady and stopped by occasionally to check up and collect the rent. The brothel remained open for close to four years and allowed my aunt to support herself handsomely and travel. In Esther's eyes her only faux pas was to trustingly leave money in the care of one of her male lovers, who lost a small fortune in a bad investment.

While my mother was telling me this, I had images of a Toulouse-Lautrec-like bordello with red velvet walls and women with feathered boas around their necks and nothing else on save for skimpy lingerie. To my dismay, I was later told that the brothel wasn't as lavish as I had envisioned. The house was sparsely decorated with a common room and some austere bedrooms off to the side. It was more like Luis Buñuel's *Belle de Jour*, where the catatonic Catherine Deneuve liberated herself in a brothel made up of tough but gorgeous Parisian women.

Though I was never able to philosophize about the pros and the cons of prostitution with her, I sensed that Esthercita viewed prostitution as acceptable—as long as a woman chose it for herself. But I strongly doubt if she would have ever prostituted her own body. Still, she openly enjoys talking about the dynamics of the relationship between men and women, telling dirty jokes, and she has kept an openly gay man as one of her lifelong best friends. She never had children or remarried and always barks at me about the absurdity of marriage. Had my aunt lived in a small town, it would have been hard for her to escape the stigma of allowing prostitution in a building she owned. But since she lived in the big city, she was able to dabble in the risqué without many ever knowing her secret.

Because I have other choices to support myself financially, I find that prostitution can be degrading—it seems like a violation of my sense of intimacy. But I've come to accept that Tía Esthercita did what she had to do to establish herself in Colombia as a woman with high aspirations in the 1950s. Because she was involved in what people considered a scandalous endeavor, she liberated herself from the conservative confines of Bogotá society. Her financial and social independence gave my grandmother first the shelter and then the courage to escape an abusive husband and run away with her two daughters to the United States. My own mother continued Esther's legacy by divorcing my then-conventional macho father and going back to school, getting her bachelor's degree and ultimately buying herself a shiny new white Camaro. These are the women that helped frame my understanding of feminism.

My Two Mothers

I have always viewed the women in my family as anomalies among Latinas. Because I was born in the States and raised in a white suburban neighborhood by my liberated mother, I wasn't subjected to the traditional traumas of most Latinas. Many of my other relatives and *amigas* had to come to terms with living under a constricting, role-playing roof: "father qua head," "mother qua helper." My mother's most famous speech, which she gave often, was about how I should never rely on men. Her own mother had supported herself and her two daughters as an immigrant in the United States by working factory jobs until she remarried again in her late forties. My *abuelita* exacerbated an already bad pneumonia while working packing foods in the freezers of a Howard Johnson's in Queens, New York. She developed a lung disease that took her life at sixty-one while she was still full of vitality. Motherless, my mom at age thirty-six was now truly on her own.

Sometimes I see my mother as two women: my mother from the North and my mother from the South. "A woman must have a career to support herself, Adriana, because you can never rely on any man," she insists. In my teens I thought her declarations of independence were simply antimen campaigns from an embittered woman looking for love—especially because I found the opposite sex so intriguing. Though I have seen my mother cry over a broken heart, she has always practiced what she preaches—she has traveled the world and made her voice heard in her community. This was my mother from the North talking during the take-home Burger King dinner conversations we had in between her full-time job and night classes at the local university. At that time she was studying for a bachelor's, and I watched her blossom while reading about "zipless fucks" in Erica Jong's *Fear of Flying* and reveling in her art classes—a skill she also picked up from my grandmother, who painted right up to her premature death.

My mother from the South showed me how to dance and feel beautiful. I marveled in watching her and her stunning single Colombian-American girlfriends dance to the sounds of the *cumbia*. My mom would seductively place one hand on her belly and let the other dangle out in front of her, pulsating to the scraping rhythm of the *guiro*, a percussive instrument made from a gourd that is used in many Latin American countries. Mom, being young and charming, attracted plenty of American men into our lives who showed us their versions of the good life—but all of them were intimidated by Mom's no-bullshit streak and love for debate. While nobody in my circle of adolescent friends had the experience of recognizing their own mother as a sexual being, I was well aware of her uniqueness. Sensing my awareness, Mom thought it best that I learn about my own body and the wonders of sex through books like *The Joy of Sex* and *What's Happening to My Body*, which she placed in my room one day. Talking would have been a nightmare, but she knew sex was a loaded weapon for someone like me, who hadn't yet read the manuals.

Unlike many Latinas of my and previous generations, I didn't have to confront *marianismo*, the counterpart for machismo. Symbolizing the primacy of the Virgin Mary in the female role, marianismo describes the self-sacrifice and rejection of pleasure women subject themselves to so they can please others, especially the men in their families. It is the belief that Latinas should live in the shadows of their men—father, boyfriend, husband and son. My parents' divorce had the effect of liberating me from marianismo, although I didn't realize it until my adolescence. They split up when I was eight, so my father didn't get to witness my tumultuous sexual awakening firsthand.

My desperately concerned mother threatened me on several occasions with a trip to a Catholic boarding school in Colombia, which would set me straight. My mother and I knew this was pure theater (though I had visions of myself in a habit), because both of us regarded churchgoing as merely attending weddings, funerals and baptisms. But what really triggered my latent *marianista* tendencies were my mother's threats to call my father and tell him about my sexual escapades with the paperboy. The notion of having my father find out that I had a raging libido seemed worse than any convent. Having been made to feel dirty by my mother and those stubborn as ink hickeys on my neck, I still enjoyed being Daddy's little girl on my weekend visits with him. Latina guilt or not, I was also protecting a father who had been wounded by my mother leaving him. In the end she never called him, however, and I never set foot in any convent or preppy private school.

Years later, in my sophomore year of college, my father and I finally had it out over my overnight stays with a boyfriend. Fueled with the seedlings of early feminist scholarship, I told my father that I was not a virgin and called him a dinosaur for thinking that any one man was worth so much that I would sacrifice myself and wait till I was married. "I'm here to have fun too, Dad," I said. I still cringe at the way he looked at me in disgust. It took a while before we were ready to talk again, but when I explained that I was living in a new era for women that he was not accustomed to, it was one of the most redemptive moments of my life. "Things have changed, Dad!" I insisted. Sitting there pale and with a tightly clenched jaw, I think he finally understood how being born in this country and living apart from him had had an irrevocable effect on me, his only daughter.

Looking for a Feminism of a Different Color

Educated in American schools and universities, I recognized the legacy of white superstar feminists like Gloria Steinem, Betty Friedan and Germaine Greer. Though at times their styles were overheated, they were crusaders for equal rights, bra-burning privileged white women who took on a firestorm of antagonism for their revolutionary consciousness-raising. I greatly appreciated all they had done for American middle-class women, but I wasn't sure if enjoying the company of men was a central part of their brand of feminism. I much rather enjoyed the guiltless sex of Erica Jong and the vixens and vamps depicted by Camille Paglia, who praised the brazen behavior of the unholy popstar Madonna. I was part of the early '90s generation of lipstick feminists and the post '80s backlash on "ugly feminists." We shaved our legs and armpits and made calculated remarks like: "I'm not a feminist, but . . ." We were not sure of what we really wanted, but at least I felt safe being vague. Most of the time I was still fighting battles for the respect of my boyfriends, professors and bosses.

At the same time, I indulged in being fashionably slim and "exotic" on my East Coast college campus. Though I was never called a "slut," at least not to my face, I engaged in casual sex with pseudo-intellectual men and enjoyed the game of conquest without experiencing much remorse when rejected. Surrounded by mostly Jewish men from suburban towns, I started to realize that being a goy excluded me from ever being taken seriously for marriage. I had begun to feel like I did not completely fit in. I felt like an other.

As mainstream feminism inspired me to rebellious heights, I looked to the writings and efforts of Latinas and women of color. Aware of the plight of Latinos living in the United States, issues of race and class began haunting my thoughts the more I lived in the real world, away from that fantasy land of intellectual nurturing called academia. As a freelance writer, I made it a point to visit various cities in Latin America—Caracas, Rio de Janeiro, Santiago, San Juan, Mexico City, Medellín, Cali, Bogotá, Buenos Aires and Havana. I knew it would be necessary to know firsthand about the everyday lives of

Latin American women to begin to compare the differences between women's issues in Latin America and what Latinas in the United States were struggling against.

It was in the essays of Xicanista writer Ana Castillo, about the censorship of mestiza women on both sides of the borders, that I found a voice to help me understand the unfair treatment that darker women receive. Though I never had to bear direct abuse, reading Castillo's words in *Massacre of the Dreamers* made me think of how my grandmother's health deteriorated as a result of working in a factory. I was made aware that if I had to emigrate from Colombia today, I would be facing similar challenges to those of any immigrant woman of little means coming to the United States to find work. Castillo spoke loudly, stating the ugly facts about how Latina women were the lowest paid women in the country. None of the white feminists I had come across had mentioned the women of color working class. She chronicled Latinas' long and infuriating battles with machisimo and the hypocrisies of Catholicism's Madonna/whore syndrome. While the white feminist movements had their own mother goddess to pay tribute to, Castillo spoke about the spiritual and mystical womanhood found in indigenous earth religions through her writings on *brujas* and *curanderas*, or wielders of magical healing. I felt trapped in the steel cage of my hometown of New York, and my only outside experience with earth religions had been on my journeys to Latin America. Castillo spoke about the traditions of our ancestors and adapted them into messages of loving oneself, empowering the dormant bruja in me. She was the first author I had seen on the cover of a book who was striking, fierce and oh so Latina.

While my experience up till then with the mainstream middle class tended to separate me from many women of color, my contact with this new feminism brought me back into closer contact with my own ethnicity, my own self. Reenergized by my new vision of the world, I began seeking women of color who were interested in discussing literature and this new consciousness we were feeling. Through these women of all shapes and sizes, I was inspired to start writing stories of my own. And only through the writing was I able to connect the dots to the women in my family.

Today my home is decorated with kitschy Latina icons. I have photos of Frida Kahlo, a Virgen de Guadalupe light switch, representations of the female orishas from the Yoruban pantheon, and a painting of Anima Sola, a folkloric legend pictured in handcuffs condemned to withstand the eternal flames of purgatory. These symbols imbue me with a female power solely with their visual presence. They are emblems of the pleasure and pain of womanhood, society's misinterpretation of us and fear of our sexual energy. It surprises me how Frida's image has drawn even white women to worship her. Perhaps it is because of her ferocious brow, her unabashed hirsuteness, her bisexuality and her dark eccentricity—qualities in opposition to the ideal of the American woman. My bookshelves are replete with texts that investigate the lives of legends like Argentine ruler Evita Perón, La Malinche (the Spanish conqueror Hernan Cortes's indigenous translator) or Sor Juana Inés de la Cruz, a Mexican woman who entered a convent just so that she could educate herself at a time when women were denied higher education.

And I'm fascinated by the lyrics of the Colombian rock group Los Aterciopelados. Androgynous lead singer Andrea Echeverri possesses a melodic yet husky voice that taunts machos by proclaiming herself to be a *chica difícil* (difficult chick), a *cosita seria* (serious little thing) not wanting to be *la culpable* (the guilty one) or not wanting to ruin her figure with a baby. Her songs are about the quotidian life of women in Latin America, whose reputation is always at severe risk of being tainted. Astrid Hadad—a Mexican, Mayan and Lebanese singer—combines performance art with feminist lyrics in her album *Ay!* Crooning campy *rancheras*, she performs onstage in a Virgin de Guadalupe costume that depicts *la virgensita's* famous radiating aura. With ironic detachment, she addresses serious problems like domestic violence in songs like "Me golpeaste tanto anoche" (You beat me so much last night). Why do I bask in such dark humor? Maybe because it brings out the surrealist double-meanings of machismo while reminding me of the contradictions of being a progressive woman in love.

My North and South American Ways

Latin men have long put Latinas on pedestals, convincing them they had all the power while in reality the women were in men's possession. To this day, Latinas from South America still gain power in politics, society and in their careers for being beautiful, poised and for not having a tarnished reputation. It is our cliché: We love our men— and they *really* love us. For ambitious women in the United States, being beautiful will only jeopardize their reputation in any professional field aside from Hollywood. I don't come from a long line of

Protestant cool, suffragette movements and the 1960s feminist revolution. My heritage is hot Catholicism, where men and women are so intricately tangled that feminism becomes a dirty word. My mother and Tía Esthercita would never have used the F-word to describe themselves, afraid it would have meant they were lesbians or man-haters. I, as a modern feminist, straddle the contradictions of U.S. and Latin American identities—I'm not curvaceous and polished enough for Latin American standards and I'm too sexy and well-dressed for white-American standards. As a U.S. Latina, I can dance and think my way out of any situation, but for my sisters in the South, the economic chaos in Latin America is still inhibiting their movement toward sexual equality.

My family's history has undeniably affected the person I have become. I know that Esthercita's wild streak and my grandmother's brave trip from the South to the North severed the patriarchal cord that strangled the women in my family for centuries. Today, in wartorn Colombia, where prostitution runs rampant, the number of young women bearing arms is increasing, and more and more women are being forced to head families and businesses because their men are getting killed off.

Tía Esthercita is not as rare a specimen anymore. She is buddy-buddy with my mother, who visits Bogotá often. I love looking at current photographs of white-haired Esthercita, who can hardly speak anymore but still manages to do it all with her big brown eyes and shoulder-heaving laughs. There is one photo I own of Tía and my still quite sexy mother, who is approaching fifty, that fuels me—I am lucky to have them both as my feminine guides. Through them I have learned to be a liberated woman by emulating both their North and South American ways. Tía still has a gentleman caller, and you bet, he is married and she has known him for more than forty years. Both my mother and Esthercita have had their sorrow, their bouts of loneliness and unsupportive lovers. They have had some women tsk tsk them for their brazen behavior, and others become inspired by their ways. I say *muchisimas gracias* to these difficult *chicas*, my Tía, grandmother and mother, for never being silent, for being happily unmarried, for enjoying sex and for never suffering in pain like so many have. I thank them for showing me a new kind of feminism, one that includes plenty of pleasure.

Love Clinic

Soyon Im

"Don't have sex," warns my mother. It is Sunday morning and we are on the phone—11 A.M. her time, 8 A.M. mine. If I don't answer her call, she'll imagine a couple of disastrous scenarios, and I'm not sure which is worse for her—the thought of me lying underneath a wrecked car or a man. Once a week we talk, and every week she tells me not to have sex—sometimes at the end of our conversation, in lieu of saying good-bye.

My mother has been trying to keep me from sex since I was in elementary school. In fifth grade my friend Jenny had a slumber party and I wasn't allowed to go. "A girl shouldn't get used to sleeping at other people's houses," my mother said. The first time she suspected I might go astray was when she caught me slow dancing with David Kim. I was fifteen and David was the first Korean-American guy that I ever liked. We met at one of those six-week SAT prep courses that cost hundreds of dollars and convenes during the weekends in some glass-and-steel corporate park. My parents made me attend the classes in the hopes that I would score a 1400 and get into an Ivy League college.

David played tennis regularly and he'd often come to class right after practice, his gym shorts hanging easily on his tall, lean frame, the sides of his hair damp with sweat, his face slightly pink. You could tell he was still warm from exercise. During our tedious lessons I'd take furtive glances, relishing his beauty. *David has hirsute, indomitable legs,* I wrote in tiny letters in my notebook, using the new vocabulary we were learning by rote. *My boredom is abated by David's pulchritude. David is sanguine and virile.*

David actually lived only five blocks away from me, but because we were on opposite sides of the neighborhood's school district lines, we went to different high schools, which was a good thing. If we'd gone to the same school, he'd have known that I wasn't one of the cool kids, and he would've probably never spoken to me, except maybe to ask a question about homework or something dweeby like that. He certainly wouldn't have invited me to a party at his house.

The party was small; there were eight or nine teenagers drinking wine coolers in a dimly lit half-basement. Wham! was on the stereo, and at one point David asked me to dance. "Careless Whispers," a slow number, was on. He started by putting his hands behind my shoulders, then eventually dropping them around my waist. We weren't so much dancing as hugging each other. I'd never stood so closely to a boy before, and the warmth of his body was exquisite. He didn't kiss me, but every once in a while, he'd nuzzle his chin against my neck and I'd feel a tingle run all the way down my spine. We held each other like that for about twenty minutes when all of a sudden, my mother walked in.

What followed was a scene from a bad soap opera. She grabbed me by the arm, marched me up the steps and out of David's house. Outside, she slapped me across the face. "Do you know how girls at parties like that end up?" she asked. Then she shouted, "They get pregnant! They get herpes and they don't know who the father is!"

My mother had a long career as a gynecologist. I marvel at the irony of how she spent each day dealing with other people's sexuality while denying mine. Then again, she did her residency in a Bronx hospital and saw every ugly disease close up. Sitting behind the metal stirrups of her examining table, she discovered the intimate details of thousands of strangers. Patients confessed to her secrets they wouldn't share with their best friends. *My period is late. I have an itch down there. He gave me warts.* At night, in front of the TV, she'd read medical journals filled with photos of infected genitals turned pimply and black.

My mother's clinical exposure and her Korean conservatism made a fearsome combination. Like an evangelist, she tried to instill the fear of sex in me, thunderously lecturing on the calamities that befell sinners. Sex led to disease; sex led to death; and inescapably, sex led to more wanton sex.

The more she pressed, the more I had to go against her. As a teen, I was determined not to stay a virgin or marry early. I read women's magazines like *Cosmopolitan* and fantasized about an older, grown-up me having lots of sex with lots of different men. A few articles on G-spots, multiple orgasms and the appeal of blue-collar men convinced me that I wouldn't have to settle for less-than-stellar sex. I was a fuck-me feminist before I'd had my first kiss. In my mind sex wasn't just about love or hormones, it was a key to my own identity. Sex represented a freedom that my mother had never experienced as a Korean woman—and there was no way that I was going to become like my mother.

Nor was I going to be like so many girls at school, ebullient when they were dating and then sobbing for days and weeks after they'd been dumped. I observed many guys who, in contrast, shortly after breaking up with a girlfriend, took up with another. How was it that they seemed so unfazed? Why did guys seem to have so much more control in relationships? Why did we girls allow them the power? Why did my mother give in to my father?

At the time I wished my mother would file for a divorce. My parents hadn't lived together for more than ten years and I didn't see the sense in them staying married. When my mother, brother and I moved to the United States, my father decided to stay with his corporation in Korea. He visited us for just a few weeks each year, and my mother essentially became a single parent. When I was sixteen, my father left his company and finally joined our family for good. It was a bad arrangement. He constantly picked on my mother and dismissed her views on just about everything. "Bird brain," he'd utter in a poisonous tone that sickened us all. The worst was when he demanded money. Not having any work in the United States, he sought out doomed business ventures and expected my mother to provide the capital. She didn't want to give up her savings—the money she'd earned as a doctor since coming to the United States—but he always got his way.

I'm ashamed to say I wasn't supportive. I hated my father for weakening my mother, but I hated my mother more for not leaving him. At eighteen I left for college, thinking I was escaping my parents. Unfortunately, I left something crucial behind. Two weeks into my first semester, my mother came across an old diary in my room. She read it and discovered that I wasn't a virgin. During the ensuing fight, she repeatedly yelled, "You betrayed me!"

I betrayed her? What about my father? Why was I the one being punished? Feeling angry and exposed, I retreated to my studies, devouring books by feminist thinkers. Olga Broumas, Naomi Wolf and Susan Faludi became my new role models. I befriended other women emerging from repressive pasts. Guilt-free sex was our credo as we hopped into bed with both genders. I dreaded the holidays when I had to go back home.

While feminism gave me a community of other like-minded women, it didn't give me any clues on how to resolve two very different cultures, how to be both Korean and American, how to speak to my own mother. By the middle of my first year of college, my mother had started calling me on Sunday mornings to remind me not to have sex. At first I gave a good fight and tried to explain to her that being sexually active was acceptable behavior for someone my age and that few people of my generation believe in the good girl virgin stuff. After a while, I realized it was easier to lie.

• • •

A decade later I continue to live a secret life, as duplicitous and conflicted as a gay person acting straight to co-workers. I answer my mother's phone calls, assure her that I'm not having sex while my boyfriend lies in bed next to me. I might be in love, but I am deathly afraid of sharing that joy with my mother. Of course I want to tell her the truth, but every time I try, we end up yelling at each other.

How do you talk about love and sex with someone who thinks nothing positive of dating? My mother never experienced the kind of first date where you eat dinner, watch a movie and kiss at the front door. When she came of age in Korea, men and women weren't free to date without scandal surrounding them. When she was twenty-five, my mother's dates were arranged by elders and consisted of drinking tea and shaking hands at the end. By the third meeting she would decide whether she wanted to marry her date. I imagine that for a man, the process is not unlike interviewing for a job. Only those who are well-educated, well-connected and who promise success need apply. There was no opportunity for the couple to spend time and really get to know each other, fall in love and have sex. There was also no opportunity to discover the flaws of a seemingly perfect spouse or the many little ways in which they might not be compatible. That is, until after they got married and it was too late.

Yam-ja-neh is a Korean word used to describe women. It means nice, sweet, compliant. I've heard it applied to me many times by my parents' friends, who don't know shit about me. They meet me at dinner parties or wedding receptions, and because of the way I dress or the way I do my hair, they pronounce me yam-ja-neh and offer to set me up with their sons and nephews. I feel fifteen all over again, except now I have my mother's consent—not to have sex but to meet prospective suitors.

Geography doesn't matter when it comes to Korean matchmaking. My father's golf buddy gives me the phone number of his son in Chicago. (That's only, what, two time zones away from my home in Seattle?) "He graduated from MIT and is working as a software developer," the man pipes. My parents smile, encouraging me to take the number. For them it's the same game played years ago, when they were comparing test scores and college acceptances. Except now my parents are losing face, because I dropped out of premed to study writing. "Our daughter—we don't really know what she does. Let her tell you herself," my mother says to the programmer's father, who continues to check me out. I look yam-jah-neh to him, but if the truth came out, I'd be out of the race. Which is fine by me. I mean, I'm not really going to call this geek in Chicago, so what's the difference?

"Thank you," I say to the man as I take his son's number. I act out the role of the good daughter for my parents; it's the least I can do for turning out the way I did.

"Don't tell anyone about that ju-che-gi," my mother tells me. *Ju-che-gi*, which means fool, is what she calls my ex-boyfriend, Ian, whom I dated for two years. Ian is Dutch and for the first year of our relationship we lived together in Holland. He came with me when I returned to the United States and we lived in a studio in Queens, a mere twenty-minute drive away from my parents. Because of our living situation, there was no hiding him. It was my most significant relationship, not only because of the duration but because of his contact with my mother. For a while she even liked him.

When I ask why I shouldn't tell others about Ian, she answers, "Men won't like it if they find out you've been used." Because I didn't marry him, Ian is shameful, and the two years I spent with him must be rewritten for others who may not approve, the random golfers and doctors we meet at Korean functions. As if I were one of her patients, my mother keeps my history confidential, striking out the love of my life like a disease.

Is it foolish to think that as we both get older, we'll come to accept each other? Despite all the difficulties we've had, I still long to share more of my life with my mother. If we can't agree on things, I want her at least to know why I make the choices that I do, including why I fall for the men I do. Lately, I've started telling her a bit about my boyfriend—while letting her entertain the idea that I'm not having sex with him. It's better this way than not communicating at all.

Every once in a while, she surprises me and gives me hope. "I know American people carry on differently, but aren't you tired of all this dating?" she asked me recently. I could argue that it's better in the long run to learn from many different relationships, but as a commitmentphobe who attracts other commitmentphobes, I have to admit that all those dinners, movies and STD tests have lost their novelty. Yes, Mom, I'm tired of dating. I'm tired of the minirelationships that expire like milk. I'm tired of the breakups, even when they're "mutual" and "amicable." When my last boyfriend/potential husband/potential father to your grandchildren dumped me, he said, "I like you a lot, but I'm not sure if I can love you." He may as well have sent me a form letter. *We have reviewed your resume and while we are impressed with your experience, we do not have a suitable position that fits your qualifications. Thank you very much.*

Even though I want a long-term, loving relationship, I wonder if I can truly sustain one given my track record. At the end of our conversation, my mother withholds her usual mantra. Instead, she says, "Just be careful who you get involved with. You've got a lot more to offer than you think."

I could say the same for her.

Dutiful *Hijas:*
Dependency, Power and Guilt

Erica González Martínez

It started before I was born, before my mother was born, and before her mother was born. We were groomed to be caretakers, to carry the world on our shoulders without swaying and then humbly accept accolades *(que buena)* for it. We were an impossible fusion of Wonder Woman's strength and La Virgen Maria's sanctity and sacrifice. *Que Dios te ayuda* otherwise. Yes, I am a dutiful daughter, but it stresses me out. There, I've said it, but I don't exactly feel relieved. I feel guilty for thinking it and saying it. I hear those expressions echo in my head—*After all she's done for you . . . cria cuervo y te sacarán los ojos . . . la abandonaste.* I feel ungrateful *y como una hija mala* (like a bad daughter).

I was reminded of my place as a dutiful daughter on a recent trip to Puerto Rico. Even though I traveled alone, as usual, I still got the same question from my family. *Why didn't you bring your mother?* I had invited her because I felt guilty about going off to enjoy myself while she hadn't traveled in a few years. But she had declined. In Mami's hometown, as always, I was introduced and identified as *la nena de Norma.* My name, if even mentioned, was secondary. I found this funny—and very telling—to the point that I would outright declare, *Yo soy la nena de Norma.* I had to belong to someone and that meant Mami, since I wasn't Erica, *fulano-de-tal's* wife, because I was single.

Aside from the question and introduction—both of which had centered around my mother—there were two other comments that clearly painted the role of daughters as social security. An older woman I came across talked about how she was organizing her finances in preparation for her golden years: *Ya que solo tengo dos varones, que puedo hacer.* The mother of two boys, she had savings in lieu of a daughter. On another occasion an elderly male relative complimented me on my independent spirit. When I thanked him and told him I wasn't in a rush to get married or have kids, he responded with, *Pero quien te va a cuidar cuando te pones vieja?* Giving birth to a daughter was the equivalent of buying life insurance. A daughter would be there to take care of the parent in old age.

I am one of many dutiful daughters. For example, my twenty-four-year-old *amiga* who was raised in South America feels like a return on an investment. When she finished her undergraduate degree, it was demanded that she immediately fly back to the nest to take care of her mother, grandmother and brother. Initially, this had only meant being physically present. Now there are financial expectations beyond contributing to household expenses. While she would like to have her own home, her sense of obligation—imposed and self-imposed—is a block. *Their attitude is, "If you're not serving a* husband, then you're serving us." *I would leave but I would feel so guilty; I wouldn't feel at peace.* Interestingly, her brother is exempt from this responsibility.

Another friend, who is twenty-nine, until recently had her life dictated by her predetermined role. *My mother overdepends on me. It's reversed—I am the parent, she is the child. I see other parents not depending on their kids and the kids have the opportunity to go out in the world and find themselves. I had to know who I was from early on.* When my friend went away to school, her relatives wanted to know why she couldn't attend a local college, but her brother wasn't reproached and guilt-tripped for also enrolling in a university hours away. He was free to go; she was free to stay. *He's not a girl, so he's not expected to do the same.* Years later, with her decision to relocate, my friend received the same accusations from her family. *They feel like I'm deserting my mother. They say I am the only thing my mother has. I feel guilty about leaving her, like I'm not being a good daughter.*

We love our mothers. We want to be there for them and want them to feel comfortable in knowing and relying on that. What is problematic is the double standard; the patriarchal definition of what it means to be a "good" woman; the reproduction of a superior-inferior power dynamic via culture and religion; the marginalization of women, in particular women of color, in the economy; and the emotional dimension of guilt. These factors are all intertwined to produce a situation that deserves a space for conversation and reflection.

• • •

Ave Mareeeahh!

Marianismo is the crux of our existence.[1] Although the book *The Maria Paradox* inadequately simplifies this mother-daughter dynamic as a clash between "old" and "new" worlds, it offers a solid explanation of marianismo. Using the Virgin Mary as a point of reference, marianismo defines women as obedient servants who "happily" sacrifice themselves for everyone else's good. In marianismo, it is a woman's duty to be subservient and submissive, not to make decisions for herself.

Among the ten commandments of marianismo listed in *The Maria Paradox* are: "Do not forget a woman's place. Do not be single, self-supporting, or independent-minded. Do not put your own needs first. Do not wish for more in life than being a housewife." [2]

I was taught to defy marianismo, however. My friends and I were overencouraged, if not pushed, to pursue university degrees. Our mothers saw education as a vehicle for liberation from economic dependency, typically the factor that kept them in unhappy relationships. My parents spared no expense or effort when it came to education for my sister and me. Getting a college education was mandatory for us even though it contradicted some tenets of marianismo. In college I, along with the women I am still close to, began to be exposed to the work and boldness of feminists and womanists. I learned about the concepts of "voice," "the personal being political" and the "masculinization of nationalism." I read enlightening work by Julia de Burgos, bell hooks, Angela Davis and Assata Shakur.[3] I interacted with amazing professors, like Micere Mugo, Linda Alcoff, Alicia

Vadillo and Terri Northrup; and I was inspired by the mothers who fought against police brutality in New York City and the accomplishments of the Latin Women's Collective, a now-defunct organization that focused on developing Latinas as leaders.

Even though I grew up knowing that Gloria Steinem was dedicated to women's rights and recalled the ERA (Equal Rights Amendment) posters, my first real understanding of feminism came through the women who looked like me and who spoke to me culturally and politically. They were committed to liberation, of a colony or of one's self. As a Puerto Rican, these questions of race, class and national liberation were critical to me. I subscribed to bell hooks' definition of feminism:

> Feminisim is not simply a struggle to end male chauvinism or a movement to ensure that women will have equal rights with men; it is a commitment to eradicating the ideology of domination that permeates Western culture on various levels—sex, race and class to name a few—and a commitment to reorganizing society . . . so that self-development of people can take a precedence over imperialism, economic expansion, and material desire.[4]

I understood that I was a Puerto Rican *woman* and that the woman part of me couldn't be a backburner component. The patriarchy was real and reflected in many of the political campaigns in which I participated. Learning how to identify and address sexism was a process. Pointing it out was on many occasions dismissed, passively agreed with or responded to defensively with examples of female political martyrdom. I saw how sexism—or rather, not dealing with it proactively—could cripple political work. Instead of feminism being linked to race, class and national liberation—and made part of our daily work and progress—it was mostly relegated to panel discussions.

Nationalist Lolita Lebron wore a skirt when she and her armed comrades charged the U.S. Congress in 1954 to defend Puerto Rico's right to be a sovereign nation. In 1915, Luisa Capetillo, a feminist and socialist who organized workers in Puerto Rico, was arrested for wearing pants in public in Cuba. Both Lolita and Luisa inspired me. I was driven by the ultimate freedom of my people and myself. These ideals came into conflict at home, however. It was easier to organize a rally against a tuition hike or get involved in a movement to free political prisoners than to face the painful contradictions of who I was raised to be.

Growing up, my sister and I had *muñecas* and knew to cross our legs when sitting down. We also had an easel, a Starsky and Hutch set, race cars, a cash register and a Fisher Price doctor's kit. An ex-air force boxer, my father taught us to shoot a BB gun at empty Nestlé Quik cans and how to snap a punch. According to my mother, getting married and having kids was not a priority, and philandering husbands were unacceptable. But the premise of marianismo (women as servants), along with the aspects of suffering and guilt, were ingrained, both inside and outside of the home.

Suffering Will Make a Good Woman Out of You

I had a striking introduction to women's suffering in Catholic elementary school. I had picked up a book about Saint Rose of Lima. Even though I was little, I understood she was Latina because she was from Peru and Peru was in South America. That meant she had some kind of link to me because she spoke Spanish while all the other saints seemed to be from Europe. As I read the paragraphs on the bottom of the pages and looked at the pictures on top, I was both horrified and fascinated. Saint Rose stuck a pin in her head and slept on rocks to prove her commitment to God. She rejected the advances of Satan—who was drawn both as a hideous giant and a tempting stud, not the Red Devil-*pique* figure. I was amazed at the things Saint Rose did to herself. Soon after reading that book, I was petitioning for something or trying to repent for being "bad." I made myself suffer. I wasn't brave enough to resort to rocks, so one night I threw barrettes and bobby pins all over my bed and slept on them. I wanted to serve God but I didn't want all the pain involved. Yet I understood that the more you suffered, the more saintly you were, which makes you closer to God and yes, *superbuena*.

In church, women were elements of the equation. The statue of the Virgin Mary watched us or waited to be adored. Her greatness came from bearing a special child and being chosen to do so by an almighty being, assumed to be male. The nuns, the Sisters of Mercy, sat in the front pews during Mass and ran the elementary school. The women directed the choir, cleaned the rectory, cooked for the priests and responded to inquiries. But after God, always assumed to be male, the priest was central. He had the power to celebrate the Mass, and in the name of "Him," absolve us of our sins. The deacons, typically men, were next in importance. Making a church or school function, as the nuns did, wasn't enough to merit leading a Mass. As classic dutiful daughters, they had the role of servitude. This male-oriented hierarchy in the church followed the patriarchal organization of society. It also was a reality in my family.

In our house, there was clearly a chain of command. My father, a Vietnam veteran and police lieutenant, was the *jefe*. My mother, a former beautician-salesperson-receptionist-daycare worker, was next in line. My sister and I were the subordinates. I was the boss by virtue of being older. My mother was by no means quietly compliant, but my father was frequently the decision-maker, an entitlement that came from being the man and the breadwinner as well as having a college degree, compared with my mother's high-school education. Mami raised us and maintained our home while Papi earned the money and paid the bills. When this structure and organization was ruptured, we were faced with redefining our positions.

Transferring Dependency

My parents split up after twenty-six years of marriage. I was twenty-two and had just graduated from college. Although the breakup was not a surprise, my mother was unprepared and panic-stricken by the thought of having to survive on her own. She had worked for years before and after marrying my father, but a major stroke at a young age had rendered her physically unable to handle many tasks. She could not contribute an income to the household. Despite raising us and taking care of the house, her work had not been acknowledged as such because it did not yield money. In the computer age, she wasn't ready to reenter the job market. My mother had been deeply frustrated at her dependency on my father. As a result of her physical limitations and her concerns about raising us properly, her life was in the home. She had been unable to establish herself beyond a mother or a wife. This is by no means saying that being a mother and wife aren't wonderful things. But they are aspects of the self in relation to others. My mother was *la mama de . . . la esposa de . . .* but maybe she wanted at times to just be her, in her own right.

Paralyzed by fear, my mother attempted to transfer her dependency on my father to my sister and me a time when both of us were coming into our own as independent adults. This dependency wasn't necessarily always financial but in the realms of decision-making, organization and action. She had always overdepended on us emotionally. We were her world and would get chastised for doing things like staying out late as young adults (translation: staying away from her). Our relationship was already troubled by the power dynamic of the parent as superior and the child—even an adult daughter—as subordinate. Although my mother in her proud, *jibara*-never-ask-for-anything way would not tell me that I had to be the "man" of the house, the pressure was there. At times I felt like I had to be her missing husband or parent.

I did not shy away from being there, but I was uncomfortable with her asking me for direction or to make decisions for her. Although she initially and understandably felt devastated and confused about the end of her marriage, I wanted my mother to understand that there was the potential of her emerging from this crisis as a new woman. I wanted her to recognize that she could finally take some ownership of her life and make choices based on her own well-being and desires, and that she deserved and had the right to do so.

In the long divorce process, my sister and I responded as we should have—with support, love, assistance and patience. But there were many occasions when we had to hold our mother by the hand to do something like make a phone call to a bureaucrat. She preferred to have my sister or me deal with any task she found intimidating. When we didn't comply, she acted wounded, not seeing, at least at first, that we were only encouraging her to become self-reliant and establish her own identity, much in the same way she had encouraged us over the years. We had been taught to be the best and that we were capable of doing anything by the same woman who was now floundering at what she saw as the frightening prospect of independence, or rather, having to go it "alone" and fearing that she would fail. My mother grew up in poverty in Puerto Rico—a poverty rooted in the United States' domination of the Puerto Rican economy. The possibility of not being able to afford the medical care she needed or to cover her bills was scary. She wasn't operating from the perspective that she came from a long line of survivors who did what they set out to do—to make life a little better for the next generation.

It was emotionally enervating for all of us. But understanding that this was a space and time for my mother to grow and do things according to her own wants and needs, I gave her tough love. We said no to some requests and yes to others. However we reacted, there was always a level of guilt.

Judge, We Find *la Hija* Guilty

We have been trained to feel guilty for being less than perfect (even though as a wise poet once told me, there is no such thing as perfection). Even on occasions when my mother doesn't give me a pitiful look, I project guilt. I can never do enough for her. After all, she carried me for nine months, dedicated herself to my well-being and has been my biggest cheerleader. How could I ever repay her? But is that even the point? We sustain our guilt by constantly trying to compensate for feelings of inadequacy about being less than "perfect," less than *La Virgen*, showing our subscription to a *marianista* philosophy. The logic is that I am a *good* person when I *serve* her, and that must be 24-7.

Conveying to my mother that my love for her does not diminish when I don't do what she wants was a challenge—for both of us. Giving myself permission to say no to her—*que Dios me perdone*—and not feeling like a bad person for doing so was a breakthrough. All of the sacrifices she made so I could have a better chance would be in vain if I did not bring to the table the knowledge and experiences I had gained. That scenarios of living and power could be different and not necessarily doomsday-negative, even in your fifties, was what I offered. We painfully go back and forth, more often than not trying to exorcise ourselves of some residual issue and climbing to a new plateau.

As a politically conscious, single woman, I have the internal critic as well as the external cultural judge evaluating whether I'm acting like a selfish, individualistic *gringa* or a community-building and respecting Latina. Whenever my twenty-four-year-old friend appears to do something that doesn't have her family at center, she gets the old *Eso es una cosa Americana*. We both agree that our sense of community and family is a part of who we are, but not breathing and living family as the core of our beings every single minute of the day doesn't make us sellouts or *Americanas*.[5] Claiming our own voices does not mean that we forego our people's survival strategies and remarkable principles of sharing and looking out for one another.

The issues of class and economics are rarely divorced from any aspect of our lives. Most of my friends struggle to pay their rent, living expenses and student loans. We're not affluent women who can support another person's entire financial needs or hire attendants and housekeepers. Our mothers, approaching their retirement years, find themselves out of the male-as-principal-breadwinner structure to which they were accustomed. Our mothers also find their role of caretaker disappearing. What do you do when what you have based your identity on—caretaking—is no longer a need? How do you become emotionally and economically independent? How do you carve your own identity? How does a buena daughter help out of choice and love, not guilt?

The fears are valid. The fear of being alone. The fear of not having a purpose. The fear of not being able to afford basic necessities. The economy is not striking up the band for women in their fifties with limited skills. If professional Latinas make fifty cents on every dollar an Anglo man makes, imagine how a Latina with limited earning potential survives. An article in the *New York Times* described how older women are finding themselves in the predicament of entering their golden years but having to stay in the workforce as a result of divorce. This is attributed to women who spent years raising children but not having pensions of their own. Even older women who are able to land jobs now have to delay retirement as they play catch-up with someone who worked a lifetime.

As a dutiful daughter, I felt pressured. I wanted to take care of my mother, to tell her that she could just kick up her feet and relax because I had everything under control. This not being the case, however, I couldn't help but feel inadequate about not meeting my own *supermujer* expectations. I also was afraid of feeling selfish or of being labeled as such for not putting her happiness before mine. This is why I would agonize over having to inform her or my family that I wanted to go away to school or to rent my own apartment. Then I would feel resentful about the comments or looks I would receive.

I didn't want my mother to correlate my not being physically present in her house with not being in her life. And I was afraid of having every aspect of my life revolve around what would make my mother happy. I know that my decisions about school and the apartment were the right ones, but it doesn't mean the guilt and anxiety disappear forever. On a few occasions when I haven't been able to reach my mother, I have imagined the worst and chided myself for not living with her, for not protecting her enough. I have felt that if something happened to her, I would be full of regret for not being as dutiful as I could have been, for not preventing something bad from taking place. Yet us living together would roll back our relationship.

Although my mother was somewhat better off than some of her pals in similar situations—she co-owns her house and receives financial maintenance from my father—she will have to pay for astronomical medical insurance and household expenses by herself. She also doesn't feel comfortable with just relying on maintenance that could not be there one day. This insecurity led her to enroll in a course that provided computer training and job readiness to people in her age group. Not quite a tech nerd, Mami is now more proficient at Microsoft Excel than I am. But finding work hasn't been easy. Sometimes she doesn't meet the criteria of prospective jobs or feels she is denied an opportunity because she is older. Other times, jobs aren't right for her needs. Besides technological skills, the program Mami participated in allowed her to develop a network of friends and her own life. To my delight, she would hang out with "the girls," dictate her own comings and goings and excitedly recount her day to us. She enjoys volunteer work, where her contributions are valued and appreciated and tries to revisit goals she had once set for herself. My mother has created an opening that allowed for self-development and fulfillment and expanded her experiences beyond the world that was prescribed for her as a dutiful *mujer*.

Our mother-daughter relationship is a work in progress. We—Mami, Sis and I—struggle through new ways of being in the world that will help redefine what kind of mothers and daughters we will be in the future, and what kind of sons, daughters and grandchildren we will raise.

I especially thank Mami, Melinda, Blanca and WILL (a collective for women of color writers) for making this essay possible.

Femme-Inism:
Lessons of My Mother

Paula Austin

My mother taught me everything I know about "feminism" even if she didn't think she was teaching me. She taught me to work hard, to be hard, to fight mean, to fear love (to question love). She taught me the meaning of honor and retribution and fear, and pain that goes way back. She taught me what she knew. She taught me about desire and sex and sensuality. How to flirt, be coy and demure. How to be femme, a high diva, show off my cleavage. How to be looked at, how to be invisible and afraid. How to survive, to stay alive. She taught me what she could. About women's power and authority.

Reflections

I was four years old when my mother brought me and my three older sisters to the United States from British Guiana, a small Caribbean country on the northern tip of South America. The United States offered a different kind of access to higher education and the ability to change one's economic class, if you could play the game. My mother, Ena, had grown up in colonial British Guiana during the

157

1930s. She lived in rural Bartica, where people were poor and Black and struggled to feed their children. My grandmother washed the dirty laundry of rich, white English people seven days a week. She stood all day at the washer board and basin and then later at the ironing board. My grandfather had left his family when my mother was ten years old. As a child, my mother scrubbed floors to help her mother. My mother's education ended at the sixth grade. She says she "never had a head for school or book-learning." She couldn't keep any job that she got. By the time she was sixteen, she had already had two nervous breakdowns and had been raped by a friend of the family. My mother eventually learned to self-medicate with alcohol. She also learned to do hair and sex work.

Ena's idea of strength lay in the power of her sexuality. Looking good and getting what you needed. On her limited budget she was always clean, well groomed, sexy. Heaving breasts, round wide hips hugged in by a long-line brassiere and girdle. Her hair wound up on the top of her head, pressed and shining with hair grease. She knew how to "get" things—money, kerosene to light the lamps and food for her children. This was her work, to survive and keep her girls alive, while her husband—twenty years her senior—supported his other family across town.

Through her sex work my mother found reason to feel accomplished, adequate, of use to her family, sending her sister, Lucille, to school and feeding Lucille's children as well as her own. Ena found a means by which she could control both her life and her body. Even after my mother married at twenty-one, she continued to have several "boyfriends." There had always been men who coveted her, and she used this to her advantage at a time and in a country where dark-skinned, poor women like her had few opportunities outside of telephone operator, secretary or teacher to make money. Colonialism, imperialism and white supremacy created an economic separation between light-skinned Black women and white women as smart women of leisure and dark-skinned Black women as thick-headed laborers.

In 1984 I was sixteen. I was a junior in high school, in love with my best friend, Jennifer. This is the same year that Susan Brownmiller published her book *Femininity*. I did not read it until two years later when I was taking a women's studies course at my liberal arts college in New York City. (It was unheard of that I would go away to college—only white kids did that. So I lived with my mother in Flatbush, Brooklyn, and took the subway to school and work each day.) Brownmiller discussed a femininity rooted in heterosexuality and a female-to-female competition for male attention. She talked about femininity as a type of "feminine armor," not a suit of metal in the traditional sense but rather an overstated and distorted display of weakness that was comforting and safe to men.

As a child, I often watched my mother from the bed. She would take out each clip from her hair and rings of long, pressed black hair would unravel down her head. She brushed it hard, and back, and pinned it up and to the side. Then she twisted the back in a French roll and brushed a little bang behind her ear and pinned it there. She pulled on her control-fitted panty hose over her shapely thighs and ass. Over her hose she put on her girdle and fastened her long-line brassiere. Sometimes I would have to help pull the hook and eyes together behind her.

I often watched her do her makeup in front of the small mirror that sat on a tiny square table across from the bed I slept on, in the bedroom I shared with my mother and sister. She would dab some foundation from the bottle into her hand and smear it evenly across and around her face. She used concealer around her eyes and covered that with powder. She wore black eyeliner, above and below her lid, which she administered with a pencil. She wore eye shadow and mascara. Lastly, she lined her lips, using some shade of burgundy. When she finished dressing, her shoes and pocketbook always matching, the room smelled like her expensive perfume long after she had gone.

This was her ritual each day, the donning of her costume. This was her feminine armor, her feminist attire. This was the very thing that brought her strength and power. I could tell this by the way she stepped out onto the street in her blue polyester floral dress that hugged her hips and thighs, her strong calves shaping down into her white pumps, her ass and pocketbook both swaying. Her sexy gait was evidence of her prowess, and both she and I were proud. She was unknowingly modeling for me.

When I was eleven or twelve, I was punished for wearing makeup. I would wait until my mother was out of the room at bedtime and I would sneak an eyeliner pencil from the makeup drawer to under the bed. In the morning I would pretend I was looking for my shoes and slip the eyeliner into my pants pocket, sneaking it out of the house.

Somewhere between the apartment door and the building's front door down five flights of stairs, I would hurriedly apply the makeup, lining my eyes with the blue pencil and combing on the black mascara I had stolen from Woolworth's. I was never delicate enough. I was rough, rushed and heavy-handed. Once applied, as hideously as it may have looked, I stepped out from that apartment building. Out onto Ocean Avenue in Flatbush, where I was a poor Black girl, living in someone else's apartment in an all-white neighborhood, where my family was seen as "the help." And at eight in the morning, on that street with all of its white faces staring down at me or not seeing me at all, I walked with my head high and made it to the bus stop without flinching. It was my armor, too.

My Radicalism

My introduction to what "feminism" was and what it could mean for me as a woman of color came when I was twenty. At my private, predominately white college, we read many things, including *This Bridge Called My Back: Radical Writings by Women of Color*. It was the first time I saw in print something I could identify with, the intersection of history, culture, oppression and identity. It was a rite of passage for me. That year I came out as lesbian, as visible in terms of my Caribbean culture and heritage, as an abused daughter of a wounded, alcoholic mother. Until this point my existence as a chunky, curly-haired, brown-skinned, large-chested girl had been very much about how to remain unseen. I felt ugly, undesirable, unlovable. During summers as a teenager, in the heat of my Brooklyn neighborhood—which was changing from Jewish affluent to Puerto Rican/West Indian work-ing class—I had felt large and uncomfortable in my T-shirt and shorts as well as in my own skin. Now in college I began to see myself and the world differently.

There I worked with five white women in a student group. We organized around "diversity" issues on our campus. I learned about leadership, voice and coalition-building as we worked on racism, sex-ism and homophobia at our school. We read and wrote together, staged actions, hung up signs and held caucuses, panel discussions and consciousness-raising groups. I learned about internalized oppression, not so much about racism as about sexism, and under-stood it to be at the heart of my desires for invisibility during those teen summers. Understood it to be at the heart of my sense of myself as ugly and undesirable—and simultaneously sexually perverted. (At this time I was being unhappily sexual with random men at my job.)

This internalization of all the destructive messages I had gotten over the years—which I continued to receive—about brown, round women was at the heart of my short stint of trying to deny my femme self (after I had come out) for a more politically correct (and accepted, by my white lesbian friends) androgynous presentation of myself. Still, in many ways this was an idyllic time: social activism and diversity work in a relatively safe environment. I wouldn't know the real impact of patriarchy and its intersection with racism, sexism and homophobia until I left school.

After graduation I stayed in New York and found a job working as a secretary. I wanted to teach but wasn't quite sure how to do it and I needed to support myself. I wanted to move out of my grand-mother's apartment, which was downstairs from my mother's employer's apartment. It was this life, after school, where I would face my reality without the built-in support of women from college, with whom I had become accountable for fighting against injustice. There were mornings on the subway, being felt up and doing noth-ing except enduring it. Sexual harassment at the gym, and being too ashamed to even feel my indignation until much later. Without the anger and righteousness of my women friends, how could I remem-ber that I had a right to my own body, a right to say no? What a priv-ilege it had been to be able to sit and talk about these things, to scream our rage, to write essays. What would I do with this new sen-sibility? Out here, alone.

My mother had known racism. She understood its existence as a fact of life, a given. It wasn't something changeable, moveable. It was some-thing to be maneuvered around, waded through like muck and mire. It wasn't even something necessarily to be talked about. And she moved through it slowly, her pace crippled by clinical depression, little education and hard work from an early age. I think she found some strength in doing hair and sex work. She always said to her daughters, "You have two things against you: you're Black and you're a woman. Nothing is going to be easy." She would urge us to get our education so that we would not have to "depend on a man." My sister and I would cringe at hearing ourselves referred to as "Black," certain that it wasn't a good thing. Often in the same breath my mother would urge us to marry white men, so that we would have babies with "good hair."

. . .

My Armor

I always admired my mother's sense of what was powerful about herself: flirting. I remember hearing my mother on the phone or watching her with company. She flirted with everyone. It seemed a completely natural way of interaction. What I learned, listening to my mother's sultry voice—placating, or asking questions like a little girl, giggling, sighing, her eyes wide and suggestive—was that women who had this skill had power. Did the men, and women, she used this on know what she was doing? Did they allow themselves to be manipulated, or distracted from the task at hand? I don't know—not even now when I use my powers of flirt and distract.

It is moments like being stranded on the highway with a flat tire that what I have learned from my mother becomes necessary. I am on my way back from the beach with a white lover who looks like a boy. I am in a long cotton dress, slits up both sides, flip-flop high heels, hair in a curly pom-pom on the top of my head. We are somewhere between Durham and Wilmington, North Carolina. I am a Northerner with all kinds of frightening stereotypes about the South, all of which come into play when I am stranded on the side of the road at dusk.

We trudge across the highway to what looks like a road toward town or houses, at the very least. We end up at a bus repair shop. A man with a deep southern drawl and greasy overalls emerges from the back of the shop to greet us. My lover is concerned about her baseball cap and butch appearance. I am concerned about being Black. Will I be raped or lynched? Will they realize the person I am with is not a boy? Even with all my fear, there is no question between us that my femme affect is the safest bet here. I ask to use the phone, saying we have broken down. My girlfriend nods, smiles, stands idly by. The man directs me to the phone and I call AAA. I tell them I have a flat tire. "I can't seem to get those screwy things off, you know, they hold the tire in place?" I say. The tone in my voice is of distress and silliness. I shift my weight from hip to hip, smiling at the greasy man as I wait for them to dispatch a truck. My girlfriend does not speak.

There is no real reason for me to maintain my femme performance on the phone with the AAA customer assistant. I am not really being paid attention to by the garage attendant. Still, I am deep in character, and it brings me a sense of control in the midst of this danger, as does the two-inch elevation from my shoes and my lipstick. The donning of my armor helps to hold at bay the anxiety and panic until it can be safely expressed later in the arms of my lover or with my friends.

Off the phone I talk more with the greasy man about the "screwy things" that we could not seem to remove and the jack, which we couldn't get to work. When the tow truck arrives, we squeeze into the front seat with me next to the driver, a white man with a thick drawl and the smell of stale Coke and cigarettes permeating everything in the truck. He has had to move aside several girly magazines to make room for us. We drive ten miles before we can get back to the highway. In an effort to distract him from too much observation about the Black woman and white woman in his truck, one of whom looks suspiciously like a boy, I chatter. More conversation about the "screwy things."

"Lug nuts," he says.

"Oh, is that what they call them?" I giggle. "I just don't know a thing about changing a tire. And what is that?" I point toward the fields of crops we whiz by.

"T'bacca."

"Ohhh, really, is that what it looks like?" More giggling. My lover's leg is anxiously pressed up against mine.

We finally make it back to my stranded car. The tow truck guy hoists a large jack from his truck, upon which he begins lifting my car. I flit around him. "Man size," I say, referring to the jack suggestively. I am aware of my play-acting, feeling powerful in the skill of it. He is responding to it. I think it brings comfort to him. I look the part, like my Mama taught me.

The line is thin between empowerment of "femme" and its potential self-destructiveness. I wonder if it was like this for my mother. She turned to sex work out of necessity. This is not something I have to do. Femme brings with it what we have learned about what it means to be female and woman in this country and culture. As many times as I have felt empowered by it, I have also found the power of my femme affect slipping away, leaving instead the ways I feel defeated, inept, unable to handle difficult situations. Rationally, I know these to be the messages of the oppressors and colonizers. Still, I have competed with other femmes for the attention of butches and transgender men. I have both claimed and loathed the titles of Jezebel and

Hoochie Mama after having an affair with a woman who already had a wife. And even though this particular relationship was damaging, my femme self finds pride in having been able to steal this woman away from her partner, if only for a moment. Sometimes I hate that part of me.

Femme-Inism

I have felt left out of feminism mostly because it leaves out women who looked like my mother—traditionally feminine, of color, poor, powerful despite the impacts of oppression on her psyche. It leaves no room for women who find their power through a perceived powerlessness. Amber Hollibaugh—lesbian sex radical, ex-hooker, gypsy—says that it is no accident that there are so many femmes with a history of sex work. She talks about sex workers moving in the world differently than other women, with their heads held high. Men looked at my mother when she walked down the street, and she never looked down or away. This display of blatant subjectivity flies in the face of what we are taught as little girls, how to be a "good girl."

My femme dance *is* reassuring to men. But there is also power, art, objective, resistance in it. For my mother and myself, colonization and the battle against it poses a contradiction between appearances and deeper survivals. Joan Nestle, author and founder of the *Lesbian Herstory Archives* and general femme hero, has said, "There is a need to reflect the colonizer's image back at him yet at the same time to keep alive what is a deep part of one's culture, even if it is misunderstood by the oppressor, who omnipotently thinks he knows what he is seeing."[1]

For me and my mother our femme existence and our femme performance have been the ways in which we have found pleasure in our bodies, wide-assed, round and brown. Bodies that society teaches us to scorn. To ignore the way in which femme reclaims ourselves is to seriously diminish our resistance. It is this resistance that is at the heart of my "femme-inism." My mother's feminism was limited, mixed in with very traditional West Indian and Catholic views of gender and sexuality.

There is no language that can create an understanding of how my femme identity and "feminism" function in me as one, with no space between them. The same way race, gender, sexuality and class exist simultaneously in me, and how who I am is the filter through which I see everything. The same is true for my femme-inism. Maybe it is how I can reclaim my mother's high-femme practice in a more empowered way. To survive, I had to allow myself to be who I am, constrained for a while by the lesbian feminism of the 1970s, which rejected both butch and femme as a "heterosexist imitation of the oppressive gender roles of patriarchy." Even though I came out as lesbian femme in the 1990s, when folks had begun to write about the separation of sex and gender, making room for the possibilities of gender play as itself a political and erotic option, there was still a very large community of lesbians, young and old, primarily middle class and white, who continued to subscribe to the lesbian feminism of the early women's movement.

I have only to look at my mother to see it is possible to be both femme and feminist. For me and for many poor and working-class women who have struggled to support themselves, and their families, who have struggled to be strong through the physical and emotional manifestations of oppression and colonization. The stories my mother has told me about herself—of an outrageous girl washing her naked self on the back steps in the twilight, of a mother starting a new life for herself and her children in a different country and culture at the age of forty-two, of a woman whose empowerment knew many bounds, who did what she had to for her children to survive, a woman who somehow in the midst of her own internalized oppression trans-ferred racial and gender pride, as well as she could, to her daughters—these stories I keep alive and recount as evidence of the strength of the women in my family.

These stories are the context of my femme-inism. The monster of colonization, acculturation, prejudice, discrimination, poverty, misogyny takes shape in me as I struggle here to bring together, in myself, these two aspects of my mother, which her life only hints at—her true and deep passion and sexuality and her strength to proac-tively address the limitations of her situation.

Feminist Musings on the No. 3 Train

Lourdes-marie Prophete

I joke that my mom's and my aunt's problems all stem from the Trinity: the omnipotent rules that they accept faithfully without question, the savior man who will marry them and save them, and the Holy Ghosts—the men who are actually in their lives. I came up with that insight on the No. 3 subway train, leaving my mom's home after a visit. In transit between my mom's world and mine, insights like these pour out. If feminism is in the water I drink, my mom's herstory is the dry land that pushes me to swallow.

The actual men in their lives were helpful but more in the background: the Holy Ghosts. My mom grew up in Haiti, where she married my father and then moved to New York. He left her and returned to Haiti shortly after I was born. He sent me letters and money until he died. My aunt came to live with us a couple of years after my grandmother came. My aunt was "waiting" for a husband. Boyfriends came and eventually left. My grandmother came closest to the ideal— she married once, stayed married until her death, had children and grandchildren. She was the matriarch who raised seven children as well as nieces and nephews in Haiti. When my mother was growing up, my grandmother was effectively a single mother because my grandfather had to live far away from her and the children in the isolated country, farming and sending her money. She came to New York to help my mother raise me. She prayed a lot. She rarely talked about herself. She died when I was young.

My uncles would help out doing "manly" things, like driving my mother, grandmother and aunt places and fixing things that my mom would not even let me near because I was a girl. I noticed men were given more space and authority and took it. My mom said that men drink beer, so we had beer in the fridge just for the suitors and our male relatives. I was told that if I had had a father, I wouldn't have rebelled so much because he would have beaten it out of me. Some of the men in my extended family were kind and gentle, while others were hard and authoritarian. They were all in the background, peripheral to the women.

My family raised me to wait: for Catholic Armageddon, for a husband and, once I found the husband, to wait on him. I balked at this. But even as I rebelled, I was afraid I wouldn't escape from the future they projected for me. I lump all of their self-defeating ideas that no amount of discussion and reasoning could change with the first part of the triumvirate—the omnipotent rules, a hodgepodge of beliefs that were often contradictory but sacrosanct. According to these rules, the ideal for a woman was that she stay at home. A woman cooks, cleans and takes care of the children while her husband works. A woman should be obedient to her husband. They argued women shouldn't be allowed to be priests because they were too frivolous and weak. I wondered who in this network of strong women, extended family included, was frivolous and weak. Yet, these women also demonstrated their respect for females with beliefs such as that girls take better care of their elderly parents than boys do.

The strange thing about my family is that most of the time they were feminists in action. The life I have now and the choices I enjoy are due to my mother's sacrifices and her faith. Even as I condemn my female relatives' sexism, I realize they were fighters, surviving and doing things on their own every day. My mom got up and went to work, her example telling me that I could do it as well. She immigrated to America to give me a better life. The women in my life told me I had to do well in school. My mom taught me to read before first grade, which was probably the determining factor in my later academic success. When I graduated from high school, my mom and aunt got uncharacteristically emotional, remarking that it looked like I was going to make it. I have inherited from these women a very pragmatic way of looking at the world, because they did whatever was necessary to get the job done.

It is hard going and coming from my mom and aunt's home. In that journey, I leave the world I've created behind—a world that is flourishing, full of goals, joys, challenges and possibilities—to enter a very desolate world. They worry about this, they suffer from that, but even when there isn't anything pressing, there is still the dead air. Although they have pushed me to incredible heights, they themselves are stuck. I help but I haven't solved the problem. On the train to and from, I'm looking for understanding.

One of my cousins who grew up in Haiti told me I don't know Haitians. I know my family in New York, and they are a pretty unhappy bunch. She had a point. The calmest and happiest I have ever seen my mother was when we visited Haiti together. There, my extended family seemed to have lighter hearts and more everyday joy. I realized that my mother sacrificed her emotional health coming to the United States. It is hard to be a single mother and an immigrant. It is all speculation how culture, sexism, racism, classicism and personality played a part in my mom's life. What I know is that my mom's sacrosanct belief in the inferiority of women and their role in the world didn't help. It is still not helping. She survived and is surviving. However, I feel she would survive better and, more importantly, happier without that noose around her neck.

When I visited Haiti as a nine-year-old, I noticed that people spent time in each others' houses. It was very social. One of the games was to tell stories. It is hard to believe my aunt's stories of my mother going out dancing when she was young. Living in the United States made it easy for my mom's life to become small. She never made New York her home. My experiences in France and West Africa have given me a better appreciation of how hard it is to create a new life in a foreign land. People who are able to make a foreign country their home have to be bold and aggressive. My mom was bold and aggressive when she had to be in order to care for her family, but she never put value on *"pleasi,"* pleasures. Putting effort into making her life in the

United States more pleasurable would have seemed extravagant to her. Pleasure is nice if you get it, but you don't fight for it. In Haiti, knowing the language and the culture, she would not have felt isolated. It would have been easier to make connections with new people. Now, all of her friends in New York are people she had been friends with in Haiti. She has never had much of a social life in New York. She spent a lot of her free time praying, watching TV and sleeping. Religion was her succor. It also fed her tendency to keep her life small, with its concentration on passivity and the afterlife.

My mother is living for the afterlife. Once, when she found me crying about something, she said that we're not meant to be happy, that this life is about suffering, and we'll have happiness in heaven.

An important difference between my mom's personality and mine is the value I place on my own wants, needs and feelings in the here and now. She put an incredible amount of energy into raising me but none into herself. I grew up with a greater economic stability, so perhaps that is why I insisted on creating a life that met my emotional and spiritual needs in the here and now. I carry some guilt about this.

My aunt is currently suffering from many maladies, but everyone in my family agrees her trouble stems from depression. She's never married in a culture that teaches her that it is her job to be a wife. In her world she has had few choices. I wish she'd grown up in a place where she was encouraged to make up her own path and look beyond the choices presented to her by family and culture.

It frustrated me when I was growing up that if something broke in the house they'd lament that if only we had a man in the house, "he could fix things." I did not want them to feel helpless or feel helpless myself. So I'd go over and fix the TV or VCR or put the fan together. But they'd still go on: "Our lives would be so much better if we had a man in the house." When I'd present the fixed item to them, they'd put on a surprised smile but I knew I hadn't solved the problem. Years later I surprised them with a career playing with computer technology and the Internet.

I can understand missing male companionship, but that wasn't the way they talked about it. They talked about the "savior" man specifically within the context of social security and economic survival. I understand that when two people share a life together there are economic benefits, but those benefits were at the forefront of the way the women I grew up with talked about men. This wasn't just limited to discussions about husbands. I noticed that whenever we got into conversations about family, my mom said she wanted children because she wanted someone to take care of her when she grew older. I was ten when I asked Mom, "What does a husband do?" In her words: "He would advocate for me. People take advantage of you when you are a woman alone. He would know of opportunities and fight for us in the world."

I understood her answer better after I visited Gambia and Senegal in West Africa. The inability of most women there to achieve financial and social independence underpinned gender inequality in that region. Women were so absent from public culture in Dakar that they were hardly seen walking in the streets. I am sure they had their own culture and life separate from male society, but that male society is the one with access to the public space, the finances and the political power. A Western-educated Gambian man explained to me that there are some very strong Gambian women who become successful, and they can be very vocal, but there is a line and they will not cross it. I believe my older female relatives grew up in a similar atmosphere. They learned to depend on men to act for them. Even when they take care of themselves, they never stop emotionally or psychologically depending on men . . . like on the Holy Ghost. It seems to be another excuse to not live for themselves, to not create happiness for themselves.

I've had discussions with friends about whether people who grow up under oppression with no access to alternatives know that their situations are wrong. I believe they feel it even if they aren't able to articulate it to themselves. They may not know how to attach this background of oppression to the cause of their current situations and therefore accept it as normal, but it is there. My mom's and aunt's adherence to the proscribed female role is like an invisible noose around their necks constricting their ability to reach their potential. They live out the effects of it.

The difference between my situation and that of my mom's is degree. My mother's access to information, wealth and power was disadvantaged, and she accepted this as the natural way of the world. Her ideas about family were bound up with the idea of economic and social security. But I live in a society that gives me choices, choices that men in other countries can't exercise. It is easier for me to imagine independence without relating to family and husband. I owe a debt to the feminist movement that I can get a job, live alone and walk around in jeans and a T-shirt without getting harassed. My mom's concern about economic security adds an urgency to conversations about family that I—with my Western, highly educated background—don't relate to. At the same time, I've grown up with my own issues around gender, race and class. My access to information, wealth and power was also at a disadvantage, but I don't accept that as natural.

My impression of life growing up in a working-class Caribbean neighborhood was that you had to be very worried about surviving. Life was hard and difficult, and you had to make as much money as you could to be safe. After moving into the white, liberal arts college world, I was presented with the idea that life is a challenge or an adventure, and you must find the work that will make you happy (notice the word "happy"). I did not want the unpleasant passionless future of my upbringing, however the other future of my well-to-do classmates seemed like a fantastic dream. There was a conflict in these two realities, and I did not know how to reconcile them. I took a leap of faith. I ended up living my life searching for and creating my own happiness, despite my doubtfulness of the workability of this path. It worked for me. Armed with a good education, I had more choices then the people I grew up with. It is doubtful I will ever have to clean houses like my mom or my aunt. I realized there is not one reality, many realities co-exist.

I am conscious of the distance between my family's world and my mostly American life. I look for insight wherever I can find it to help me navigate that space. I hope to understand what happened with my mom and gain some wisdom. I get a lot of the "aha" factor when I think about how gender roles and sexism have framed my life and my mom's. The "aha" factor is when you have always felt something but couldn't articulate it until someone gives you a naming system that allows you to point at all the pieces. While in Gambia a couple of years after college, I was criticized at a market by a female merchant for being too aggressive when I negotiated the price. She said I acted like a man and I should remember that I am just a girl. I felt horrible and wondered if I had been rude when I realized her criticism that "I wasn't acting like a girl" came from her acceptance of gender roles and male privilege. By analyzing the incident this way, I was also creating a mental world where things can be different.

When I was a child, I sensed my family's fear and helplessness even when I didn't understand where it was coming from. This was their reality. My tendency was to think the problem was with me and try to adapt. I thought that if this was my reality too, maybe I need to stop fighting it and just deal. Wanting something that isn't possible hurts. But my growing feminist thought encouraged me to validate those feelings and find a way to honor them. Now when my aunt says that I dress too masculine and I won't attract a man, I still feel cornered. I also feel grounded, however, because I understand where she's coming from. I have decided on a way of thinking that puts my honest expression of self above the loss of social standing in my family.

I wasn't just fighting religious doctrine and sexist dogma but a cultural sociohistorical worldview. A teacher once described the Haitians in her class as very obedient and polite. I said that's because their families will beat them if they get in trouble. Sensing my disapproval, she said it is good that they discipline their kids. Yes, but it can be taken too far when they instill fear of authority and beat the spirit out of their children. My mom's concern that I act submissively can be partly attributed to coming from a country where people who stand up get mowed down.

My mom felt that if I loved her, I should obey her in all things and accept everything she said as the truth. When I disobeyed, she'd say, "Even a dog knows his master." As a five-year-old I had the unarticulated idea that love shouldn't be so limiting. To my Haitian Catholic mom I was a freak. Home was a battleground. My mother would say horrible things to me everyday in an effort to make me more docile. I was bad when I laughed too hard. I was bad when I disagreed with my uncle's reasoning. I was bad for running around the house. Their definition of "good" was synonymous with passivity.

One day, on the train after a visit, I realized my mother and my aunt have been too "good" their whole lives. They were the extremes. Like my mom not remarrying because as a devout Catholic she felt she was still married to my father even though he was the one who lied to her and left. The rumor about my aunt is that she had a great love in Haiti who wanted to marry her. Her family was against it so she broke it off. These women followed the rules they were taught too well, and they've paid for it. I watch them still paying for it. When I look at my extended family, I notice that the women who were "bad"—those who did their own thing—are the happiest now. Some of my cousins my age growing up in Haiti are very assertive. On the whole the female relatives of my mom's generation are more traditional, but even in that group my mother and aunt are extremes.

As a kid I'd watch my mother sit in the living room with a worried frown. I wanted her to stop worrying. I'd ask her what was wrong and she'd tell me, "Problems. Too many problems." She worried about money, my safety, our health and more. She was always worried something would knock her off the little bit of peace she had. In one such conversation, my mom mentally handed me a picture of her, my aunt, my grandmother and me on the streets of New York with no place to go. I fear she carried that picture with her every day of her life. She'd sigh, "If only I had a husband."

My aunt would take me aside periodically and tell me that her most cherished wish is that I get married soon and have a family. Even understanding her Catholicism and sexist upbringing, I want her to question this belief so I finally ask, "Why in the face of all the bad marriages do you still think that marriage is some type of guarantee of future happiness?"

"Do you want to become like me alone without anyone to take care of you?"

"Mom married with all her Catholic faithfulness and my father left her, and I'm always overhearing some family gossip about some couple divorcing."

"But you'll have the children. Even if your husband leaves you, you will have the children." Ahhh. The Haitian Catholic version of the sperm donor. My mom's response was less radical: "I'm praying for a good husband for you, he won't leave you."

In my mom's old age, she now imagines there is a man who comes into a house and moves things around. She's sure she left so and so here and now it is not here. "But Mom, why would he leave the TV, VCR and jewelry alone?"

"It's a very strange world. You don't know all the strange things in it," she says.

And of course he's a man *"musha-a,"* a mister. I believe he is the devil counterpart, a flip side of the savior, the man who was supposed to save her in the triumvirate. After waiting so long, she made up a demon to take his place.

I'm like my mom in that I want salvation. She tried to escape her existence through prayer. I don't think she believed it was possible to find happiness in this world. I've looked for salvation in love, friends, work, theater, filmmaking, writing, books and myself. It is a struggle. I've been saved in little and big ways. I wish my mother would find happiness while I'm here to see it.

Waiting is what I fear. That's what I realized on a subway ride from a visit to my mom and aunt. I'm not scared of ending up like my aunt as much as I'm scared of spending my whole life existing in that passive position. Every time they ask me about marriage, I feel my own answer to myself: If I'm not waiting, I have to find the courage to make something happen.

Thirty-Eight

Cecilia Ballí

She was twenty-one. She was, as they say in that Mexican border city, *del rancho,* from one of those scrappy ranches on the outskirts of town, which should have meant she was so shy she wouldn't even eat in front of strangers. But the boys she met at the dances in the city were always surprised to learn that she'd been raised on a farm. In their eyes she was not like the rest of them, because she wore the most fashionably daring clothes and liked to converse and go to the movies.

He was twenty-three. He didn't know too much about her, only that he wanted to dance with her tonight. You see, he was from the ranch too, but from a real ranch further down the same road that led out of Matamoros, where agriculture had paid off in big wads of cash that were traded for gaudy furniture. They had attended the same elementary school, though their family background set them worlds apart. It wasn't until he was a grown young man with a trim mustache that he watched her many times from across the bus. He was so dreamy about her that when she got off, he would take the spot where she had sat, just to feel what was left of her. Sometimes, when he drove by Rancho San Pedro on his way home, he honked in case she might be sitting by the window or wandering outside and turn.

But she was oblivious; she had promised herself not to date the young men from the ranches, whose ideas about the world frustrated her. She had grown up admiring the city lights. From her family's property, she could see them winking flirtatiously if she walked far enough into the fields. Those bright sparkles stood for all the things that couldn't be hers on this little stretch of dirt. Here, during seven years of schooling, she had lit an old rag late at night and stuck it in a can of petroleum, devouring the facts and numbers her teacher dictated because too many of the schoolchildren couldn't pay for text-books. She rose to the top of her class and even got to carry the Mexican flag once during an end-of-year assembly, decked in her cousin's pink *quinceañera* dress, since she didn't own a school uniform.

Then it was over. No free education after the sixth grade in her country, and the young women—especially *las del rancho*—had to get a job or help watch their brothers and sisters. She kept on daydreaming, thrilled when she sat by the radio and listened to it murmur all the great things humans did, like walk on the moon. On infrequent trips to the hospital in Matamoros she would adore all the female nurses in their crispy white uniforms. One day she, too, would live in the city and wear a white uniform, she believed then; maybe a chemist's lab coat. All she knew for her future was that she wanted to discover new things.

So naturally, when this young man offered her a goofy, insinuating grin from across the dance floor, she didn't understand. And she didn't really care for it either, despite his good looks and electric personality. What could he want, she wondered? To dance, he came over and confessed. She hesitated. But then, who knows why, she gave in and said yes.

"I like the word 'wi-do-wer,'" my mother said recently. She was speaking to me in Spanish, the only language she knows well, but she allowed the precariously pronounced English word to teeter on the tip of her tongue. Then she added almost defiantly: "I'm not embarrassed. It gives you personality."

She had slipped on her black-rimmed glasses to inspect the naturalization certificate she had just received. At fifty-three years, my mother had finally become a citizen of the United States. Always a witness, never a member—that had been the story of her life. I had thought about this as the solemn vocalist set off the ceremony with an overly dramatic rendition of "America the Beautiful" and the robed judge thanked the inductees for representing the very best of this country. Even though I, an American citizen by birth, have in some ways become jaded about the meaning of U.S. citizenship, that morning I found myself swelling with pride for my mother. She was a little distracted herself, flustered by the fact that everyone sped off during the Pledge of Allegiance. But when the singing woman took the microphone one last time and filled the auditorium with glass-shattering strains of "God Bless America," my mother blinked rapidly and began to fan herself.

It wasn't until we were outside, walking toward her silver pickup under the warm South Texas sun, that she began to dab her pink eyes sloppily. For the first time, she told me that when she was about eight, she'd briefly attended an elementary school in Brownsville, just next to her Mexican hometown. She wasn't supposed to be there, of course, not a child who had tiptoed across the U.S.-Mexico border *sin papeles,* without papers. She and her parents and her little brother Raul snuggled into a one-room, rat-infested shack. At the American school the students sang "One Little Two Little Three Little Indians" and "God Bless America." She was crying now because the song had brought her bittersweet memories of how tough things had been then for that skinny dark-skinned girl who hadn't belonged. Today my mother has a three-bedroom brick home to herself.

Indeed, my mother has been, for most of her life, only a partial member of her own world. She was raised a woman in a rural Mexican society of the 1950s and 1960s. As a daughter, she was expected to shoulder responsibility without questioning. As a wife, she was expected to serve without resenting. As a mother, she was expected to sacrifice without looking back. To demand that of people is to shortchange their potential as human beings. But what effect does that have especially on women, and on a woman like my mother? What does it mean for her entire sense of self to revolve around referents, for her to identify as a mother because she has a daughter, an employee because she has a job?

Soon it was difficult for her to remember just herself and the days when she had indulged in making plans, in thinking about what might make her happy. Only in recent years did my mother begin to make sense of how life had changed her and then brought her back.

Only in recent years did she begin to talk to my two sisters and me about herself—not about whom she is in relation to, but whom she is, plain and simple.

I'm not sure when Mami's dreams vanished, but they must have fluttered out the window on one of those droning forty-five-hour drives across the Interstate-10 to California. Maybe it was the time she rode a Greyhound alone because she was utterly pregnant with twins and didn't fit on the seat of our uncle's pickup, yet would have been equally uncomfortable plopped under a camper he had fastened to the bed of the truck. She still cries when she remembers how, three days into the trip and not far from the city where my father and five-year-old Cristina were eagerly waiting to meet her, the bus stopped for a two-hour layover and she walked around aimlessly on swollen feet under the miserable Oakland skyscrapers.

My mother and father began dating after he had asked her to dance that night in Matamoros. Papi and his first wife had separated some time before, so he ran off with this improbable ranch girl and married her. My grandfather, a Mexican American who had chosen to make his life on the Mexican side of the Rio Grande River, had planned to leave his ranch to his youngest son, but my father was irreverent and reckless and lost his inheritance to a brother who worked harder. Now that he was ready to settle, he was forced to begin from scratch. He claimed American citizenship, rented a small home in Matamoros and drove city buses in Brownsville while my mother bore a beautiful baby girl.

Once the baby turned one, he and my mother decided to cast their lot making annual pilgrimages to California, where there were ripe fields to pick and few labor laws. In fact, when César Chávez came by with his people urging the workers to demand an eight-hour day, my mother wouldn't hear it. Every extra hour under the sun was an additional brick on the house she and my dad would build once they settled back in Texas. In Davis they tracked down some cousins and promptly rented a tiny two-bedroom in the same migrant camp. It had no living room or air conditioner but cost just $60 a month. They figured the sacrifice would pay off in a few years.

She didn't fully know yet how to be a woman in Mexico, let alone in the United States. Yet my mother was determined to do her part to make life better. Antonia Hinojosa de Ballí became Antonia H. Ballí, and she tried not to think much of the ranch back home, throwing her blind faith instead on the idea that maintaining a good family and working hard in a strange country would get us all somewhere. For the most part, it did. Our father was quickly hired to drive a big truck that hauled tomatoes to other cities, which paid far better than hoeing and picking them, and our mom eventually became a cook at the migrant camp's preschool. They saved every penny they could and watched their daughters grow.

But life was not all easy. My mother had quickly realized after marrying my father that the man she once had worshipped saw the world differently. Although when he was feeling well he lavished her with attention and drove her to Sacramento or the grand weekend flea markets in Roseville, he often didn't understand her ambitions and believed it was his job to discipline her. It didn't help that alcohol was gnawing away the best of him. Once he grew furious because she dumped two-thirds of her weekly paycheck on a two-volume set of medical encyclopedias she wanted to read. Another time he caught her chatting with a young man out in the field as they picked side by side. It didn't matter that my mother was only asking the twenty-something-year-old what it was like for him and his girlfriend to attend the local community college.

Once they were home, Papi hit her—busted her eye like he would have busted any drunk's at the bar.

People often ask my two sisters and me what our mother did to raise such good daughters. We study, work hard, go to church and love our family. I suppose to many people that is a huge achievement. Our father died when we were young, so we were mostly raised in an all-female household. That we are now such independent women (too independent, several men have complained) is a testament to the fact that we had to learn to make it on our own—and that, once we did, we also discovered we would be just fine.

One day a close friend asked me how far my mother had gotten in school. When I told him seven years, he was amazed. In his middle-class family, he said, going to college was the norm, so there was never any doubt that he would earn a degree. But that three young women—*three,* mind you—could have gotten so far in school despite their parents' scarce education was truly admirable. I'd heard that one before, and though I appreciated the compliment, what I wanted to tell him was that we have accomplished what we have precisely because our mother didn't. Being a working-class woman whose dreams had been proved frivolous by the reality of being a caretaker and a wife, she determined early on that things would not be the same for us.

The trips to California ceased after eight years. Back in Brownsville, we moved into a small wooden home in the Las Prietas subdivision while our mother and father built our brick home. There was no contractor involved. Don Lencho, an old carpenter friend from Matamoros, put up the towering frame, and a couple of hired hands helped lay the beige-colored brick. Soon we were living on Clover Drive and just across the street from Perez Elementary School, where my twin Celia and I would begin kindergarten and Cristina, ten years old by then, could finally sit in one classroom all year long. Our mother took a job cooking for a nursing home while our father bought a used 1973 Crown Victoria and painted it egg-yellow, proudly stenciling his cab number—a bold "15" on the front fenders of his new business.

For my sisters and me, household chores mainly consisted of doing our homework. Though our mother could not help us with it, every evening after dinner she wiped off the dining room table that doubled as a desk and often slipped us a favorite snack as we worked out long math problems. When the local grocery store offered a cheap encyclopedia in installments, she carefully timed each trip so that she wouldn't miss a single volume, bringing home some eggs and milk and another $2 book packed with knowledge. After thirty-one weeks of patient shopping, the full set stood looking rather dignified on our living room bookshelf. And our mom never missed Open House nights. She might have barely understood some of our teachers, but she made sure to smile and nod her head as we translated how we were doing in school: *"Dice que soy muy buena estudiante."*

Almost instinctively, our mother knew that she wanted our lives to be different. Yet, it took time for her to figure out just what that would require. Because she had been socialized differently, childhood frills like going to friends' slumber parties and volunteering as after-school street-crossing guards were not allowed at first. But we pushed as far as we could; we had to convince her, for one, that extracurricular activities were important. When she urged us with under-the-table pinches to leave an informational Girl Scout meeting after the troop leaders began discussing expenses, my twin sister and I held back our tears and refused to get up. In the end my mom worked out a compromise so that our Aunt Letty, who made beautiful wedding gowns, stitched our Brownie dresses with fabric that was only half a shade darker than the official uniform. Trial-and-error—that is the way my sisters, our mother and I forged our relationship in the early years of my life.

The cancer was eating him up; chewing him from head to toe like an impatient dog. His hair was the first casualty. All the chemotherapy left it lying in chunks on his white pillow, so much that you could soon glimpse his pale scalp under the few sad strands that remained. Gone were the days when he would spend hours before the mirror, gelling it all in place even though he would be spending most of the day sitting under a palm tree as he waited for customers next to his yellow cab. The tumor hid behind his nose, which made the treatment for it particularly debilitating. Now our dad used the mirror to watch himself as he completed the daily routine of jaw exercises the doctor had ordered, forcing him to make exaggerated, phantasmal faces. Plus, something was rotting inside of him, we were convinced, because his disease made him smell very badly. Every morning, my mother would have to coax me in the hallway, quietly so that his feelings wouldn't be hurt, to walk to his bed and kiss him good-bye, as my sisters and I had always done before running off to school.

Two years after we settled in Brownsville, after our father turned thirty-six and his sinus problems grew increasingly worse, we had made that fateful trip to a Harlingen clinic where the doctor announced that he was seriously ill. Our mom and dad had taken the news together, and though they said little, they understood that in too many cases cancer meant death. So much for taking care of my credit, Papi had muttered as they walked out glumly. When he saw his three daughters outside, though, he had tried to appear cheerful, and since fast food was a treat, he announced that he felt like eating a really big hamburger. In reality, he was devastated.

Our father received an immediate dose of radiation and then had to attend checkups in Houston every few months. In between, he drank himself to sleep and laughed in cancer's face. *"El cáncer me hace los mandados,"* he would brag. Once, on his way to the bar after some drinking, he lost control of his car and took the fence of our elementary school. The next day Celia and I said nothing when our classmates gawked at the open playground. He cursed and slammed doors and threw things when he felt like it, then tried desperately to make things up the next morning. It was his way of coping with his downfall, with the fact that, deep down, he understood life was cruelly slipping away.

Five years our mother bore it all stoically, calmly even. Cristina had always insisted that she take us to church, and just before they found my father's cancer our mom had found God. It was like being in love all over again, only with someone else who was much more understanding. She didn't want to fight our dad anymore. Where before he could drive her so mad she would pray that he might die, now she felt nothing but compassion. She made the long trips with him to the hospital, spending hours embroidering Mother Goose pillows for us while he slept. One day, when our father said he wanted some *caldo de pollo,* she rode the only bus she knew all the way to a Mexican neighborhood on the other side of Houston where she could find the chicken broth he was craving. "The patient prefers Spanish foods," the doctor had noted in his file. By the time she returned four hours later, the patient had fallen asleep.

Before our father died, he wept regretfully and pled for forgiveness. Then he was gone. Our mother asked the mortician to dress him in the only suit he owned—the brown one he had bought for himself at the Salvation Army store he often rummaged to kill spare time on his trips to Houston. Though she wept a little, she was careful to greet the many people who came to the funeral home to pay their respects. Even when she closed the coffin as he had asked her to, she was surprisingly, almost embarrassingly, composed.

It was weeks later, when she had returned home and we were off at school, that she cried. She cried long and cried hard, letting her pain fill the walls of her empty brick house. Cried for the times the nurses had poked him blue in search of a vein, cried for the days his anxiety attacks had gotten so bad he had sworn his flesh was falling off his bones. In those tears went the long nights by his hospital bed, the hot trips to California, the day he had asked her to dance. Seventeen years later, it was just her, her and three daughters and an undetermined future. No husband. No job. No guarantees. She was so young to be left alone; so old to be initiating her life. She was thirty-eight.

But after all the sadness had been emptied and God had answered her prayers for peace, my mother's uncertainty turned into resignation. Then, to exhilaration. For the first time in her life she began to feel like an independent adult, and the sensation was liberating. She knew immediately what would come next: She would work hard and take care of her daughters. That is what she already knew how to do, only now it would be on her own terms.

It did, however, take our mother several years to become happy and confident again. After our father's death she was embittered for some time and was known to proclaim dramatically to my older sister: "I was a happy child and a happy teenager, but ever since I got married I've never known happiness." She still became hysterical every now and then and would burst with the smallest provocation, like the many times Celia nagged from the back seat of the car because

Cristina was blocking the stream of air conditioning with her arm. Mami would begin screaming and wailing unexpectedly, pulling over to the side of the road until her sobs gradually subsided and the silence grew so thick we were suffocating.

Slowly, she began to piece herself back together. She had applied for a job cooking in public schools; a year after our father died, she was hired. One day, she was driving by one of the school district's buildings and noticed a line of people who were preparing to take a general equivalency diploma exam. Although our mom hadn't sat in a classroom in thirty years, she took the test and received a high school diploma. I remember when she bought her own car for the first time and posed with us for a Polaroid shot that was tacked up on the dealer's wall—four smiling women and an equally proud 1988 charcoal gray Plymouth Reliant.

That car was her little mobile home for the next six years, the place where she spent many hours in a school parking lot waiting for us to emerge from a late choir rehearsal or student council meeting. When we had concerts or an awards assembly, she always sat near the front, making every effort to appear interested despite the ungraceful sounds of our awkward sixth-grade band. She made only $9,000 a year working full time, so when I cried to her that I was the only clarinet player who was going to attend the all-state band tryouts with an old horn, she made mental calculations for days. Finally, she charged my top-of-the-line Buffet clarinet to a credit card.

What could a Mexican mother possibly teach her three daughters about American feminism? I was in college and still didn't know what it meant to be a feminist. I mean, I figured it had something to do with advocating for women's rights generally, so I was tempted to count myself in. But I didn't know what it *felt* like to be a feminist— how to perceive myself, what to say I believed in, how to treat men. For the past seven years I had watched my mother be both a man and a woman. She was the person who always made sure there was hot food on the table and asked how we were doing in school, who mowed the lawn on cloudy mornings and patched up the plumbing when it was leaking.

So I took a class. It was about the welfare system, and all of the students in it were women. Most of them were white except for a few other Mexican Americans who lived with me in Casa Zapata, the Chicano theme dorm at Stanford University. We talked about poverty and its effect on women. We talked about single moms and why the odds are stacked high against them. There was a feeling of urgency and self-righteousness that excited me. But a sort of ritual also seemed to emerge. When somebody offered a bold statement, the rest of the women nodded fiercely in agreement. There was a strange, implicit consensus I hadn't experienced in my other classes. As a final assignment, our professor had us debate two sides of an issue; that was a tough one for everyone. We all believed that women have the *right* to work, that they shouldn't have to take care of the babies *and* do everything around the house, that in fact they should be *paid* for that labor, that their office salaries should, at the *least,* be equal to those of men.

Then we talked about abortion. Of course, women should have

the right to choose. I shrunk in my chair. Having been raised a Catholic, I felt passionately at the time that no baby should be killed. But then I wasn't really a feminist, was I? I was disheartened. I took my B+—feminism can be graded, after all—and abandoned feminist activities at Stanford. I did come to understand later that gender, race and class are inextricably linked, and that I was being a feminist in other ways and through other associations. My best learning, though, occurred outside of school, with my two sisters and our mother. In our family, the future was always a fuzzy cloud the four of us poked together, discussing different approaches, testing boundaries, negotiating philosophical commitments. We learned what it meant to be feminists side by side, not hierarchically.

And we learned something else, something about sacrifice. For American feminists, feminism and sacrifice don't quite fit together. Since we have long presumed that when a sacrifice must be made—such as leaving a job to raise children—it is the woman's duty to make it, feminists often claim that we should not have to give up ourselves for others. Yet many women writers of color have reminded us that sacrifice and motherhood go hand in hand. From the moment a woman conceives her child, she offers up part of her body for something bigger. So, if feminists should not sacrifice, but mothers must, does it follow that mothers cannot be feminists? What my mother showed me is that sometimes, we improve our lot as women together and through each other. Suggesting that women are only fully realized when they have an important job, a wholesome family and spiritual well-being assumes that they have access to a decent education, to daycare, to money to pay somebody else to clean the house, to a few extra hours to spend on fulfilling pastimes. It denies the many achievements of all those other women—working-class women, immigrant women, women of color, single mothers—who work wonders with the little they have.

Because one of those women raised me, I now claim two feminisms as my own. There is the feminism that serves as my ideology, the one that is sharp as a knife and that I can bring out at dinner or in the coffee shop when I have serious discussions with friends and colleagues. It is the feminism that argues that women make special contributions to the way we educate children, the way we understand our communities, the way we organize our government and manage our relations with other nations. It is a set of intellectual understandings that is fundamental to my life, to the goals I set for myself professionally. It is the reason I look at the institutions around me, the culture that produced them and decide that our job freeing women from the tentacles of gender is far from complete.

Then there is the feminism that I can't keep in a box, that I can't fully articulate. It is the feminism that is more disposition than discourse and that doesn't even call itself feminism. It is the stubborn self-instruction that despite the setbacks, I have to keep trudging forward; the quiet assurance that even if things went terribly wrong, I would survive. This feminism measures achievement in everyday victories: a sister's new job, a redecorated room, a clean credit report. It celebrates the company of cousins and aunts around the kitchen table and cherishes our opportunity, finally, to complain, to laugh, to sing.

I spotted other women like my mother at Stanford, women who had spent most of their lives in silence. When the mothers of some of my middle-class friends came to visit, they treated all of us to an elegant dinner or brunch and suggested how we might deal with professors, what classes we should consider taking and which kind of jobs would pay us more. When my Chicana friends' moms came, they usually hid out in their daughters' dorm rooms and smiled shyly when strangers walked by. Yet, far away from home, we found comfort in each others' mothers, women who had been role models not because of the words they spoke or the rights they claimed, but because of what they had surmounted and what they had given up for their daughters. In their survival we discovered strength; in their sacrifices, boldness. Their accomplishments as women had been colossal when measured across generations. Through their individual silences they gave us a collective voice.

"When you three began to learn is when I began to learn," my mother once told me, oblivious of the fact that the same had been true the other way around. What people who think my sisters and I are *too* independent don't understand is that almost everything in our family is a group project, that one person's accomplishment belongs to everyone else. Our mother didn't get to be a chemist after all—didn't even get to middle school—but she has three college degrees hanging on her wall with a few more graduate degrees coming. And they are all hers as much as they are ours. Our mom is a social worker, a journalist, a soon-to-be lawyer. Even as young adults, we continue to seek her help and her company. It is not just that her experiences help us put our own challenges into perspective; it is that they reside deep inside of us. It is that a little ounce of her is with us always, making us the women we want to be.

My mother had to swallow the consequences that came with choosing a different life for her daughters. When Cristina insisted that she had to leave Brownsville to get a social work degree, our mother was hesitant but she half-heartedly packed up the Reliant and drove her first-born to San Antonio. Walking into the dorm where my sister would be spending the next several years, my mom's heart wilted when she saw the other students sitting around the lobby. The scene was painfully familiar: they reminded her of sad relatives waiting in a hospital waiting room. Three years later, our mom forced a smile and waved goodbye from the tiny Brownsville airport as her twins flew away to New York and California. She later told me that she had wept the night before as, for the last time, she ironed my long-sleeve cotton shirts just the way I liked them. Like my father had liked them, too.

But a new kind of life, one that she had longed to know as a child, opened up to our mother when we left. Over endless late-night phone conversations, she sympathized with our bureaucratic dilemmas, asked about our new friends and reminded us to eat well and sleep plenty. She came to visit me in California, where we climbed the sloped streets of San Francisco and revisited the migrant camp in Davis that had served as her first home in the United States. When I spent a semester in Puebla with a Mexican exchange program, she made the eighteen-hour bus trip with me, exploring places she'd never explored in her own country. She took lots of pictures of places only her imagination had toured, later carrying them in her purse to show her co-workers. In 1996, Celia took her to New York. Our mom was horrified by the crazy driving and the subways where people stared, so she insisted instead on walking dozens of blocks at a time to see the city. Then, on a sticky July morning, they decided to visit the Statue of Liberty. My mother knew very little about the scores of immigrants who had passed before that same spot for generations. But as a child the monument, which she had seen in books and on television, had represented the glitzy life of New York—a cosmopolitanism this little girl from the ranch had always wished for herself.

Standing there in her broken-in walking shoes, her unruly black curls dancing as the ferry crossed her over the cold blue waters to Ellis Island, Mami choked up and her body was covered with tingles as she contemplated that majestic stone woman for the first time. Miles away from the empty fringes of Matamoros, Antonia H. Ballí had finally seen the world.

Going Through Customs

Chappals and Gym Shorts
An Indian Muslim Woman in the Land of Oz

Almas Sayeed

It was finals week during the spring semester of my sophomore year at the University of Kansas, and I was buried under mounds of papers and exams. The stress was exacerbated by long nights, too much coffee and a chronic, building pain in my permanently splintered shins (left over from an old sports injury). Between attempting to understand the nuances of Kant's *Critique of Pure Reason* and applying the latest game-theory models to the 1979 Iranian revolution, I was regretting my decision to pursue majors in philosophy, women's studies *and* international studies.

My schedule was not exactly permitting much down time. With a full-time school schedule, a part-time job at Lawrence's domestic violence shelter and preparations to leave the country in three weeks, I was grasping to hold onto what little sanity I had left. Wasn't living in Kansas supposed to be more laid-back than this? After all, Kansas was the portal to the magical land of Oz, where wicked people melt when doused with mop water and bright red, sparkly shoes could substitute for the services of American Airlines, providing a quick getaway. Storybook tales aside, the physical reality of this period was that my deadlines were inescapable. Moreover, the most pressing of these deadlines was completely non-school related: my dad, on his way home to Wichita, was coming for a brief visit. This would be his first stay by himself, without Mom to accompany him or act as a buffer.

Dad visited me the night before my most difficult exam. Having just returned from spending time with his family—a group of people with whom he historically had an antagonistic relationship—Dad seemed particularly relaxed in his stocky six-foot-four frame. Wearing one of the more subtle of his nineteen cowboy hats, he arrived at my door, hungry, greeting me in Urdu, our mother tongue, and laden with gifts from Estée Lauder for his only daughter. Never mind that I rarely wore makeup and would have preferred to see the money spent on my electric bill or a stack of feminist theory books from my favorite used bookstore. If Dad's visit was going to include a conversation about how little I use beauty products, I was not going to be particularly receptive.

"Almas," began my father from across the dinner table, speaking in his British-Indian accent infused with his love of Midwestern colloquialisms, "You know that you won't be a spring chicken forever. While I was in Philadelphia, I realized how important it is for you to begin thinking about our culture, religion and your future marriage plans. I think it is time we began a two-year marriage plan so you can find a husband and start a family. I think twenty-two will be a good age for you. You should be married by twenty-two."

I needed to begin thinking about the "importance of tradition" and be married by twenty-two? This, from the only Indian man I knew who had Alabama's first album on vinyl and loved to spend long weekends in his rickety, old camper near Cheney Lake, bass fishing and listening to traditional Islamic Quavali music? My father, in fact, was in his youth crowned "Mr. Madras," weightlifting champion of 1965, and had left India to practice medicine and be an American cowboy in his spare time. But he wanted *me* to aspire to be a "spring chicken," maintaining some unseen hearth and home to reflect my commitment to tradition and culture.

Dad continued, "I have met a boy that I like for you very much. Masoud's son, Mahmood. He is a good Muslim boy, tells great jokes in Urdu and is a promising engineer. We should be able to arrange something. I think you will be very happy with him!" Dad concluded with a satisfied grin.

Masoud, Dad's cousin? This would make me and Mahmood distant relatives of some sort. And Dad wants to "arrange something"? I had brief visions of being paraded around a room, serving tea to strangers in a sari or a shalwar kameez (a traditional South Asian outfit for women) wearing a long braid and chappals (flat Indian slippers), while Dad boasted of my domestic capabilities to increase my attractiveness to potential suitors. I quickly flipped through my mental Rolodex of rhetorical devices acquired during years of women's studies classes and found the card blank. No doubt, even feminist scholar Catherine MacKinnon would have been rendered speechless sitting across the table in a Chinese restaurant speaking to my overzealous father.

It is not that I hadn't already dealt with the issue. In fact, we had been here before, ever since the marriage proposals began (the first one came when I was fourteen). Of course, when they first began, it was a family joke, as my parents understood that I was to continue my education. The jokes, however, were always at my expense: "You received a proposal from a nice boy living in our mosque. He is studying medicine," my father would come and tell me with a huge, playful grin. "I told him that you weren't interested because you are too busy with school. And anyway you can't cook or clean." My father found these jokes particularly funny, given my dislike of household chores. In this way, the eventuality of figuring out how to deal with these difficult issues was postponed with humor.

Dad's marriage propositions also resembled conversations that we had already had about my relationship to Islamic practices specific to women, some negotiated in my favor and others simply shelved for the time being. Just a year ago, Dad had come to me while I was home for the winter holidays, asking me to begin wearing *hijab,* the traditional headscarf worn by Muslim women. I categorically refused, maintaining respect for those women who chose to do so. I understood that for numerous women, as well as for Dad, hijab symbolized something much more than covering a woman's body or hair; it symbolized a way to adhere to religious and cultural traditions in order to prevent complete Western immersion. But even my sympathy for this concern didn't change my feeling that hijab constructed me as a woman first and a human being second. Veiling seemed to reinforce the fact that inequality between the sexes was a natural, inexplicable phenomenon that is impossible to overcome, and that women should cover themselves, accommodating an unequal hierarchy, for the purposes of modesty and self-protection. I couldn't reconcile these issues and refused my father's request to don the veil. Although there was tension—Dad claimed I had yet to have my religious awakening—he chose to respect my decision.

Negotiating certain issues had always been part of the dynamic between my parents and me. It wasn't that I disagreed with them about everything. In fact, I had internalized much of the Islamic perspective of the female body while simultaneously admitting to its problematic nature (To this day, I would rather wear a wool sweater than a bathing suit in public, no matter how sweltering the weather). Moreover, Islam became an important part of differentiating myself from other American kids who did not have to find a balance between two opposing cultures. Perhaps Mom and Dad recognized the need to concede certain aspects of traditional Islamic norms, because for all intents and purposes, I had been raised in the breadbasket of America.

By the time I hit adolescence, I had already established myself outside of the social norm of the women in my community. I was an athletic teenager, a competitive tennis player and a budding weightlifter. After a lot of reasoning with my parents, I was permitted to wear shorts to compete in tennis tournaments, but I was not allowed to show my legs or arms (no tank tops) outside of sports. It was a big deal for my parents to have agreed to allow me to wear shorts in the first place. The small community of South Asian Muslim girls my age, growing up in Wichita, became symbols of the future of our community in the United States. Our bodies became the sites to play out cultural and religious debates. Much in the same way that Lady Liberty had come to symbolize idealized stability in the *terra patria* of America, young South Asian girls in my community were expected to embody the values of a preexisting social structure. We were scrutinized for what we said, what we wore, being seen with boys in public and for lacking grace and piety. Needless to say, because of disproportionate muscle mass, crooked teeth, huge Lucy glasses, and a disposition to walk pigeon-toed, I was not among the favored.

To add insult to injury, Mom nicknamed me "Amazon Woman," lamenting the fact that she—a beautiful, petite lady—had produced such a graceless, unfeminine creature. She was horrified by how freely I got into physical fights with my younger brother and armwrestled boys at school. She was particularly frustrated by the fact that I could not wear her beautiful Indian jewelry, especially her bangles and bracelets, because my wrists were too big. Special occasions, when I had to slather my wrists with tons of lotion in order to squeeze my hands into her tiny bangles, often bending the soft gold out of shape, caused us both infinite amounts of grief. I was the snot-nosed, younger sibling of the Bollywood (India's Hollywood) princess that my mother had in mind as a more appropriate representation of an Indian daughter. Rather, I loved sports, sports figures and books. I hated painful makeup rituals and tight jewelry.

It wasn't that I had a feminist awakening at an early age. I was just an obnoxious kid who did not understand the politics raging around my body. I did not possess the tools to analyze or understand my reaction to this process of social conditioning and normalization until many years later, well after I had left my parents' house and the Muslim community in Wichita. By positioning me as a subject of both humiliation and negotiation, Mom and Dad had inadvertently laid the foundations for me to understand and scrutinize the process of conditioning women to fulfill particular social obligations.

What was different about my dinner conversation with Dad that night was a sense of immediacy and detail. Somehow discussion about a "two-year marriage plan" seemed to encroach on my personal space much more than had previous jokes about my inability to complete my household chores or pressure to begin wearing hijab. I was meant to understand that that when it came to marriage, I was up against an invisible clock (read: social norms) that would dictate how much time I had left: how much time I had left to remain desirable, attractive and marriageable. Dad was convinced that it was his duty to ensure my long-term security in a manner that reaffirmed traditional Muslim culture in the face of an often hostile foreign community. I recognized that the threat was not as extreme as being shipped off to India in order to marry someone I had never met. The challenge was more far more subtle than this. I was being asked to choose my community; capitulation through arranged marriage would show my commitment to being Indian, to being a good Muslim woman and to my parents by proving that they had raised me with a sense of duty and the willingness to sacrifice for my culture, religion and family.

There was no way to tell Dad about my complicated reality. Certain characteristics of my current life already indicated failure by such standards. I was involved in a long-term relationship with a white man, whose father was a prison guard on death row, an occupation that would have mortified my upper-middle-class, status-conscious parents. I was also struggling with an insurmountable crush on an *actress* in the Theater and Film Department. I was debating my sexuality in terms of cultural compatibility as well as gender. Moreover, there was no way to tell Dad that my social circle was supportive of these nontraditional romantic explorations. My friends in college had radically altered my perceptions of marriage and family. Many of my closest friends, including my roommates, were coming to terms with their own life-choices, having recently come out of the closet but unable to tell their families about their decisions. I felt inextricably linked to this group of women, who, like me, often had to lead double lives. The immediacy of fighting for issues such as queer rights, given the strength and beauty of my friends' romantic relationships, held far more appeal for me than the topics of marriage and security that my father broached over our Chinese dinner. There was no way to explain to my loving, charismatic, steadfastly religious father, who was inclined to the occasional violent outburst, that a traditional arranged marriage not only conflicted with the feminist ideology I had come to embrace, but it seemed almost petty in the face of larger, more pressing issues.

Although I had no tools to answer my father that night at dinner, feminist theory had provided me with the tools to understand *why my* father and I were engaged in the conversation in the first place. I understood that in his mind, Dad was fulfilling his social obligation as father and protector. He worried about my economic stability and, in a roundabout way, my happiness. Feminism and community activism had enabled me to understand these things as part of a pro-scribed role for women. At the same time, growing up in Kansas and coming to feminism here meant that I had to reconcile a number of different issues. I am a Muslim, first-generation Indian, feminist woman studying in a largely homogeneous white, Christian commu-nity in Midwestern America. What sacrifices are necessary for me to retain my familial relationships as well as a sense of personal auton-omy informed by Western feminism?

The feminist agenda in my community is centered on ending vio-lence against women, fighting for queer rights and maintaining women's reproductive choices. As such, the way that I initially became involved with this community was through community projects such as "Womyn Take Back the Night," attending pride rallies and working at the local domestic violence shelter. I am often the only woman of color in feminist organizations and at feminist events. Despite having grown up in the Bible belt, it is difficult for me to relate to stories told by my closest friends of being raised on cattle ranches and farms, growing up Christian by default and experiencing the strict social norms of small, religious communities in rural Kansas. Given the context of this community—a predominantly white, middle-class, college town—I have difficulty explaining that my feminism has to address issues like, "I should be able to wear *both* hijab *and* shorts if I chose to." The enormity of our agenda leaves little room to debate issues equally important but applicable only to me, such as the meaning of veiling, arranged marriages versus dating and how the north-south divide uniquely disadvantages women in the developing world.

It isn't that the women in my community ever turned to me and said, "Hey you, brown girl, stop diluting our priorities." To the contrary, the majority of active feminists in my community are eager to listen and understand my sometimes divergent perspective. We have all learned to share our experiences as women, students, mothers, partners and feminists. We easily relate to issues of male privilege, violence against women and figuring out how to better appreciate the sacrifices made by our mothers. From these commonalities we have learned to work together, creating informal social networks to complete community projects.

The difficulty arises when trying to put this theory and discussion into practice. Like last year, when our organization, the Womyn's Empowerment Action Coalition, began plans for the Womyn Take Back the Night march and rally, a number of organizers were eager to include the contribution of a petite, white belly dancer in the pre-march festivities. When I voiced my concern that historically belly dancing had been used as a way to objectify women's bodies in the Middle East, one of my fellow organizers (and a very good friend) laughed and called me a prude: "We're in Kansas, Almas," she said. "It doesn't mean the same thing in our culture. It is different here than over *there*." I understood what she meant, but having just returned from seven months in the West Bank, Palestine two months before, for me over there *was* over here. In the end, the dance was included while I wondered about our responsibility to women outside of the United States and our obligation to address the larger social, cultural issues of the dance itself.

To reconcile the differences between my own priorities and those of the women I work with, I am learning to bridge the gap between the Western white women (with the occasional African-American or Chicana) feminist canon and my own experience as a first-generation Indian Muslim woman living in the Midwest. I struggle with issues like cultural differences, colonialism, Islam and feminism and how they relate to one another. The most difficult part has been to get past my myopic vision of simply laying feminist theory written by Indian, Muslim or postcolonial theorists on top of American-Western feminism. With the help of feminist theory and other feminists, I am learning to dissect Western models of feminism, trying to figure out what aspects of these models can be applied to certain contexts. To this end, I have had the privilege of participating in projects abroad, in pursuit of understanding feminism in other contexts.

For example, while living with my extended family in India, I worked for a micro-credit affiliate that advised women on how to get loans and start their own businesses. During this time I learned about the potential of micro-enterprise as a weapon against the feminization of poverty. Last year, I spent a semester in the West Bank, Palestine studying the link between women and economics in transitional states and beginning to understand the importance of women's efforts during revolution. These experiences have been invaluable to me as a student of feminism and women's mobilization efforts. They have also shaped my personal development, helping me understand where the theoretical falls short of solving for the practical. In Lawrence, I maintain my participation in local feminist projects. Working in three different contexts has highlighted the amazing and unique ways in which feminism develops in various cultural settings yet still maintains certain commonalities.

There are few guidebooks for women like me who are trying to negotiate the paradigm of feminism in two different worlds. There is a delicate dance here that I must master—a dance of negotiating identity within interlinking cultural spheres. When faced with the movement's expectations of my commitment to local issues, it becomes important for me to emphasize that differences in culture and religion are also "local issues." This has forced me to change my frame of reference, developing from a rebellious tomboy who resisted parental imposition to a budding social critic, learning how to be a committed feminist and still keep my cultural, religious and community ties. As for family, we still negotiate despite the fact that Dad's two-year marriage plan has yet to come to fruition in this, my twenty-second year.

This piece would not have been possible without the faith, trust, love and amazing editing skills (thank you ramz!) of good friends and family, nor without the awe-inspiring work of my fellow feminist activists working for social change in the prairies and Flint Hills of Kansas and the mid-west. Infinite thanks to the womyn of WEAC, RD, MK, PK, DH, Kee, M&D for your limitless support and kindness.

"Because You're a Girl"

Ijeoma A.

It was a Sunday night in Lagos during the African Cup series. In these parts, we lived by soccer. Often, you'd hear the tale of the lover who threatened his sweetheart because she walked past the television, obstructing his vision for a precious second while the Nigerian Eagles were playing. Indeed, soccer was serious business.

This year, Nigeria had made it to the finals, and tonight's game was going to be watched by *everybody* who was *anybody* that knew *somebody*. I couldn't miss this game for the world. We had an earlier-than-recommended dinner, and before long, all of us—two brothers, five cousins and myself—littered ourselves around the miniature TV screen to witness this lifetime event. It was then that the unmistakable voice of my mother burst through the bustle, with a distinctly familiar hint of irritation: "Ijeoma, when exactly did you intend to clean up?"

"Only me?" I responded. "Could one of the boys help this time? I don't want to miss the game. *Please!*"

"Ije! You're a girl and we're raising you to become a woman some day. Now, stop being stubborn and go clean that kitchen up!"

My heart ached. Ten people were a lot to clean up after, especially on a finals night. As I dug through a bottomless sink of dirty dishes, the boys and my parents were in the living room, screaming, yelling and cheering. I felt so small. I was alone, with filthy mountains of blackened pots and kettles surrounding me in that small, somber kitchen. Once in a while, one of the boys would stop by and ask me where he might place an empty glass he had just used so that I wouldn't forget to wash it. I would use such opportunities to ask "Who's winning?!" Then I was alone again, sulking at soccer ball-shaped saucers that constantly reminded me I would be spending the core of the Eagles' game cleaning up in the kitchen; because I was a girl.

Although I was raised in Nigeria's capital city of Lagos, most of my guardians (my parents, uncles, aunts and older cousins) were raised in the rural villages of Eastern Nigeria. As a result, my upbringing was not as diluted of traditional customs as is typical in the big and populated cities of Nigeria. My parents, uncles and aunts had Four Commandments incorporating what a woman's responsibilities were to her family:

1. Her office is the kitchen.
2. She is responsible for all the chores in the home.
3. She is accountable for the children and their actions.
4. And, of course, she must pledge complete and total allegiance to the man in charge first, before herself.

I know my guardians believed that they were looking out for my best interests by molding me in accordance with these ideas. Frankly, I can understand why. In our society, it is considered every woman's destiny to be married one day and have children. Deviations from that fate usually ended up in an unhappy everafter of spite and loneliness. Being a woman in her late twenties with no suitors to pop the Question seemed the greatest shame a woman could endure. Thus, by raising me in accordance with these Four Commandments, my guardians hoped to ensure that I would not have to endure the mockery or the pain of being an old unmarried woman. However, despite their good intentions, I was never able to appreciate this way of life wholeheartedly.

Everything in my childhood substantiated the need for women to submit. The stability of our society depended heavily on it. Fairytales were laden with morals of submission, as well as forewarnings against the girl who talked back, or the wife who tried to be the second captain on a ship that demanded just one. Before long, like other girls I was convinced that something bad would happen to me if I rocked the boat. I decided that I would dutifully execute anything my family demanded, since I didn't want the same fate as the girls in those tales who dared to go against our customs. My family's approval was all that I lived for, and I wanted my parents to be proud of me. But, whenever I was alone, I'd often catch myself wishing that I were born a boy.

As I observed my family's dynamics, it became evident that my brothers and cousins didn't have the same "duties to the family" as I did. Every morning, I had to get up early to dust and sweep. I would get in trouble if breakfast weren't ready by the time the boys got hungry. It was also my responsibility to ensure that my younger brother bathed and dressed himself appropriately for the day. Of course, I had to do the dishes when everyone was done and *then* get myself ready in time for school or church, depending on what day it was.

I really wanted to be a good daughter, but at night I would dream that I could wake up a little later the next morning, and like a boy find my breakfast already waiting for me. I would take off my slippers and tease my toes with the fresh feel of a dustless floor that had already been swept and mopped . . . just like the boys did each morning. At times I would gather the courage to inquire about the discrepancies in the division of labor, but would be silenced with an abrupt: "It's a woman's job to do those things." Whenever I persisted, I became the subject of corrosive criticism that was sometimes accompanied by some form of punishment. Thus, I learned to conform and embrace the life that had been carved out for me.

On the surface I was the good girl that my family wanted me to be. I grew content with my predicament as I got older and even impressed my parents with my devotion to serve. Deep down, however, I despised my submission. I hated taking orders and cleaning after people. I usually had to consciously press my lips firmly together, so I wouldn't say "inappropriate" things whenever I was assigned a chore, or if one of the boys complained about his meal. One night, I was doing the dishes while the rest of the family enjoyed a sitcom in the living room. A cousin then came into the kitchen, slightly irritated that there were no clean glasses available for him to take a drink. He then instructed me to hurry up with the dishes when I suddenly snapped at him, "Well maybe if you learned to wash your own dirty dishes I wouldn't ever have to listen to you whine like that over a glass!" Neither of us could believe what I had just said. As expected, I was reported, and then punished for my impudence.

On another occasion, I had just baked some chicken to accompany the Sunday lunch my mother had prepared. According to our customs, the heart was a part of the chicken that could only be eaten by the oldest man at the table. As I placed the poultry pieces neatly in a serving dish, something made me swiftly snatch the heart from the dish and toss it into my mouth. It tasted really, really good, but suddenly I became afraid. How would I account for the missing heart? What was going to happen to me? I promptly decided that I would blame the merchant who sold us the chicken. At the table, I swore that he must have taken the heart out before selling the bird to us, because I didn't recall seeing it with the rest of the chicken. Fortunately, everyone believed me.

In my day-to-day experiences school became my refuge, an oasis in the midst of all the mindless house cleaning and cooking. In the classroom I didn't feel so passive. Despite my gender, my teachers often sought my insight in resolving problems that they used to test the students. I was encouraged to develop my own ideas, since productive class discussions depended highly on the individuality and diversity of the students. Something about school made me feel "great" about myself. I would suddenly become more talkative and would volunteer my opinions in various situations without the fear of reproach. It seemed my teachers were not as focused on gender as my family, and I often wondered about that irregularity. They were more interested in a student's ability to absorb their teachings and then use them in productive ways, irrespective of gender. They made me believe that being a girl wasn't really a factor in my ability to answer a test question, and I found this new way of thinking rather refreshing. In the classroom, gender didn't rank the boys higher than the girls. Instead, it was your academic excellence that earned you your respect and the teacher's favor. If you had an interest in student leadership, or if you wanted membership in exclusive school organizations, your grades were inspected, and it was those grades that earned you your rank.

For me, this was ample incentive to excel. Although I had little power over my predicament at home, I had a magnitude of control over my school performance, and fortunately my efforts didn't go unnoticed. Before too long, I was appointed Class Captain in primary-3 (equivalent to the third grade in American schools). As a Class Captain, I was in charge of the classroom's cleanliness, but in very different capacity than at home. In the classroom, I *supervised* the cleaning, and I *assigned* the different chores to my fellow classmates. In school, I had the ability to enforce the change that I was powerless at creating in my own home. I made sure that the boys worked just as hard as the girls, and I ensured that their hands got just as dirty from sweeping and scrubbing the floors. Thereafter, I would take my shoes off and indulge my feet in that nice feeling you get from walking on a really clean floor.

Ijeoma A.

As Class Captain, it was also my responsibility to enforce the School Rules on my peers. Since I was in charge, I would momentarily forget about my family's ideals of Woman's submission to Man. Whenever I spoke, my words had to be obeyed since I embodied the school authorities in the classroom. As a result of my position, I was always the first in line for school assemblies and field trips, the first to be seated at important school functions, and even the first to receive my report card at the end of each trimester. At home my place had always been after the boys. But in the classroom, I was Number One; ahead of the other girls, and of course before the boys. I valued my relationship with the other girls, however, given my background, male respect had a closer resemblance to the "forbidden fruit" and so I tended to focus more of my efforts on obtaining it. This taste of power made me feel that I could potentially transcend my fate of becoming a family Cook and Maid in my future husband's house. I suddenly felt like I could achieve more with my life: do great things, make a lasting difference.

As I became an adolescent, the demands on my time seemed to increase exponentially, especially in conjunction with my academic obligations. Since I received little help, I often found myself grumbling about all the "because-you're-a-girl" rhetoric. Whenever I lamented openly, my mother and aunts would try to comfort me: "You're a big girl now and you may marry soon. These are the things your husband and his family will expect of you, and we're only preparing you to handle them." I really hated to hear that. If my forty-eight-hour days were indicative of my life with a husband, then I didn't ever want to get married. Of course, the family hated to hear that. Still, as a minor I had to fulfill the demands of my family.

By my senior year of high school, my resources were stretched as thin as they could get. I pressured myself to do well in school because I was very addicted to the prominence my previous grades had earned me in the student government. My father also pressured me to score only the highest grades. He had gotten so accustomed to my excellent performance in earlier years that he was unwilling to accept anything less during my senior year. Nonetheless, I was still expected to fulfill all my "duties to the family." No one seemed to understand that in order to keep stellar grades, it would be helpful to have fewer chores at home. "If you don't do them, who will?" was their response. I believe my situation was exacerbated simply because I was the "only" girl in a large family of men. Perhaps if I had a sister or two, one of them could have covered for me while I studied for exams. Maybe then, my sessions slaving in the kitchen while the boys watched the TV would not have been so lonely and harrowing.

During this year my father revealed his plans to educate me abroad. To gain admission to an American college, I had to satisfy several other academic requirements in addition to my schoolwork. No one seemed to empathize with me, and so I began to see my father's intention to send me to the United States as my ticket out of these stressful conditions and an escape from my future as a "good wife." This thought motivated me to excel academically despite the odds and to earn admission and a scholarship to attend Oberlin College in Ohio.

Ijeoma A.

• • •

After arriving in America, I was not quite sure how to proceed with my life. For the past seventeen years I had become accustomed to someone else telling me how and when to live. Now, I was suddenly answerable to only myself—a role I had never learned to play. I found myself waiting for someone to tell me my chores. After living in a cage all my life, I guess I found this new environment a little too big to live in. Despite the liberating utopia that America represented, it took me a long time to let go of my previous life. How could the world suddenly expect me to take initiative when it had always trained me to receive my opinions from others? Sometimes I felt the sudden urge to do something really outrageous, like sleeping in for a couple of extra hours in the morning. "Would someone come to scold me and yank me out from under my blanket?" I would wait and see. If nothing happened, I would get up and leave my bed unmade indefinitely. Then I would wait again. Would my roommate report me? Perhaps my parents would be notified of my misbehavior and then force me to return to Nigeria. I would then become afraid and return to my room to make the bed.

I was taken aback as I learned that my roommate was messier than I was; she claimed she had always been that way. How could her parents tolerate that? Didn't they worry that she would never find a good husband? As I opened up to her, I was stunned by everything she shared about herself. She had never had to clean her brother's room. "He does that his damned self," she said, a bit surprised that I had thought that she had ever waited on him. Also, she had never cooked

223

in her life. She probably couldn't even tell you how to boil water, yet she wasn't ashamed.

Slowly I fell in love with America. Sometimes I would hang out with the boys, just so I could say "No" to them. Whenever I felt really bold, I'd say, "Do it your damned self," just like my roommate. Once, I cooked an African meal for some of my American friends. I didn't make anything complicated, simply because I didn't want to generate too many dirty dishes. I wasn't sure I could handle the same loads as I used to in Nigeria. To my surprise, however, one of the boys offered to do the dishes when we were done eating. I paused and then said, with my accent, "Yeah, do it your damned self!" He thought that was funny and so we laughed about it.

Gradually I found myself saying and doing things I wouldn't have dared to in the past, in West Africa. I finally felt light and free. I was able to focus on my studies without needing to rush home and cook lunch. I now had "leisure" time to sit around and chat with people from all over the world. I could sleep in longer, and I could experience "idle" moments when I simply did nothing. I could make boys clean after themselves, and I could do it with authority. And sometimes, just to be cheeky, I would even make them clean up after me. I really loved this new life that I was allowed to live.

Whenever I returned home for the holidays, I always underwent psychological conflicts within myself. My family had missed my cooking. They missed me too, however they had also missed my services. After two semesters of being my own master, I had to readjust to being the passive daughter they had been used to in previous years.

Once, I told a cousin to do something "his damned self." I was very frustrated. It wasn't easy reassuming my domestic role, especially after a whole year of retirement. He was livid. Before long, the rest of the family clamored around me, inquiring about what possessed me to say something like that. I remained quiet and listened to them answer the question for themselves: "She's gone to America, and now she has forgotten about her heritage." "Why did they send her there? Now look at what she is becoming." "She thinks she is American." My father returned home from work and, of course, I was spoken to sternly. I was never to repeat that behavior again.

But had America really changed me? I vehemently oppose that theory. It is true that as I progressed through college, my relationship with my family clearly experienced a metamorphosis. Although I was still respectful of my elders, I gradually became less restrained in expressing my true sentiments in various situations. I no longer followed orders passively as I had in the past, and little by little, I acquired the audacity to question them. Of course, I didn't always have my way, but at least I made it known that I was not always happy with the kind of life that *they* felt was right for me. This perceived impudence was not always welcomed, and I was repeatedly accused of disregarding my homeland's traditions and thinking that I was now an American.

But my theory is that America introduced me to Me. Growing up, I had numbed myself to the dissatisfactions I felt in a society that favored boys. My only option was to conform, so I brainwashed myself into thinking that I was happy. That was the only way I knew to keep a level head. I lived an emotionally uncomfortable life plagued with internal conflicts. It was always my reflex to suppress my true opinions on the gender inequalities for the fear of reproach from a conservative society that I loved more than myself. Each time I felt violated because one of the boys was being treated like a first-class citizen at my expense, a voice inside me affirmed that I was being treated unjustly, but I would dismiss it as the voice of a wayward extremist. America helped me realize that all that time, I had been dismissing myself, choosing instead to embrace the beliefs of a society that taught me that I was inferior to my male counterparts. American society was conducive to nurturing that part of me that didn't believe that I was weaker by virtue of my gender. America didn't change me, but rather it simply allowed me to discover myself.

As I continued to enjoy this growing sense of empowerment, I became acquainted with American feminism. Quite frankly, I didn't know what to make of it. It surprised me that any American woman could be discontent with the gender conditions of the same country I credited for liberating me. America felt like the Promised Land, and I wondered what else an American feminist could want. In my patriarchal background, women were considered the property of the male breadwinner. My aunt's husband, for instance, would use her as a punching bag without compunction after say, a stressful day at work. As a young woman I choked on these realities; my hands were tied when it came to protesting how my uncle handled my aunt, whom he considered his "property." At least in the United States my aunt could have been shielded from battery since her husband might have feared the threat of arrest. Thus, from my first perspective, America was surely the feminist's paradise.

It was interesting to learn later that many years ago, America's situation was quite similar to the current one in my natal country. I find this encouraging since it indicates that my people may one day embrace some of the values I now enjoy in America. Therefore, I do support the feminist and womanist movements in the United States, simply because these were forces that drove the change in America. I may eventually participate in the U.S. feminist struggles; perhaps I will gain some insight into what it would take to effect change in my country. For now, however, I am still living my American dream. I am so addicted to the freedoms I have enjoyed here, and I hope I can keep them, irrespective of the country in which I finally decide to settle down.

Today I am an independent woman working in the United States. I am very happy with my life, and I feel more fulfilled than I ever have. Occasionally, however, I find myself missing home. There are many aspects of the Nigerian society, besides the gender inequalities, that I failed to appreciate until I came to America. I miss the Nigerian sense of community; the security of knowing that I can depend on my next-door neighbor to worry if she doesn't see me for several days. Here in the United States, my neighbor of two years still isn't sure whether or not I have children. Come to think of it, we don't even know each other's names. I also miss Nigerian food, the obstinate devotion to family, and the festive celebrations. I miss home. However, irrespective of how nostalgic I get, I know deep inside that America is the best option for me right now. I have deviated so much from my childhood's domestic and subservient lifestyle that I don't think it will ever be possible for me to adopt it again. The only way I could return to that life would be to erase the past six years I spent in America. Without those years I would never have tasted the sweet wine of independence that has gotten me drunk and addicted today.

I think that my family is gradually coming to terms with the person that I have become. I wouldn't say that my relatives are thrilled, but they recognize the futility of compelling me to marry a man from my community who is attached to its "good wife" values. They know that I will probably tell him to do his cooking and laundry his damned self, just like I have already told some members of my family to date. However, I wouldn't necessarily conclude that an American would make the perfect companion for me either, since he may not embody the Nigerian values that I love and miss.

It is difficult to predict what the future holds for me, since I am very much in the middle of the two worlds that have molded me into who I am today. I have decided that I will go anywhere destiny takes me, provided that I have primary control over my life and that my opinions count, despite my gender. Anything less would not be a life for me. I have worked and struggled very hard to become the intelligent, independent and strong woman that I am today. I absolutely

Ijeoma A.

cannot ignore all that I have endured and achieved by settling for a passive life as Adam's Rib. Some may choose to call me a rebel, but I am simply a woman searching for a happier life. One in which I am allowed to love myself, and not sacrifice that love in favor of a society's values.

Bring Us Back into the Dance
Women of the Wasase

Kahente Horn-Miller

The singing begins and your attention is on the beat of the drum, the sound of the rattle, and the men's voices captured in song. A great feeling of empowerment overwhelms you as you go round and round. Pure energy is created as your feet glide across the floor. Your heart soars as you dance and dance. You feel as though you could dance forever. It is as though you are in another place, another time. You see others around you with faces uplifted, a look of utter joy and abandonment on them. A young girl goes to the middle of the floor. She picks up a cane and bangs it down on the wooden planks beneath her feet. The music ceases and the dancers stop and stand with heaving chests. You can almost hear their hearts pounding along with yours.

The young girl begins to speak, everyone's faces turn, and all our attention is on her. In a loud voice, she says: "Thank you! Thank you for finally listening to us!" Her fist is clenched to her chest as she speaks, then her arm sweeps the crowd, her palm open. It is as if she wants to include us in this feeling that she is trying to project with her words. Though we already know what she means. She is thanking the older generations for *listening to what the young people have been trying to say. She is thank-ing them for bringing the Wasase back so that she may dance and become strong again.*

She pounds the stick on the floor again, even stronger this time, as though her words have given her strength. A great war whoop is called out by all the dancers as they begin to dance again, their energy renewed. I dance too. I feel it too. I look around me and see the walls and windows of the Longhouse crying in happiness, for we are unified, at least for this moment in time. We all know and feel that we are of the same spirit. We are Onkwehonwe—the original people.

As a Kanienkehaka—the English call us Mohawks—I was raised within the Longhouse tradition. I live in the community of Kahnawake and I am now a mother of two girls. As my daughters get older, I see and feel their enthusiasm for life and all that it has to offer them. They do not know yet of the challenges they will experience. I think of all those things I must try to protect them from, or rather, teach them about so they can have the chance to make up their own minds. Little do they know of what the world is like in all its diversity. I struggle with it myself. I am a student—of life in general and now formally enrolled in the institutions of the culture that colonized my ancestors—working for a master's degree in anthropology. I am training in ethnography, and as I worked on one account of my community, I came to under-stand the dynamics within and surrounding the social problems young people here face. This is my story.

It began in September 1997, when a local thirteen-year-old girl attempted suicide. This woke up many people in the community. I—along with other mothers and fathers, aunts and uncles, sisters and brothers and grandparents—was compelled to think about the future and what it offers young children such as my daughter (my second daughter had yet to join us). The suicide attempt made people look closely at their children, as they tried to decipher the messages the kids were communicating through their actions. Drugs and alcohol are not new to any indigenous community, including Kahnawake. This young girl's action forced a response, however. The initial question that everyone asked was: "How do we begin to combat this problem?" This appeared daunting, so the question changed to: "How do we get the energy to start?"

One woman in the Longhouse community—the keepers of our traditional ways—looked through the "Warrior's Handbook," written by Louis Karoniaktajeh Hall. She hoped it might give some direction. Karoniaktajeh, who passed away in 1993, is considered the philosophical father of the Rotiskenrakete, the Warrior Society. He was instrumental in revitalizing Kanienkehaka spirit and identity through his writings and paintings. In his book she found this passage:

> To fight any kind of war one needs courage, gumption, knowledge of the enemy and strategic planning. The biggest single requirement is FIGHTING SPIRIT. People with fighting spirit shall not become casualties of a psychological warfare. How does one acquire fighting spirit? . . . Our ancestors discovered the secret long ago. All their men were

great warriors. One hundred percent. How did they do it?
. . . One method that has come to us is the War Dance.
Our ancestors brought up the spirit of the people by the
War Dance, even those who did not dance. . . . Since it
works, it should be performed at every opportunity.[1]

The idea of having a War Dance (known as the Wasase) seemed like
a good way to start. She approached others in the Longhouse with this
idea. Her suggestion was met with a positive response, so the process
of planning the Wasase began. I was part of this planning process. I
wanted to be involved in this movement to provide a future for my
daughter and the youth of our community. The Wasase was set to take
place on the Kahnawake Mohawk Territory in Quebec, Canada, in
October 1997, but during the preliminary stages some people began
to question the women's participation. As women, we wanted our
roles more clearly defined. We could not see ourselves as merely providing support for the men during the ceremony, which meant
remaining outside the Longhouse. This was our battle too. The survival of our children, our sisters, our brothers—we were fighting for
our community. We wanted to dance.

And so it was decided that this issue needed to be brought before
the participants in the Wasase ceremony. We would decide together
what the best solution was. On the day of the event, we met. It
became obvious that reactions were all over the place. We young
women were adamant about our right to dance. We felt justified
about what we were doing. A few of the older women supported us.

But others insisted that the women's role was to stand on the side and provide moral support for the men. The men listened. It wasn't really about them, and in our tradition men do not impose their ideas on women. They shared what they knew about the history, the meaning and the past uses of the Wasase ceremony, but none of them got up to pass an opinion one way or the other. This was our issue.

As is the way in our traditional decision-making process, we threw in our opinions and our personal experiences. As people listened to our stories about drugs and alcohol and the other problems that confronted us, we began to convince everybody of our honesty and sincerity. Eventually the other women saw what we saw—that as mothers, sisters, daughters and community members, we had a legitimate and powerful role to play in this war that we were fighting. We had proven our case. They understood! We did it! We were going to participate!

Suddenly, everyone awoke to the realization that we had come to one mind, we had reached consensus, without anyone formally announcing the decision. Our voices had been acknowledged. The energy in the Longhouse began to increase as the men and women stretched their legs after such a long day. The time for deliberation was over. People talked about dinner, the kids, who needed a ride, and they gathered their stuff to leave the Longhouse and prepare for the dance. As I left, I realized this was the first time I had ever felt the full power of the Kaienerekowa, our Great Law of Peace, in action as my mother had described it to me. Knowing and seeing are two different things, especially where the Kaienerekowa is concerned. Anyone who does a bit of reading or listening can understand it as a governing philosophy, but you cannot fully comprehend its power and the role that our women play until you participate. This was the first time that I had ever felt the strength of the Kaienerekowa at work. And I carry this with me now—an image of the sun shining through the Longhouse windows on our people, the memory of our energy on that late afternoon as new life came into our old traditions. The women of my nation stepped onto the warpath of greater empowerment for all Onkwehonwe.

We were going to dance.

I am a strong Kanienkehaka woman, but I do not consider myself a feminist. Even though many of the early American feminists were inspired by my culture, my experience has been very different from that of women in the dominant society and I don't purport to understand feminist theory. But I do understand the Kaienerekowa. As a young girl, I was taught by my mother to question everything. This feeds the anthropologist in me, but it is also a key to our traditional culture. We are taught to take nothing at face value. We have to listen to what the natural world is telling us and take the time to understand it, including our roles as women in the natural order of things. We know that if we don't do this, our people won't survive. Everything must be considered, everything is linked. We must think for seven generations to come.

I realize now just how much this has become part of my nature. I must understand things at a deeper level, otherwise I don't feel complete. But, because of my unique position, my identity constantly shifts between scholar and participant, between my duties in Kanienkehaka society and the externally defined field of Iroquois studies. Sometimes it is hard to maintain a clear focus on what I am doing as a researcher; however, my experience is the lens through which you are looking now. As I describe the world I see, I become a role model, challenging the abusive image of the squaw, changing attitudes, empowering my people so they can appreciate and be appreciated.

After the Wasase ceremony was over and I sat in front of my computer screen, I thought back to the discussion in the Longhouse. I knew that some of the women felt that it was just "not right" to dance with the men. They compared it to letting men join the Women's Dance. But what did this mean? As women, couldn't they see that we too have an important role to play in the particular kind of warfare we were engaged in? I thought that perhaps they were not sensitive to our current situation of being surrounded by the colonizer's society. But perhaps I was just being patronizing to think this way, not giving them the full credit they deserve as "survivors" of a sort. Perhaps the women who objected to our participation just did not know how to reconcile dancing in the Wasase with their traditional roles as they understood them.

What is our culture? And what is adaptation? At first I felt frustrated, for what seemed clear to me was in actuality not so neatly defined. As I asked myself these questions, I decided to look back into the history of the War Dance and of my people to figure out what had brought us to the current debate. In doing so, I realized that this aspect of history needed to be understood and rewritten from a Kanienkehaka woman's point of view. Below are some of my reflections.

For us, performing the Wasase was a means of strengthening us to fight a metaphoric war against drugs, alcohol abuse and the increasing number of suicide attempts in our community. The Wasase is a ceremony that we adopted from the Sioux more than two hundred years ago, and Kanienkehaka communities had used it when we needed to feel empowered in modern confrontations: in 1974, when we took back Ganienkeh in upper New York State, and in 1990, during the Oka Crisis in Kahnawake, when the guns of the Canadian Army were pointed at our women, children and grandparents. Where the term *wasase* comes from is not known, but it means renewal, and its ability to bring new strength to our society was already evident during the discussions before the ceremony. Then we danced, continuously, with the men in an outer ring surrounding the women in a center ring. This still lives in my mind. We dance while rattles are shaken. We respond with whoops and hollers while a wooden cane is passed from hand to hand until a person feels the need to stop the dance and speak their mind. There is a loud thump as the cane is hit onto the floor. Everyone stops and listens. Then we all respond in acknowledgment and the dancing continues. This goes on until the first daylight, allowing everyone's emotions to be displayed in full view, giving all those present a chance to recognize their mutual commitment to the confrontation.

The specific circumstances of the Wasase's origin have been forgotten. It is this spirit—the unity and energy that is created—that survives. This spirit and strength exist in all of us, in our selves, in our relationships to the land and to each other. No one can take that away from us. It exists in all our cultures. It is just a matter of finding the right tools at the right time to allow the release of this power at the moment when we need it most. It is at these times, when we are most challenged, that we can feel most empowered. And at this particular time, our women needed to feel our strength. By incorporating women into the War Dance, we were keeping pace with the changes in our society, just as we have always adapted our ancient traditions to fit the different types of situations we have encountered.

As I considered what the ceremony had accomplished, I became even more acutely aware of the oppression that we Kanienkehaka have suffered. I grew up with a limited understanding of the history of my people and did not begin to take an active interest in learning about our past until I was working on my undergraduate research papers. At that time I was searching for meaning in my life and trying to understand the treatment my people received during the Oka Crisis. During this incident we fought the neighboring town's proposed expropriation of our ancient burial grounds for the expansion of a golf course. As the issue escalated, we found ourselves surrounded by Quebec Provincial Police and the Canadian Army. We knew then that sovereignty and our very survival as a people was at issue.

I had spent my childhood away from the Kahnawake community and the issues that involve being Onkwehonwe, the original peoples.

My mother had been a prominent participant in the civil and native rights movements of the 1960s, but she took time out to raise her daughters away from the spotlight. I had no idea of who she was as an activist and a Kanienkehaka woman. "I did not want to limit your development by making you feel you had to fit a mold. I wanted you to be free," she said when I asked why she had never told us about any of this. So she lived and raised us as she had been taught in the Longhouse culture, and we observed.

During the summer of 1990 my mother was doing research in the Kanesatake Mohawk Territory in Quebec to complete her master's thesis, and she ended up behind the barricades during the Oka Crisis with my two younger sisters. I was in a state of turmoil. I had no idea of her previous involvement in such things. I could not comprehend why she was staying there or why she would keep my young sisters with her. I felt like shouting to the world to let everyone know how angry I was. I did not understand where my anger came from. But differently from any other time in my life, I wanted to tell people I was Mohawk. I felt a sense of real connection, stronger than I had ever felt before. When my mother came back to Ottawa after the crisis was over, I began to see another side of her. She was more vibrant, with a sense of purpose. One of her brothers from behind the barricades offered me healing and showed me a deep spiritual side of indigenous identity that I had never encountered before.

With his gift I began a long journey of self-discovery, though I was still accompanied by confusion about who my mother really was. As she prepared for her many court battles resulting from her political participation, I headed off for university. When I began my first year of studies, I was still angry and burdened with a sense of loneliness. I felt a need to reconnect with my identity. I decided to do this through my schoolwork. I began to orient my courses toward "Iroquois" topics. I often phoned my mother, who began to teach me what she knew. If she couldn't explain something properly, she faxed me pages from books and newsletters circulating in Kahnawake.

As I began to understand more, I felt a different kind of pride in who I was, a pride based on knowledge and understanding. I finally began to see who my mother is as a Kanienkehaka woman. Without us realizing it, she had raised my sisters and I in the traditions of the Haudenosaunee, the precontact confederation of the Kanienkehaka, Oneida, Onondaga, Cayuga and Seneca nations, which has been widely referred to by the colonial name of the Iroquois. My mother taught me to stop and think about everything before making a decision, as is done in the Longhouse. She taught me to be confident and straightforward, to believe that "Hey, I'm a Onkwehonwe woman, and I'm equal to anyone. I can look after myself!" She taught me respect for others and their voices, for other cultures and other nations, for elders and the most fundamental thing: that I must think about how anything I do will affect the seven generations to come. In a sense, my sisters and I had become my mother's ultimate contribution to the movement.

Many remark upon visiting Kahnawake today that it does not look like a reserve. Yet we are constrained by the typical limitations that frustrate the existence of every reserve. Our traditional life was governed by two very important principles: sharing and reciprocity. With these tenets severely limited by government interference over the years, we have lost much of our communal way of life. The Longhouse is the center of our traditional ceremonies. Many older people have returned to the Longhouse after experiencing a lifetime cut off from Kanienkehaka ways, for when they were young, it was illegal to continue the traditions of our ancestors. Through education and church indoctrination, through all the negative stereotypes and assumptions evident in Hollywood films and popular music, they were forced into another way of relating to the world. My people were not allowed to speak our Kanienkehaka language, to have Kanienkehaka names or to practice Kanienkehaka beliefs, including our songs and our ceremonies.

My own mother was not allowed to use her given Kanienkehaka name, Kahn-Tineta. It is a name whose full meaning cannot be translated into English. Does it mean "she stands in tall grasses," or "she makes a fresh path across a green field"? Does it signify her birth in the spring? Or the memory of some member of our clan who had passed away? Her school teachers did not consider the value of the culture she inherited. She was forced to use the generic Christian name Mary, given to her by the nuns at school. At seven years old, she came home from school crying because she had been told she belonged to a dying race.

All of this had a detrimental effect on generations of our women. I realize now that in some ways those women who questioned our right to participate in the Wasase were resisting the effects of Western influences on our culture. European understanding, of our society and of their own, is skewed by male-centered cultural biases. It is worth remembering that the role of Haudenosaunee women did not automatically change after contact. Women continued to do the same things. We had a well-defined and important function in our culture. It is becoming more apparent to all of us that the church and the colonial state worked together to weaken indigenous societies. These colonizing institutions realized that our status had to be changed if they were to break our traditional worldview and teach us "civilized" European ways. As the colonizers imposed their legislation on us—deposing our governments, imprisoning our men and sending our children to residential schools—the bitterness of these lessons has been incised into our oral history.

The mother of the girl whose suicide attempt inspired our dance told me about her family's experience: "My father was always sort of a Longhouse, but we had to hide. Cause they'll get you arrested. You get arrested if you are Longhouse. And everybody is so afraid of you, as if you were a criminal. It's still like that. I don't know when it's going to stop. They're still like that. If you're a Longhouse." The church and the state could not change the physical reality of our lives, but in many ways they changed our thinking, which has been more damaging.

With all of this sad history in mind, it is easier to understand why some women felt impelled to question our participation in the

Wasase. But the fact that they felt free to speak up and raise their concerns shows that some of our old spirit has survived. Our ancestors kept something alive. Through the Wasase and our use of the Kaienerekowa to solve the questions surrounding it, we were all empowered. Many of our women are single mothers like me, and in our society our connection with our children is most important. We all support each other. As I raise my children in the Longhouse tradition, I have come to see that the aim of our constitution is to ensure a balance of power and peace. I am proud of the strong role we women have to play in such a dynamic system. Our social importance is not dependent on any particular man. Our philosophy places us at the very center of the nation, reflecting our procreative powers, which mirror the life-giving strength of Mother Earth. We are the foundation of everything. We give birth. We raise the children. We carry our clan titles. We are the caretakers of the land. We are the rational mind of our traditional government. We advise the men and appoint them to office. We deliberate about when it is time to go to war, and we provide the calmness and stability that are needed to survive.

Since I took part in the Wasase, I have come full circle. There was a time when I did not understand who I was or where I came from. As I raise my children and move ahead in my academic career, I see now just how much my mother taught me. She showed me by example. Through participating in our old traditions and writing about them, I have had my eyes opened to my history and future. I now see that we already have the tools we need to succeed and to be able to work together. Our power comes from our men and women participating together in the social and spiritual Kanienke-haka traditions. Our ceremonies create a sense of openness and unity, and with unity comes empowerment, which is necessary not only in times of war but also in everyday life. No feminist theory is as powerful as the philosophy entrenched in the Kaienerekowa. The Wasase helped us find the strength and unity needed to provide a future for the seven generations to come. It showed us that we can all be a part of the dance.

Ladies Only

Tanmeet Sethi

It is a small photo. You know it is an older print because a white, scalloped border frames the black and white image. My mother and father stand on a hill with a view of the city of Seattle behind them. They are newly married, but they are complete strangers. It is 1963 and my mother wears a sari and large sunglasses, with her hair in a beehive. It was her first time in the United States. Her father wanted a son-in-law who was industrious and able to stand on his own feet. That is how my mother came to this country. It was a short trip back to India for her husband, a three-day engagement and a three-day wedding. And just like that, my mother was transported to a land where she had no friends or family. There were no Indian grocery stores or Indian restaurants. There was no e-mail then. It was an ordeal to even make an international call. My mother says you have to make home wherever you are. This is what she did. And she thrived. I think of this whenever I hear anyone call Indian women "weak."

It is another Sunday morning; I have the routine down now. I am only twelve but I know all the guru's names in order and can play the har-monium in gurdwara. My religion is Sikhism and this is my place of worship. I feel at home here. At the same time, I never know how to explain my church to my American friends. Women on one side, men on the other. We all sit on the same floor, and my mom tells me that is because, in God's eyes, we are all equal. Why can't we sit together? That is just the way it is, she says. I remember seeing a phrase in one of my schoolbooks—"separate but equal"—and I think I understand.

Her brown baseball cap contains her long, flowing, black hair in a bun. She would not be caught dead back home in the pink-and-brown striped shirt and brown polyester pants that complete the outfit. It is a Baskin-Robbins, not a fashion runway by any means. Every ten-year-old child's dream and it is my reality. My parents own this childhood ecstasy and my mother spends her days here, scooping out the thirty-one flavors for the local Louisianans to enjoy. In that outfit I suppose it is hard to recognize my mother. I think most customers are com-fortable enough with their assessment of her as a foreigner of some sort. They wince at her Indian accent and dark skin. Most assume she is Latina and start to use their rusty high school Spanish with her. They seem offended when she tells them she does not understand what they are saying. Others just speak very slowly, and for some reason loudly, assuming she will have a hard time understanding them.

I am embarrassed by the way they look at her, like she is an alien of sorts. I wonder why they cannot see what I see. A woman who left all that was familiar to her to come to a foreign land where she is always an outsider. A woman who learned an entirely new way of living at an age when most of these people's educations were done. A woman who left an upper-class family in India to work for a living with her husband in America. A woman who had to constantly explain her background because no one but her husband understood her memories. For a while I thought she was invisible. But then I realized that these people were blind.

A graceful artist performs the classical dance of Bharatnatyam and we study her, transfixed. Black kohl outlines her eyes in bold, dark borders. Her hair is tied back with garlands of jasmine strung through the curve of her braid. Shining gold necklaces and bracelets outline her form. Heavy bells adorn her ankles and sing her dance with every step. Her outfit is a juxtaposition of fuchsias and bright blues on a silk background that fans out in a peacock splendor when she bends her knees. She bows to the Mother Earth first to ask for advance forgiveness for the upcoming steps and leaps. Her hands are poised in distinct positions, changing with every step, for they also tell a story in their own tongue. The orchestra frames the dance with its *raag*, chosen specifically for this story-telling adventure. As she makes defiant moves with her long, elegant fingers and her graceful, bell-covered feet, she transports us along a heavenly story of the gods and goddesses. The spectators, both men and women, are entranced by her gestures and powerful stances. Riveted to their seats, they hang on her every word. She speaks and guides with her steps. As she moves, she acts as our teacher and we all listen.

• • •

My grandmother's key chain is no ordinary key chain. Its chiming sound is subtle but pervasive. Made of sterling silver, it hung ornately on my grandmother's *salwar* and always made an unmistakable sound everywhere she went. The ringing filled my childhood memories of my grandmother's house in India. It hung a few inches long, with three rows of silver bells and a paisley-shaped border. Salwars do not have pockets, and its hook was an ingenious way to attach it to her body. It held the keys to all the doors and all the cupboards, where she kept her most precious silk garments and jewelry, the jewelry she was given as a new bride. The jewelry that she divided between her four daughters, two daughters-in-law and eight granddaughters before her passing six years ago. She gave me a set of earrings that hang delicately like chandeliers. They are made with pearls, garnets and rubies and reflect brilliantly off my brightly colored *lenghas* and saris. When I wear them, I think of how many weddings and parties they have attended. But my most prized possession of my grandmother's is her key chain, because now I wear it, hooked onto my waist. As I move, its bells move in a rhythm that comforts me in a way I cannot explain. Maybe I am in awe of its power. I remember how my grandmother held the unique ability to open parts of the house. She was the ruler of that house's treasures and now I hold the key to mine.

"What do you do for a living?" he asks innocently.

"I work in a hospital," I say. (I don't think strangers should be privy to my personal life, so I am purposefully vague.)

"Oh, so are you a nurse?" Of course he thinks that. This is my standard response from the average white American man. Always assuming I fit the stereotype of a woman.

"What do you do for a living?" This time asked by an Indian man.

"I work in a hospital," I say.

"Of course you are a doctor; all good Indian daughters are." This is my standard response from the average Indian man. Always assuming I live only to please others.

The women on the other side of the room chatter in a rumbling buzz of animated sounds. It takes a while before I hear fragments of their debate. "Poor thing," I hear and then, "What will become of her?" I see my cousin try to leave the room inconspicuously, but not before I catch a grimace of shame on her face. She is twenty-four and unmarried, an unthinkable prospect to many of our female elders. She has not mentioned any stress to me about this during my summer vacation there. Maybe she is embarrassed, I realize. Maybe she thinks I, a still unmarried twenty-eight-year-old living in the States, will judge her as well. Suddenly, I wonder what they think of me. By now, they must either think I am gay or that I have a sordid past that has blemished my record. I think about my cousin and the pressure that lies on her to find a suitable match. What does she want to do, or has anyone even bothered to ask? A flurry of thoughts come to mind and I want to run to my cousin and comfort her. "You should do what you want to do. There is more to life than getting married." But I hesitate. How can I impose the ideals of an American culture in which she will not live? But how can I allow her to be castigated by her culture for being human? I struggle with the realization that we are sisters, but sisters separated by more than miles.

Everyone *oohs* and *aahs* at this picture, my body painted with intricate patterns of *mehndi,* or henna, as Americans call it. It is the night before my wedding. My family and friends dance around me in a blur of lush colors and sounds. A woman paints curved lines and paisley prints on my hands and feet. She paints the letters of my husband's first name, hidden delicately in the texture of the flowing design. Tradition states that on the wedding night, the husband should look for his name. If he cannot find it, the wife has eternal control of the house. It is a tradition steeped in old thought, where the wife has to win power in the house.

But even in modern times, it makes for romantic foreplay. I had always dreamed of the ceremonial mehndi pattern I would choose, as a Christian girl dreams of her white bridal gown. The origins of this ancient ritual lie in the decorating of the bride, to make her beautiful for her new husband. It is my tradition. It is chauvinistic, some could say. I know they would say that if they did not think the henna was so hip. Now, so many women have adopted the trend of wearing henna tattoos. It makes me angry that they frivolously wear these designs without understanding their origins and then tout their feminine power, as if they are stronger than other women across the world. I suppose they can be selective when they want to be.

• • •

It is only a few minutes before my wedding. I am looking out the window, dressed all in red. I thought this day would never come. I chose my own spouse and met with resistance. It seemed hopeless at times. But, eventually, my parents accepted us lovingly, unconditionally, and here I stand. I am weighted down by gold, gold on my arms, gold hanging from my ears, gold on my neck, even on my fingers and toes. There is a gold *tikka* on my middle part and a red *duputta* over that. It is heavy but not a burden. It is what women in my family have done for generations. I wear the weight of my culture and class and enter another cycle of my womanhood. My mother adjusts my *kurtha*. She stands behind me with a beautiful lavender and gold *salwar-kameez*, her face shining brighter than my jewelry. The picture is in black and white, but I can still see all the colors. Every time I look at it, tears enter my eyes. My mother, standing behind me in support; that is where she will always be.

They look so innocent, sitting on the bed, all girlishly joking with each other. It is hard to believe that this is an Indian brothel and that these women have to sell themselves for a living. They represent all cultures of India, from the fair-skinned Punjabi women of the North to the darker women of Madras. They all wear ornately colored saris and various gold ornaments. They explain their lives to me. They are like any other group of women who have to choose a profession for survival. They are excited to have a visitor, especially one who does not want anything from them but their stories.

It is a hot and humid day in Mumbai, as most are; the women

wipe the sweat from their foreheads with the colored borders of their saris. They tell me why they moved to the red-light districts, their individual stories. One young girl tells how her in-laws threw her out because of an insufficient dowry. Wracked with shame and fear, she could not go back to her home. That would spell failure for her younger sister's chance of marriage. Another was beaten by her husband for her infertility, another almost burned by her in-laws for the darkness of her skin. I sit in amazement of the stark honesty with which they tell their stories. They are all so welcoming to me, an outsider in many ways. We sit on the bed and laugh like friends while they explain the inevitability of their arrival to Falkland Street, one of the largest brothel districts in this massive city. The stories continue but all have a common thread. These women, without education or any money, followed their only recourse. Prostitution was an escape for them, a way to sustain their independence.

I am here on a medical assignment, to provide HIV education and prevention for Indian sex workers. I ask them if they are scared of HIV. They tell me that they refuse customers unless they bring a condom. Here, unlike their previous homes, they wield power with a small rubber ring. They express admiration that I am a doctor. But I have more admiration for them. Here they are, a reconstructed family, founded on a mutual understanding of what it takes to claim a life of one's own.

The picture is a sad but common one. It is black and white with no borders. Two women are in the foreground. One lies on an examining table, belly exposed, as the other leads a device over her abdomen. The device slides over cold gel and the ultrasound screen displays the motion of a sometimes amorphous shape through a black and gray haze. But the woman on the table is still. Her face stares intently at the active life on the screen, the life that is nurtured by her womb. Her face is motionless, almost paralyzed with fear. She has dreaded this moment, which for some may have been a time of anticipation and excitement. She torments herself with the question that will follow this. Is it another girl?

She already has two daughters at home, which is quite enough for her husband and in-laws. This time they are not taking any chances. She cannot "waste" another nine months in the production of a non-male child. They would choose an abortion instead. Plenty of other families took this recourse and so would they. They would have an abortion. They, not she, would make this obvious choice with her body. They, not she, would decide to end this process that she had started. As she lies there, demoralized, she wonders how her mother-in-law in particular could deny the rights and emotions of another woman, of another mother. She is not just an incubator or a vessel through which a lineage can be sustained. She is a woman. She is a mother. She is a thinking and living being. Her resistance and frustration mount. She vows to break her stillness one day and thus break the chain.

The *burkha* is a black, amorphous cover, leaving only the eyes visible. It drives most Western women crazy. For some reason they always ask me how I feel about it, even though I am not Muslim. I suppose to them I look close enough. Today I sit in a café with two Western women who are disturbed by the burkha. I explain to them that it is a tool of oppression in some countries and in others, some women choose to wear it. They shudder at this thought as they sip their lattés. One is encased in makeup and wears a tight shirt with capri pants. Another wears a midriff shirt and jeans with her hair flowing over her neck and around her face. I explain that many women in the world use the burkha as a symbol of power, as a statement of their value system. Women who wear the burkha refuse to be judged by their body or face. They want to be seen as another being, not as a sexual object. In this way, the burkha can be a tool of empowerment.

The women across from me listen with blank faces and confused stares. They argue that it is their right as women to wear what they want and how they wish to wear it. I agree and feel that this is precisely my point. I realize that these women in front of me are oppressed in many ways by society's perception of what a beautiful woman is. They respond to the abundant images of barely clad women with "perfect" bodies and fine-tuned makeup. They sit before me as conformists to their own cultural values. They sport the latest fashions and revel in their sun-soaked glows. I pity them; their oppression is so subtle they cannot even recognize it.

It is a warm day and the beads of sweat fall down my patient in labor. It is the morning after a twenty-eight-hour shift and I should be home in bed. As a resident, your bed is your best friend and you want to visit it any chance you get. But this patient only speaks Punjabi and the nurses have asked me to stay and help with translation. Although I have not slept for the whole shift and am exhausted, I want to stay and help this woman. I think of how terrifying it must be for her to go through this painful process without the ability to communicate with the medical personnel.

She is near the end of labor and her screams escalate. Her husband is here, but he sits on the opposite end of the room, acting as though he has no idea what his role is. He, too, speaks no English and sits dumbfounded by the intensity of the image before him. I remember my mother telling me that they never allowed men in the delivery rooms and that is why Indian men are not sure what their role is in childbirth. But I cannot empathize with him as he watches his wife yell out "I am going to die" in our common tongue. I rub her back and think of what must be going through his mind. How can he not comfort her as she agonizes before him? I go over to him and lead him to the bed. I place his hand on her back and show him how to rub her and give her some attention. He looks lost, as if this is not something he has ever done. He obliges me for a while. But when I leave for a minute and return, I see he has found his old seat again, his seat of comfort where he has no obligations.

The nurses remark that it must not be part of his culture to comfort her. I wonder if this is the same culture to which I belong. Is it a culture in which an individual is able to show no consolation to his partner in a time of distress, one in which roles are so segregated that even during one of the most important events of their marriage, he will wait for her to finish her job before he starts his? In response to her cries I hear him mumble under his breath, "You will be fine!" Again, I lead him over to her, place his hand on her body and tell him that he is not to move this time. He should sit here, caress and support her. He stares at me and shows offense at a young woman directing his actions. But he does oblige. How could he not? I am not trying to impose some feminist rhetoric on him. I am merely instructing him on how to be human and that transcends all cultures.

A child is born in India. She is a beautiful, innocent bundle brought into this world as a testimony to two people's love and commitment. She is the couple's fourth daughter, and they are overjoyed that she is healthy and happy. They were hoping for a son, but they are just pleased to have been blessed with another life. They understand the ability of women to succeed in the home and society, to build strong families, to sustain communities. They appreciate the gift they have given to the world and sing its praises. This is the snapshot I hope to take one day.

I am indebted to all of the phenomenal women in my life who create a model of strength and dignity and to my husband who persistenly pushes me to sustain that model.

I Sold My Soul to Rock and Roll

Kristina Gray

I never knew her name. I still don't. But I remember I wanted to be her friend so badly back then. Maybe I still do. At the time she was the only black girl at Suitland High School with purple streaks in her hair and the rock and roll swagger to match. Even in our overcrowded school of twenty-seven hundred other mostly black students, she stood out. I'm sure the other kids noticed. But I was in awe. I studied her every move and wished that somehow I, too, could one day be just as punk as fuck. I used to rehearse what I'd say to her if we ever ran into each other in the bathroom. I would compliment her new hair color, then lean over and whisper, "Your secret's safe with me." We didn't know each other at all, of course, save for the occasional awkward glance shared in the hallway between classes. But I was on to her. I could tell she was just like me. Another black girl who knew the joys of power chords and thrashy, rock-fueled angst.

I used to dream about us skipping school together, slipping out of the doors by the gym, so we could spend all day listening to the Breeders and old Joan Jett records. We'd make our own zines, swap faded vintage

257

T-shirts and in hushed voices we'd admit that Tupac wasn't really that cute anyway.

We never did skip school together. I never even got up the courage to say hi to her. Instead, I spent that last year in high school admiring her from afar, secretly wishing I could share my love of the Sex Pistols with someone, anyone.

It's not easy being a brown-skinned girl in love with rock and roll. Listening to "white music" has always been akin to treason in the black community. Never mind that we were the architects of much of what is today labeled rock and roll. My CD collection makes me a sellout. Like most black people, though, I've always been around white music. I bounced around to Culture Club when I was young just like every else, and my mom still owns her "Girls Just Wanna Have Fun" record. But while other black folks regarded the music as mere novelty or Top 40 fodder, I fell head over heels. As a kid, I watched MTV religiously, absorbing just as much *Headbangers Ball* as *Yo! MTV Raps*. I knew how to do the running man and could quote Eric B. and Rakim. But I also loved singing Guns N' Roses into my hairbrush-turned-microphone and perfecting my Billy Idol-inspired sneer in the bathroom mirror.

I learned early on that I had to keep my rock and roll tendencies a secret. Nice black girls just didn't listen to Faith No More. I was supposed to spend my pre-teen years swooning over bubblegum boy bands on the cover of *Right On!* and copying the dance moves I saw on *Soul Train*. I tried to like Bobby Brown. I really did. And I wanted so badly to learn the words to Salt-N-Pepa songs. But as much as I wanted to fit in, I took a perverse pride in knowing I could go back and forth between black and white worlds barely noticed. I wasn't passing so much as sneaking, blurring racial lines as I embarked on my own covert rock and roll mission. By day, I was humming Boyz II Men. But by night, I was rocking out to heavy metal from inside the privacy of my quiet suburban bedroom with its pale pink walls.

Presumably, I had nothing in common with the longhaired white boys whose music I was beginning to lust after. I rarely, if ever, understood any of the lyrics or high-pitched growls coming from their mouths. But somehow I identified with the screeching guitars and badass attitudes from bands like Poison and AC/DC. At the time their music felt like raw energy, more potent than anything else my eleven-year-old ears were used to. Rock and roll was as wild and explosive as I wished I could be. The music transported me from my docile world of piano lessons and Judy Blume books into a make-believe land of high kicks and big hair. For the first time, I learned it was OK to get loud and get angry—at least in my bedroom. Rock and roll was showing me how to scream at the top of my lungs. It was rowdy. Out of control. And it reeked of white male privilege.

Bands like Bon Jovi were middle-class guys born with the innate understanding that they owned this world. Even as a kid I could tell these were white boys in the purest sense of the word. They flaunted their entitlement all over my MTV in skintight leather pants as they strutted across the screen belting out disposable pop songs. Of course, it would be years before I actually had the words to describe what I first noticed back then. But no amount of women's studies courses or feminist literature would ever be able to fully explain what I had already instinctively detected at the age of twelve. These boys had the luxury to forget about color, culture and class every single day of their lives. Perhaps I believed that through their music, I could vicariously forget about race, too. For a few brief moments each day, I could step outside of my brown skin, unzipping it like a heavy winter coat. I'd turn up the music and dream not of being black or white, but a rock star.

It was almost like being in a state of complete racelessness. Part of me loved it. For once I didn't have to worry about being too black or too white. I wasn't expected to be the model minority from the family with an eerie resemblance to the *Cosby Show*. Nor did I feel pressure to be a finger-wagging, neck-rolling, tough-talking sista. I was just there. Pumping my fist and throwing up the devil sign to a Def Leppard song.

But no matter how hard I tried, I was still an outsider, equally as unexpected as uninvited. What had begun as "race music," made for and by people as dark as me, had now transferred ownership into the hands of white boys and girls. And even though it was still OK for those same kids to listen to rap and r & b, I was not supposed to be rocking out to their music. Black girls had no place in the rock and roll hierarchy. I knew white men were the guys in charge. That much was clear. Their job was to piss off parents, wear the flashiest outfits, play the hardest riffs, do the hardest drugs and fuck as many (white) girls as possible. Women? They weren't in the band. They were "with the band." White girls were groupies who flung panties on stage and gave blowjobs on crowded tour buses. I didn't know where black girls were supposed to go. After all, I never heard my story in any Van Halen song. Rock and roll, at least in its current incarnation, had not been built with me in mind.

It also had not been built with budding feminists in mind. Growing up in a black household, I never heard the F-word used too much. Like my love of Mötley Crüe, most black women in my life saw feminism as a white thing. It wasn't meant for us and it didn't include us. But even though they couldn't quite quote Gloria Steinem, the women in my family led by example, showing me how to defiantly make my way in a world that told black women we didn't matter.

Their unique brand of proto-feminism served me well, too, as a kid. That is, until I sat down to watch the newest Warrant video. In an instant, I unlearned everything my mother and grandmothers and aunts had taught me all along. It turned out being a girl had nothing to do with being fearless or beautifully independent. Being a girl meant having perky breasts and long blond hair. It meant being seen and not heard. Weak and thin. Sexy but not assertive. Boys liked you better that way. We were merely accessories wrapped around the lead singer's arm.

I didn't want to believe it. These were not images of women I was used to seeing. These girls seemed so frail, like vacant automatons designed to service early nineties rock gods. They were nothing like the women in my life who had always juggled work and family but never once referred to themselves as "working mothers." The women

I knew fought to desegregate their local schools so their daughters would have access to the same education afforded to white children. The women I knew cleaned white women's homes so their own could afford to eat. The women I knew had seen men leave but had somehow managed to keep their families intact. I wanted to be strong like them. I wanted their round hips and weathered smiles. I didn't want to be like the bikini-clad girl in front of me gyrating to a never-ending guitar solo. She didn't seem interesting at all. But I couldn't help but be intrigued. Something told me she commanded more attention than I ever would.

Luckily, by the time I got to middle school, grunge had come along and kicked metal's shiny ass. It wasn't so cool anymore to have girls with bad perms shaking their asses on MTV (that was left to the hip-hop videos on BET). In high school I ditched Metallica for Elastica and secretly dreamed of being like the alternateens I read about in *Sassy*. Rock was still the music of teenage rebellion, but kids weren't just fighting for their right to party anymore. We were moody and cynical and fed up with dead-eyed suburbanism. Like other kids my age, I took solace in the warbled words of Nirvana's "Smells Like Teen Spirit." But I knew no matter how many flannel shirts I owned, I would never completely relate to Kurt Cobain or the rest of the alternative nation.

When I went away to college, I figured I was destined to finally meet other black girls who would nurture my inner bohemian. Instead, I found segregated cafeteria tables and white girls who crowded into my dorm room just to watch me braid my hair. In an effort to blend in with the girls around me, I began trading in my rock and roll for waifish girly folksters. Eventually, I realized the music was as whitewashed and bland as the girls I wanted to be like. I grew tired of muted sounds from willowy blondes and went back to the loud, raucous music I'd always loved.

By then I had already declared myself a feminist, but now I wanted to be a riot grrrl. I started listening to women like Sleater-Kinney and Bikini Kill, who rocked harder than any of the boys on MTV. I wanted their razor-sharp cool and suddenly felt empowered by their buzzing guitars and throaty moans. They were everything girls weren't supposed to be. They were brazen, loud-mouthed and opinionated. Just by getting onstage, they were making a powerful feminist statement. Finally, someone was singing about everything I never had the guts to say.

When I discovered the riot grrrl scene, I felt that much closer to being accepted in my own little rock and roll world. I had missed the movement the first time around, falling into it only by accident years later. I thought it was strange, however, that the scene had started right in my own backyard in Washington, D.C.—a city that is predominately black—and I was just finding out now. How come it took riot grrrl nearly ten years just to reach me? Why hadn't its message been spread around to the rest of "Chocolate City" and its very black surrounding suburbs? Didn't the girls I grew up around who lived in Section 8 housing and were pushing baby strollers by the age of fifteen deserve a revolution grrrl-style, too?

At first I thought I would find salvation in punk rock feminism. Instead, I found myself once again on the outside looking in. Despite the movement's shortcomings, the music was still liberating, and it felt so good to finally reclaim my voice, my body, my agency. I didn't want to get my ass grabbed at hip-hop clubs anymore. I didn't want to hear "Show us your tits!" at another arena rock concert. I wanted to be as brave and defiant as the women I was seeing onstage.

In between listening to bands like Bis and Jack Off Jill, I took women's studies classes at my tiny liberal arts college. I loved being surrounded by so many beautiful young women of different shapes, sizes and colors and felt so very safe in those classes. But I also felt bogged down by all the rhetoric and theory, eventually deciding it was all way too out of touch. I didn't need another book on white male capitalist heterosexist patriarchy. I could just blast X-Ray Spex's "Oh Bondage, Up Yours." I remember sitting in class one day listening to my sixtysomething professor discuss the word *bitch.* She explained how there was no male equivalent for the word nor was there was a word in the English language to describe aggressive women other than bitch. I raised my hand and asked, "What about riot grrrl?" She didn't have an answer so much as a wrinkled look on her face. Then she muttered, "No one really uses that word" and stared back down at her lecture notes. But I wanted to use it and hear other young women use it too.

Around the same time I joined my college's women's group. I participated in Take Back the Night and made shirts for the Clothesline Project. At a local middle school I mentored eighth-grade girls, who confided in me about abusive fathers and older boyfriends who went too far. I also started making my own zine, turning cut and paste words into my own photocopied manifesto. Where riot grrrl and rock music in general had failed, I was creating my own little community inside the pages of zine after zine. I didn't have to be invisible anymore. I didn't have to feel underrepresented or alienated. I didn't have to explain myself if I didn't want to. I could put an article about being pro-choice next to one about hearing my favorite jungle DJ spin at a rave. I could talk about walking through slave castles in Ghana in one breath and making mixtapes in the other. For once I wasn't restricted to stereotypes or tokenization. I could tell my story and represent the full spectrum of what it means to me to be a black girl.

I realize now there must be tons of other girls just like me out there who make their own zines and listen to "white music." I'm not ashamed of my record collection anymore. In fact, I love flaunting my rock and roll ways. I am a young black woman who calls herself a feminist and loves to shake her hips at sweaty punk shows. Sometimes that makes people uncomfortable. But I like knowing that I'm crashing the all-boys club and raising some eyebrows. In a two-tone world where people are only allowed to act either black or white, I am proudly checking the "other" box. Rock and roll doesn't just belong to white boys anymore (or, to a lesser degree, to black guys like Bad Brains and Lenny Kravitz). Black women are allowed to do more than rap about our "ill na na" or moan our way through slow jams and gospel songs. We've been rocking and rolling since the days of

Memphis Minnie and Etta James. Besides, according to *Time* magazine, white kids now buy 70 percent of all hip-hop music, so I think I have the right to a Le Tigre CD.

Questions of authenticity still haunt me, though. These days I wonder: Did I really like Warrant back then or was I just trying to act white? Did *anyone* actually like Warrant back then? Sometimes I still feel like I have to constantly prove my indie cred to white kids, who automatically think that because I'm black, I can't possibly understand rock and roll. And when I hear people talk about "the scene," I feel out of place. As much as I love the music, keep up with the newest bands, live by the do-it-yourself ethic and wear all the "right" spiked bracelets, I still don't feel that I'm part of any larger community. Let's be honest. No matter how progressive it claims to be, the scene is still ruled by white boys with guitars. Of course, there are those who would argue that there is nothing stopping black kids like me from going to rock shows. The same well-intentioned types who scratch their heads and wonder, "Why aren't there more people of color at punk/riot grrrl/indie shows? We'd like more to come, but they never do." But we don't need an invitation. We just want to feel welcome.

I'm used to the laughs by now, the weird looks, being the only black face at a show. I think things are changing, though. Last year I managed to even get my girl Tomika to come with me to a hardcore show. She started laughing once some kids up front started a pit. But then a few minutes later, she turned to me and said, "Yo, this drummer is tight." I'm also happy that today there are black women out there like Allison Martlew from the Butchies, MeShell Ndegèocello and Macy Gray, who are keeping it real and keeping it rockin'.

But I'm still waiting for another thick-lipped, kinky-haired rock and roll heroine to call my own. One of these days, I'd like to see a sista who's Kathleen Hanna, Shirley Manson and Lita Ford all rolled into one. A black girl who rocks. Maybe I'll just have to pick up a guitar and do it myself.

Lost in the Indophile Translation
A Validation of My Experience

Bhavana Mody

I had zoned out at some point during the conversation, eyeing the variety of cat food products on his sister's bookshelf. The rest of us were seated on the couch while he was grounded on the floor, waving his arms around, making driving gestures, vomiting gestures, turning, yelling and dancing. . . . It was more like a game of charades than a conversation, except there was zero-audience participation. In fact, I don't think I had been given the opportunity to respond once. The two other women on the couch were *oohing, aaahing* and giggling now and then. But he couldn't evoke a smile from me at this point. His question had left me feeling sick and unimpressionable.

He was an acquaintance from college who was sharing some tales with us about his recent travels to India, where he was studying Buddhism in the hills of the Northeast region of the subcontinent. He threw around gestures and statements and for the most part, I had no idea what he was talking about. I wanted to butt in, but there was no room to disagree with him. After all, he had just recently returned and I hadn't been to India in years. So whenever he looked at me, I smiled and nodded, as if in agreement. I *should* have known what he was talking about, right? I eyed the two other women. Is that what they were thinking?

My pride was on the line here. How come they weren't looking at *me* and asking *me* questions? I wanted to be given the floor. *Yes, I really am Indian. Sure, I know all the Hindu goddesses. Of course I meditate. Well, yeah, I've been to Bodhgaya.* When the truth is, I know about three Hindu goddesses, have tried meditating about twice (and failed) and have never been to Bodhgaya. Yet I didn't want them to think I was void of the Indian experience. So here I was already feeling insecure about my Indian-ness, and then he popped the question.

He smiled at me, his dreadlocks swayed forward and his crooked teeth poked through his brown wild boar of a beard. I saw his mouth move the first time, but for some reason the words didn't seem real. I almost choked.

"What did you say?" I asked, eyebrows raised. He didn't think he was implying anything when he asked it. He just wanted to be generous with his wisdom, you see.

"Do you know what your name *means?*" He grinned excitedly, eager to share the knowledge. I blinked a couple of times. The other women were eager too. They turned their heads toward me for the first time, but not their bodies. He was much more entertaining than I was and they wanted to continue the charades-style conversation. I shifted uncomfortably and muttered softly. I suddenly felt shy about talking about myself.

"Yeah, it means like dream or something, I think—" I wasn't

finished. I was just starting to recognize the power I held for those few seconds when he snatched it back. They nodded and turned their eyes back on him.

"Your name means 'MED-I-TA-TION.'" He articulated each syllable as if none of us had ever heard the word before. This is when I turned toward the cat food, my eyes welled up with tears, my pride sunk, my Indian-ness disproved. And the white man in front of me carried on.

I can't tell you how many male friends and acquaintances I know, all white, all college educated, that have traveled, meditated and studied in India. And each time another white male person tells me about their time in India, I wrestle with a range of emotions, dealing primarily with race and power. I immediately begin to think of my skin color and how I was always different in the United States but how I'm also different in India.

During my small-town upbringing in Kentucky, I experienced plenty of racism, sometimes in the form of stares and at other times in more blatant forms. So in some way I do take it as a compliment when white men obsess over India. They are actually *interested* in my culture rather than appalled by it. This "interest" is a *huge* step up from my old Kentucky home, where if *I* "acted Indian," I'd be made fun of. That's probably how Indians in India feel about white tourists, relieved by the curious smiles, the cameras and the sari-shopping. The exotification is a step up from the blatant racism and terrorism that Indians have experienced both in India and in America. It is nice knowing that white men aren't out to get us, right? They're just *interested*. I know their admiration of Indian culture is well-intentioned. I even brag to my parents and relatives about the white men I know.

They are often taken aback but also proud that Americans are so interested in their way of life. "These American boys like wearing robes?"

"These American boys drink chai?"

"These American boys enjoy sitar music?"

"These American boys must be crazy."

Well, no, Indian relatives, Americans are good and they aren't all materialistic, fashionable football players that eat hamburgers and listen to Backstreet Boys and live on Melrose Place. So here I am on the one hand questioning white men for exploiting my culture. And on the other hand I want them to go to India so that they can develop a sense of respect for Indian people.

"It is good your American friends are trying to *understand about you*."

Yeah, that's it. Right there. Uh-huh. This is where the problem lies. My relatives are wrong in assuming my American friends are trying to understand me. Sure, the India-obsessed dudes (to reduce redundancy, I'll refer to these white men as "Indophiles") that go to India understand more about the "third world," Hinduism, yoga and what not, but do they really understand actual Indians (including me)? How do they treat actual Indians in this country? Like I mentioned before, I wasn't always treated so kindly.

As an Indian-American woman, my identity was and still is

challenged repeatedly. Raised in rural Kentucky, I wanted so badly to fit in. But it was difficult for my blond, blue-eyed neighbors to get past the fact that I was dark, my parents had accents and dressed "funny" and that our house was painted a bright blue, the shade of an eighties-style satin prom dress. I was *odd* and that identity stuck. Somehow, I made it through my years in that town, through preteen battles with my parents about wanting to try cheerleading instead of math team, and through being made fun of because my grandfather had a braid and wore "sheets."

I spent most of my time at home, sometimes feeling socially inept and other times simply enjoying the Indian-ness. I loved my mom's soft rotis she made regularly and my dad's old Hindi movie music he played on Sunday mornings. I loved playing games using seashells with my grandmother and singing *bhajans* with her at night. Sometimes I would parade around my room, wearing a *salwar* dress and lots of bangles.

The funny thing is, aside from the folks in my Indian home in Kentucky, I wasn't really comfortable among other Indians. I detested going to India, where I felt invaded with my relatives' comments on how I spoke, ate, dressed and studied. When I was in India, I longed to be back in Kentucky, where I could listen to my Indigo Girls tapes on long country drives or sit in my own room and read or write without interruptions, dreaming of being an actress or part of the Peace Corps.

You'd think I'd have had a sense of peace among other Indian Americans, but this was not the case either. I reluctantly attended Indian gatherings in the bigger cities with my parents, awkwardly wearing *chanya-cholis* and tripping on the *gerba* dance floor. I was intimidated by the other Indian-American girls my age who dressed and danced beautifully. I would stand there holding my choli skirt up because I didn't tie it right, while they glided and gossiped in their friend circles, discussing their bright futures in medicine and engineering.

Eventually, I landed myself in a small liberal arts college in Ohio, where I learned to feel a sense of power in my oddness. It was a school that was predominantly white, so there was no such thing as ethnic studies or Asian studies. I was lucky enough to have a Black studies class. But during my first year of college, nothing upside-downed my world as much as Women's Studies 101. I learned that maybe I wasn't so odd after all, because maybe, just maybe, patriarchal social constructions had caused the various forms of discrimination I'd experienced all my life, both as a woman and as a person of color. The other women in the class connected with me; we had a shared understanding. I was overjoyed. I embraced my new friend *feminism.*

But as I delved deeper and deeper into feminism, something was still missing. Although I was understanding more and more about gender and oppression regarding women's issues, I still hadn't come to terms with the racism I experienced and my Indian-American identity. And because there was no one to have a shared experience with, I threw it on a back burner and poked at it from time to time. For example, I drew parallels in my anthropology classes, learning about other cultures, particularly women in other cultures. Independently, I read about women in India and decided to write my thesis on that topic. When I interviewed Indian women, and they nodded their heads at me in ways that only *I*, being Indian, would understand, I felt reconnected to the culture and tradition I had always felt so distanced from. I couldn't wait to go back to India and be with my family there. In my thesis I explored ethnicity and gender repeatedly and, thanks to feminism, I could question and critique various social constructions.

And so I know something is very wrong with white men telling me this and that about India. But I don't have an official theory from which to critique them. Although I understand exotification and discrimination and where it comes from, sometimes I feel too shocked and tongue-tied to say anything. I get pissed because I don't think my experience as an Indian-American woman is understood, just as the experience of Indians in India is grossly misinterpreted. When I do say something, everyone thinks I am overreacting because nothing comes out logically.

One time I was seated with a couple of Indophile friends, and the two were exchanging stories about train riding in India. I was very attentive while they were talking because I really like trains in India. I can see how train riding in India can be enjoyable, but I'm not sure how much of a *crazy* adventure riding on a train is. The two friends kept gabbing about this and that—imitating the vendors and discussing all the CRAZY times on the trains. And then discussing all the CRAZY times in some city. All the CRAZY craziness and CRAZY adventure of travel in India. Usually, when I go to India, I see my family. Nothing terribly CRAZY. When I was seated with the two Indophiles, I felt like I had to justify why I'd never done anything as

CRAZY as they had while in India. What was my hang-up? Then I realized that "CRAZY" was a judgment: what they saw as so CRAZY was just the same-old same-old for most Indians, including my family, living their everyday lives.

I can't say I've ever had a wild adventure in India. It's very difficult for me to travel in India, as I am rarely allowed to leave the house alone. In most cases girls and women cannot travel long distances unaccompanied because it is important to be associated with a man, as a wife, a daughter, a cousin or a niece. What these Indophiles didn't seem to understand was what a privilege they had to be able to roam all over India. Women cannot travel as independently as men. And Indian women can travel even less independently. We do not limit ourselves but are limited due to the societal constraints that white men do not have to deal with. The few times when I was alone, I encountered a great deal of harassment. Most of my family in India (men and women, but especially the women) have not seen anything in India outside of their home state of Gujarat.

During this same conversation both men mentioned how they *only* ride third-class trains, where the "real" Indians are. As if "real" Indians are poor and cannot be middle class or rich. I admire that they acknowledge the poverty that exists in India rather than turn a blind eye to it. But I do not like how they glorify it. As if they're way too tough and way too poor to sit among the weenies in the air-conditioned first-class train. Well, I guarantee that if those third-class passengers had the choices my Indophile friends did, they'd be happy to be weenies. I didn't say anything, but I thought to myself how I'd be much less irked if my friends had swapped a first-class ticket with a third-class passenger—that way, both could have had a unique, once-in-a-lifetime experience. After all, we all know Indophiles can afford four extra dollars.

There was also a lot of talk from these guys about how great village life is. *Milking cows, eating mangoes, laughing all day, la, la, la.* I, too, believe in simple living, but there is a difference between *simplicity by choice* and poverty. Most Indian villagers are of the latter group. Admittedly, I had a similar perception of village life once too. Then I hung out with my family in the village for an extended period of time. They are dealing with alcoholism, domestic violence, illness, lack of education, and so on. The truth is, most people that live in Indian villages are suffering miserably. On the surface, though, when language barriers are thick, it may seem that village people are always smiling. Also, what Indophiles don't always see when they hang out with the cheerful, "hard-core" fellas in the villages is that those who suffer the most are the women, those that work the hardest are the women. But they don't talk it up with the women.

This is the real India, they seem to say. As if poverty makes it more real. Something just ain't right about the glorification of poverty by those who have a $1,200 airplane ticket in their hidden chest pouches. So that leaves the Indophiles with a very romantic perception of Indian culture. Few of these enlightened white men are aware of India's complex history and social structures, nor are they familiar with the racist stereotypes, harassment and violence that Indians and other people of color face daily within the United States.

*Dude, chill out . . . Indian people are interested in our sicko culture,
so why can't we learn all the beautiful things about theirs? It's about
sharing, not commodifying.* You see, people say that to me all the time.
*Indians come here and are taking advantage of the motels and the tech
companies. They love to listen to the Backstreet Boys and eat at McDon-
ald's. Why is it any less ethical to go to India and take bits of their culture and religion?* This is when my eyes go big and I start shouting
about power and who's got the power and how the wrong people are
getting empowered, but nobody seems to get what I'm saying.

I don't think that white men see themselves in a constant position of power. It's just an equal exchange to them. They aren't the
ones that deal with discrimination, stereotypes and colonialism. It
has never been an equal exchange. South Asian immigrants provided
the technical and medical expertise the United States was begging for,
particularly in the sixties and seventies and currently in the Silicon
Valley. Americans benefit from highly trained professionals without
having to spend money educating them. In most cases Indians leave
their homeland and come to the United States to make a new life
for themselves. Americans go to India to check it out. They've got
that ticket in their chest pouch, remember? So the exchange is not
equal at all.

Since this most recent obsession with India has begun, I can't say
that the lives of most Indians have improved. We have no greater political voice in the United States, even though all our gods and goddesses
are in all the head shops and henna is sold at beauty salons everywhere. While we deal with the reality, the white men have chosen to

deal with the fantasy. The fantasy of India. And that's exactly what it is. Ask any nonresident Indian if the India they know is the same as the India the white men know. I guarantee the two experiences will be as paradoxical as chai in Orissa and chai in Oregon.

I called my mom the very next morning after that horrible evening of charades and asked her about my name. "It means 'dream' or 'good dream,' right?"

"Yes, it does." Sigh of relief.

"It doesn't mean 'meditation,' right?"

"Well, yes, it does."

"What?!?!"

"It also can mean 'emotion' or 'thought' or 'wish.'. . ."

"But, Mom, I want to know what it means exactly."

"*Dhiku,* your name means many things. It is very difficult to translate to English." Right on, Mom. You heard it. Aw yeah. Another deeper sigh of relief.

Some things just can't be translated.

Heartbroken
Women of Color Feminism and the Third Wave

Rebecca Hurdis

This essay isn't just about an adopted, woman of color feminist; rather, it is a story about how I came to believe that I was worthy of all of these identities. It isn't just a story about feminism or solely about adoption. It is an exploration of where the mind stops and the heart follows. It is too easy to distract myself with ideas about "deconstruction" and "critical analysis," terms that lack the emotional depth to explain my experiences. The struggle is not to find one place where I can exist, but to find it within myself to exist in all of these places, uncompromisingly. To live a life of multiplicity is as difficult as it is to write about it.

All of my life I have been told the story of when my mother held me in her arms for the first time. It was late at night at the airport in Newark, New Jersey. My mother, father and two brothers, along with my grandparents and uncle, were all waiting in the terminal lounge for my plane to arrive from Seoul, Korea. There were other families also waiting for their new babies to be brought off the plane. My mother tells me that she watched in anticipation as all the escorts walked off of the plane with small bundles of Korean babies. Each time they walked toward her, they would pass by, giving the babies to other families. My family grew anxious and nervous as the flow of people exiting the plane grew sparse. My chaperone and I were the last to deplane. The woman walked toward my family and placed me in the arms of my mother. I was six months old. I clung to her, put my head on her shoulder, patted her back and called her "mother" in Korean. The year was 1975. The day was Mother's Day.

Growing up in a transracial adopted family, I was often confused by the images of the "normal, nuclear families." We didn't look like any other family I saw. I couldn't comprehend how I could love my family, feel accepted by them and believe that I belonged to them as much as my phenotypically white brothers. Yet every time I looked in the mirror, my reflection haunted me, because the face that stared back was not the same color as my family's. This awareness was reinforced by the sometimes brutal questions of others. I constantly had to explain that I really was my brother's sister. He was not my husband but truly my brother. I was not the foreign exchange student that just never left. Embarrassed by the attention, I tried to ignore the differences. I took the negativity and dissociation I felt and began to internalize the feelings. I fooled myself into thinking and acting the role of a "good little Asian saved from her fallen country and brought to the land of salvation." I began to believe the messages about being an Asian girl and about being adopted. This compliance was one of the only ways I learned to gain acceptance and validation as a child. I realized that my identity was being created *for* me not *by* me.

When I was ten years old, we moved from a progressive city in
Maryland to a small town in Connecticut. Aside from the infamous
New England fall foliage, the only color I saw was white. I suppose it
wasn't such a radical change for the rest of my family, because they
didn't need the difference and diversity I required for spiritual survival. I quickly realized the key to acceptance was to not be too ethnic, or ethnic at all. To be accepted, I had to grasp and identify with
whiteness, completely denying my Asian self. I spent my teenage years
running away from myself and rebelling from the stereotype of the
"good, cute little Asian." The only images of Asian Americans that I
saw came from the television. I accepted the misrepresentations as
real and accurate because our town only had a few people of color to
begin with. I always thought they were the exceptions to the stereotypes. We were the "fortunate ones" and we self-perpetuated the lies
about ourselves and about our people.

I fooled myself into believing that life was so great. I was accepted
and had all of the things that I thought made me just like everyone
else, yet I couldn't understand why I still carried around a sadness. I
was playing out the script that had been given to me, yet I kept feeling as though I was in the wrong play. When I would talk to my
friends about it, they wouldn't and couldn't understand. I was told
that I was making too big a deal out of being Asian and besides I *was*
just like everyone else. They thought that I just worried too much. My
friends went so far as to convince me by telling me that "I wasn't
really Asian, I was white." But the truth couldn't be denied, just as the
color of my skin couldn't either. They thought that because we were

friends they were entitled or allowed to nickname me "Chinky." They tried to justify it by saying that it was only a joke. My boyfriends were ashamed that they had an Asian-American girlfriend. They assumed they had a right to physically, mentally and sexually abuse me because they thought they were doing me a favor by lowering their standards to be with a woman of color.

I came across feminism as a first-year student at Ohio State University. I was extremely depressed at the time. Everything—my created identity, the world of whiteness that I knew, the denial of my race—that I had worked so hard at repressing and ignoring throughout my life was finally surfacing and emerging. I no longer had the validation of whiteness to protect my false identity. The world that I had understood was changing, and I was confronted with defining myself without the associations of my family and friends. I was forced to step outside of my white world, shedding my blinders to find that I wasn't white and that I had never really been so. The only illusion was the one that I had created for myself, the one that had found acceptance. But I was beginning to realize the cost of this facade.

Yes, I had a large circle of white friends and boyfriends throughout high school. Despite their acceptance, however, I was simultaneously cast as the other. I was undeniably Asian. I was the subject and the object. I was the china doll and the dragoness. The contradictions and the abuse confused me. How could my friends and boyfriends love me, yet in a heated argument spit out "chink" at me? How could they respect me, yet sing the song that had been popularized from the movie *Full Metal Jacket,* "Me So Horny?"

My first women's studies course focused on the history of the women's movement, the social context and the contemporary issues facing feminism today. We looked at issues ranging from violence to sexual orientation to women-centered spirituality to representation in music and film to body image. I began to recognize my extensive history of sexual, mental and physical abuse with boyfriends, and I started to comprehend the cycle of abuse and forgiveness. I was able to begin to stop blaming myself and shift the responsibility back to those who had inflicted the abuse. Initially I had disconnected the abuse from racism, even though it was heavily intertwined and simultaneous. It was just too large for me to understand, and it was still too early for me to grapple with race. I still was thinking that I just needed to become the "right" kind of Asian American and then everything would make sense.

I know that for a lot of women of color, feminism is perceived as being a white woman's movement that has little space or acknowledgment for women of color. I understand how that is true, but back then this class became a catalyst for change and healing. It was a major turning point in my life, where I was able to break my silence and find empowerment within myself and for myself. Women's studies offered me a place where there was validation and reason. I was uncovering and understanding how my own internalization was tied to ideologies of racism and sexism. Although the analysis of racism was somewhat limited in these courses, it served as a lead for future interests. Women's studies and feminism was a steppingstone toward striving for a holistic understanding of myself.

Initially I identified my experiences as being part of a larger discourse and reality. I named the abuse and trauma of my past and could therefore heal from it. I proudly began calling myself a feminist. I viewed feminism broadly as the eradication of sexism, racism, ageism, ableism and heterosexism. It was a social and political commitment to a higher vision for society by resituating women from the margins into the center. I began recognizing and naming what I believed was sexism. The summer after my first women's studies course, I returned home and wrote a dramatic letter to the Congregational church of which I was a member. I earnestly asked them to remove my name from their list because "I did not want to support or be affiliated with a patriarchal institution such as a Christian church." I felt this act was a rite of passage, my initiation into the feminist movement.

But I left college feeling as though there was something missing to this feminism. Professors would talk about Black feminism or women of color feminism, but merely as another mark on their feminist timeline. Little time was dedicated to really examining the intersection of race and gender. Back home I went to my local new-age store (which also doubled as the feminist bookstore) and stumbled on *This Bridge Called My Back: Writings by Radical Women of Color* (edited by Cherríe Moraga and Gloria Anzaldúa). It was the first time I had found a book that had the words "women of color" as part of the title. It was as if I had found the pot of gold at the end of the feminist rainbow. Even though I didn't find myself completely represented in the book, specifically because none of the contributors had been an adopted child, I did find my thoughts, anger and pain represented through the eloquent voices of other women of color. Their writings incorporated race and sexuality.

Reading this anthology, I realized I was entitled to feeling something other than apologetic. I could be angry. I could be aggressive. I could be the opposite of this little china doll that everyone expected me to be. Given my background, this book was life-changing. It represented one of the first moments where I could claim something that was mine; something different from my parents, my friends, my community; something other than whiteness. I remember sitting at the town beach on a hot and humid August day, flipping through the book, my mind exploding and expanding. As I sat there frantically reading, I recall looking up at the sun, closing my eyes and thanking the goddess that I had found this work. Through this discovery I had found that I was not alone. Not only was I feminist, but I was a woman of color feminist.

What makes my relationship to women of color feminism different from most other women of color is how and why I entered the conversation. I began looking at race through gender, where most have the reverse experience. This idea of entry point is crucial. I call myself a woman of color before I call myself an Asian American. It reflects how I have come to see myself and how I understand my own identity. The term "women of color" seems broadly inviting and inclusive while "Asian American" feels rigid and exclusive.

Women of color feminism took me from being a victim to being a warrior.

I am now in an ethnic studies graduate program trying to explore if women of color are within feminism's third wave, and if so, where. I began this project as an undergraduate but I had hit a wall. It was difficult locating voices that represented generation X or third wave women of color feminism. Not much had been written, as our voices were just beginning to emerge. I found women of color feminists in alternative places such as zines, anthologies, magazines and pop culture. I felt frustrated that our voices were deemed not "accredited" enough to be represented in the mainstream.

I held a certain expectation for Jennifer Baumgardner and Amy Richards's book, *Manifesta: Young Women, Feminism, and the Future.* This book markets itself as being *the* text for the third wave of feminism, and I had high hopes that it would address issues of race, gender and class sexuality. Instead, I found the specific history of white (privileged) women. This is a great book for the college white woman who has recently been inspired by feminism and wants to know about the past and how she should contribute for the future. Yet this history is complicated by the fact that the authors do not honestly acknowledge that this is their intention. Rather, they assert that this book is a history of all women, dropping the names of such women of color as Rebecca Walker and Audre Lorde.

I found it astounding that there is no extensive discussion of women of color feminism. This indicates that Baumgardner and

Richards feel as though this is a separate issue, a different kind of feminism. It is as if their work is the master narrative of feminism, with women of color feminism as an appendage. I had hoped that they would have considered such books as *This Bridge Called My Back* and Audre Lorde's *Sister Outsider* as groundbreaking, as they are deemed by most generation X women of color. These books were life-changing to me not only because their critiques have historical value, but also because what these writers were saying in the 1980s was still relevant in the 1990s. *Manifesta* is successful in creating momentum for young white women's activism through the attempt to move feminism out of academia and back into a social and political movement. But the book's greatest contribution was that it raised a need for creating a lineage for women of color feminism.

Is it possible to construct a feminist genealogy that maintains inclusivity? Does feminism still exist for women of color or is it just a "white thing?" Are generation X women of color participating in feminism? These questions propelled me to further think about the connections as well as the separations between women of color and feminism. In the exploration of the third wave of women of color feminism, I talked to several women of color professors and students at the University of California at Berkeley. Their responses and our conversations together were incredibly helpful. These women challenged me to further think about my own conceptions surrounding feminism.

I had expected that as women of color, most of these students would also identify as women of color feminists. I believed the two terms to be synonymous. Instead, I found a rejection of the word "feminism." I hear many women of color refer to themselves as such, yet they make the distinction that they are not claiming a feminist identity. Although many of the women support and stand in alliance with women of color feminism, there is still a lapse in their chosen identity. Many report to have read the popular and pivotal texts within women of color feminism and have felt moved, but their "empowerment" only goes so far.

What is it about the word "feminism" that has encouraged women of color to stand apart from it? Feminism has been indoctrinated into the academy through the discipline of women's studies. It has moved out of the social and political spaces from where it emerged. Women's studies have collapsed the diversity that was part of the feminist movement into a discipline that has become a homogenous generality. For women in the third wave then, one needs to have the academic training of women's studies to be an "accredited feminist." Once race is added to the complexity, many women of color feel as though the compromise or negotiation is just too high a price to pay to be called a feminist. Women of color's participation in women's studies and feminism still causes splintering in our identities.

Many women believe that there is a certain required persona to be a feminist. In the ethnic studies course "Women of Color in the U.S." at Berkeley, for example, students expressed feeling that they didn't have enough knowledge or background to be able to call themselves feminists. The students' comments reflect how many women of color find difficulty in accessing feminism. Often the response is that "feminism is a white woman's thing." Whiteness in feminism comes to represent privilege, power and opportunity. It rarely positions women of color as being as legitimate as the identities of white women. Women's studies has been accurately accused of treating race as a secondary oppression through offering courses about race that are separate from the central curriculum, while ethnic studies feels more comfortable as a place to discuss race and gender. But even in ethnic studies, women's experiences and histories still remain on the margins. Like women's studies, they too have had problems integrating gender into the analysis of race.

Women of color often feel women's studies is a battlefield where they are forced to defend their communities and themselves. Women's studies, the academic endeavor of feminism, has a history of relegating women of color as second. When women of color raise issues of race in these classrooms, the response from other students is often defensive and loaded with repressed white guilt. For young women of color, there is a sentiment that we must find a central identity that precedes all others. We are asked to find one identity that will encapsulate our entirety. We are asked to choose between gender, class, race and sexuality and to announce who we are first and foremost. Yet where is the space for multiplicity?

Although I am a self-proclaimed woman of color feminist, I struggle with being an "authentic" woman of color feminist. Even though I realize it is self-defeating, I worry that other women of color will look at my feminism and judge it as being socialized whiteness and an effect of adoption. The roots of my feminism are connected to my adopted mother, although I am uncertain whether she would identify as a feminist. She was a woman who wouldn't let us watch the *Flintstones* or the *Jetsons* because of their negative portrayal of women, yet she unquestionably had dinner on the table every night for her husband, sons and daughter. Most important, she raised me to believe I could be whoever I wanted to be and in that a strong woman. If feminism has been bestowed onto me from my adopted mother, then I choose not to look at it as another indicator of whiteness or of being whitewashed. Rather, I see it as a gift that has shown me not the limitations of mainstream feminism but the possibilities of women of color feminism. People sometimes question my attachment to feminism. Despite the criticisms, it has served as a compass that navigates me away from paralysis into limitless potential.

One of the reasons that my project is now at a standstill is that the conversation has changed. In the 1970s and 1980s women of color feminists seemed to be in solidarity with each other. Their essays showed the racism and classism within mainstream feminism, forcing mainstream feminism to be accountable. Today, however, women of color are focused on the differences that exist among us. When we try to openly and honestly acknowledge the differences between us, we become trapped in difference, which can result in indifference.

Women of color feminism has currently been reduced to a general abstraction that has flattened out difference and diversity, causing tension between women of color. Instead of collectively forming alliances against whiteness, women of color now challenge the opposing identities that exist under the umbrella term "women of color." It raises questions about entitlement and authenticity. It tries to suppress the heterogeneous composition of women of color feminism by trying to create a unifying term. Yet the differences of class, racialization and sexuality have arisen and persisted, challenging assumptions that all women of color are in solidarity with each other. We all come with backgrounds and histories that differ from one another and despite knowing this, we still maintain this ideal and creation of the authentic "women of color." The one that is the right class, the right race, the right sexuality. We must refuse being reduced to an abstraction. We must address the conflicts that have begun to fester paralysis instead of fostering change. But that also means that we need to revitalize women of color feminism so that those actions can begin to take place.

I see women of color feminism at this moment of indifference. I see the backstabbing. I hear the gossip. I feel the tension. We use our words like fists to beat each other down and beat each other silent. It is not pretty and certainly not productive. When do we recognize that the moment has come to move forward? I wish I had some solution of a way to "use our difference to achieve diversity instead of division." But we know that clichés are just clichés. They don't provide us with the fairy-tale endings. They don't make us feel better or more hopeful. More often than not, I think clichés just annoy us and leave us sarcastic.

It is crucial to explore and expose the problems of women of color feminism, but we also need to be weary of what we are willing to sacrifice. I think a new, third space is being created in women of color feminism. Those of us who are not easily recognized and acknowledged as women of color are coming to feminism as a place to discuss the implications of invisibility. We are pushing, expanding and exploding ideologies of multiplicity and intersectionality. We come as transracial adoptees, women of mixed race, bisexuals, refugees and hundreds of other combinations. For us, women of color feminism continues to be a living theory and a way to survive.

Talking Back, Taking Back

It's Not an Oxymoron
The Search for an Arab Feminism

Susan Muaddi Darraj

I see no reason to say that the Arab woman is less intelligent and ener-
getic and sincere than the [W]estern woman.

—Ghada Samman, 1961

My father is a feminist, although he would probably never admit it. It
is difficult to even write the two words "father" and "feminist" next to
each other in the same sentence (despite the nice alliterative sound). I
can imagine him hearing it and shrinking away from the word,
shaking his head vehemently and saying, in his thick Middle Eastern
accent that all my girlfriends find so charming, "No, no, no, not me,
thank you." And yet, despite his denial, my father has helped me form
my own unique feminist identity more than that other F-word—
Friedan.

I remember sitting in a feminist theory class in graduate school,
feeling strangely unmoved by the words of Betty Friedan and the
second-wave feminist writers. I understood their struggles and
respected their courage—there was not a doubt in my mind that it

took a lot of courage to resist Western patriarchal demands on women's lives. But these were not representative feminists. In *The Feminine Mystique*, Friedan expounds on the woes of being a mere housewife, but it seemed there was a certain level of class privilege that accompanied her position. The role of a "housewife" usually developed when there was a man to support the family, when he could do it all on his own salary. Although my mother swept the floor and cooked most of our meals, I realized that housework was not her only "work." She also worked full-time in the business that she and my father ran together.

Sitting in that class, with other women who expounded on the oppression of housework, I dared once to ask, "Who will do the housework then?" Seventeen pairs of eyes turned to me, and I continued: "If men don't do it and women don't do it, who will? It has to be done. Do you propose that we hire *other women* to come and do it? Other women who clean people's homes because they have the opportunity to do nothing else?"

Silence greeted my question, as I had expected. I realized then that most of the women in the class were upper-middle and middle-class white women—and I felt like a complete outsider. Perhaps they could understand Friedan because her brand of feminism spoke directly to their experience. But it didn't speak to mine. I didn't view housework as a mark of oppression. There was a certain sense of pride placed on a clean, welcoming home, and both my parents had always placed value on it. That was why my father spent his weekends trimming the lawn and sweeping the walkways and why my mother mopped the kitchen floor and wiped the windows until they sparkled. It was why my brothers and I were marched off to various rooms every Saturday morning, armed with furniture polish and dust rags. We all did housework. No, this version of feminism did not appeal to me. But then again, what version did? For a long time I thought that this was the only brand of feminism that existed. If that was true, I certainly wasn't a card-carrying member.

Furthermore, I didn't like the way that this feminism viewed people like my mother and grandmothers and aunts—and me, for that matter. I was tired of turning on the evening news, eager to learn news of the Middle East, and seeing women clad in heavy, black robes, their eyes lowered but barely visible behind the slits in their face veils as they scurried past the television cameras. I have been to the Middle East. I am an Arab Christian, and I know many Arab Christian and Muslim women. Some—but definitely not all—of my Muslim friends veil themselves, as do a few of the older, conservative Christian women, especially before entering a church. Why did Americans equate Muslim women with veils so completely, and why did the cameras seem to pick out only these women?

The answer was an uncomplicated one: because this was the quaint vision of the Middle East with which America felt comfortable. This vision included heavily robed and mustachioed sheiks, belly dancers, tents, camels and—of course—veiled women. This vision was, to use an orientalist cliché, a desert mirage, concocted by the same Hollywood producers who created Rudolph Valentino (*The Sheik*).

American feminists, like the rest of the nation and the Western world, had accepted the flawed image of the Middle East and Middle Eastern women without question. "Of course, they [meek and silent Arab women] are oppressed; we [liberated, assertive Western women with voices] must help them." I have heard similar statements (with the notions in the brackets implied) from white American feminists who wanted to save their Arab sisters but not to understand them. They wanted to save them from the burden of their families and religion but not from the war, hunger, unemployment, political persecution and oppression that marked their daily lives and that left them with only their families and religion as sole sources of comfort. The tone of white Western feminism—with its books about "lifting the veil on Arab women" and Arab women "lifting the veil of silence"—was that Arab feminism was nothing greater than an amusing oxymoron.

The apparent hypocrisy and condescension that white Western feminists held for Arab women confused me. I felt betrayed by a movement that claimed to create a global sisterhood of women; it seemed that the Arab woman was the poor and downtrodden stepsister in this family.

Where was my feminism?

It was my father who first taught me "feminism," who told me that I could do anything I wanted—achieve any goal, reach any height—and that he would support me in that climb. I don't remember ever feeling that my culture—and in my mind my father embodied that culture almost completely—stood in my way, although others thought my culture was a jungle of patriarchal pitfalls.

Susan Muaddi Darraj

One day my father told me a story that rocked my world. It was that of Jamila Bouhereid, the Algerian woman who had played an instrumental role in the Algerian resistance against the colonial French forces. It was one of those stories that he and his generation had heard about while growing up in Palestine, nations away from Algeria, though the story stirred them nonetheless. Bouhereid had been captured by the French and tortured in unspeakable ways, but she refused to divulge essential information about the resistance. The torture continued until it finally killed her. He told me the story during one of our many marathon conversations that usually lasted through the night, while we sat at the kitchen table, sipping coffee and eating oranges. I became obsessed with Bouheried's story and tried to find out everything I could about her. Unfortunately, there was very little information about her—or Arab women in general—available in English.

My futile search was not a complete failure, however, only the opening of a new door. I came across the names of other Arab women whose names I had heard: Huda Sha'rawi, the founder of the Egyptian Feminist Union, who had called for the ban of the veil at the beginning of the twentieth century; Mai Ziyyadah, a feminist writer and a contemporary of Sha'rawi, who called for men to free women in order to free themselves; even Khadijah, the first wife of the Prophet Muhammad, who had financed his travels, owned a lucrative business and been the first convert to Islam. I searched the Internet for information on more modern Arab women: Hanan Ashrawi, a chief spokesperson for the Palestinians; Leila Ahmed, a feminist and scholar who wrote about Arab women with accuracy, honesty and pages of solid research; and Fatima Mernissi, who sought to rediscover Islam's valuation of women.

I also searched for something that neither the Internet nor the library's shelves could offer me: a real, hard, searing look at the lives of modern, everyday Arab women. I saved my pennies and, armed with my notebooks and pens, traveled to Egypt, Jordan and Palestine over the course of a few years. I met women in my family and made some new friends. One summer, I spent three months in the West Bank, in the city of Ramallah, and studied at Birzeit University. Ramallah and Birzeit were a mere half-hour taxicab ride away from Taybeh, the small village where my parents grew up and where my grandmother and several aunts, cousins and uncles lived. Although I was thrilled to spend time with my relatives, I also wanted to meet and interact with Palestinian college women, and I met quite a few and listened to their stories. At many points and on many occasions I felt like I was looking into a mirror, at what I would have been like had my father and mother never left the political oppression and insecurities of Palestine.

One woman, a twenty-four-year-old student, told me how it was a struggle to get to the university every day, not because her father wouldn't permit it (for he actually encouraged her), but because she had to take a multipassenger taxi in which she had been groped many times by the male passengers. Another woman, also in her mid-twenties, described how her parents were proud that she had been accepted at the university, but she often skipped semesters because money usually ran low. It often was a choice of buying textbooks or letting her younger siblings go without meat for several months. She estimated that at that rate it would take another six years to finish her bachelor's degree. Another woman, who veiled herself, explained to me how as a religious person she felt compelled to educate herself for her own betterment and for that of her family.

It struck me that many of the women whom I met could be considered feminists, perhaps not by the standards of the white Western feminism that I had encountered in my feminist theory class, but by the standards of a different feminism—one that allowed women to retain their culture, to have pride in their traditions and to still vocalize the gender issues of their community. These were women whom I considered feminists because they believed in the dignity and potential for upward mobility of every woman; they wanted to erase class lines between women; they worked so that they could have choices in their lives and not be channeled into one way of life.

I realized upon my return to the United States that fall that, more than ever, I longed for a feminism that would express who I was and what my experiences were as an Arab-American woman. That feminism was within my grasp, but I discerned several obstacles that blocked my path. The chief one was the seeming universality of white Western feminism, which appears to leave no room for other visions. This caused various conflicts within me. Another obstacle to voicing my own feminism to white Western feminists was that the various traditions in my Arabic culture were indeed the markings of a patriarchal culture. Many feminist texts and discourses on the Middle East highlighted such traditions, although most modern-day societies, including that of the United States, can be accurately described as patriarchal.

One such tradition is that Arab parents are usually referred to by the name of their eldest son. Thus, a couple whose eldest son is named Abdallah would be referred to socially as Im Abdallah (mother of Abdallah) and Abu Abdallah (father of Abdallah). I am the eldest child in my family, but my parents are called by the name of my brother, who is a year younger. There is generally an emphasis on having at least one male child in Arab families, and the boys are often named after their grandfathers; my brother Abdallah was given the name of my grandfather Abdallah. As a woman, this certainly bothers me, and it strikes a sour note with many Arab women. After all, why the big deal about boys? What is so disappointing about girls? It seems to me that American feminists overly criticize this tradition, however, while forgetting that it is no different than American boys being named David, Jr. or Jonathan So-and-So, III. As far as I can remember, American girls aren't dubbed Michelle, Jr. and Jennifer IV, unless they are European monarchs, but this point does not occupy chapters in Arab feminist texts on the West.

Another unfairly beleaguered custom is that of the traditional Arabic marriage, which has wrinkled many a conversation with my American feminist friends. In the Middle East and among Middle Easterners living in other parts of the world, when a couple decides to get married, it is expected that a *toulbeh* takes place. During the toulbeh the potential bridegroom arrives at the home of the potential bride, escorted by several members of his family. The bride's family waits, and members of her extended family wait with them. The eldest male of the groom's family requests the bride's hand from the eldest male in her family. When the expected "yes" is announced (because the question is a formality, after all), the two families celebrate their upcoming union. Of course, this is a patriarchal tradition, one in which a woman is viewed as a person who should not answer for herself. Again, is it different than in American culture, where it is considered a sweet gesture and a romantic leftover from traditional times for a man to ask for the bride's hand from her father? And don't fathers still walk their daughters down the aisle and "give them away"? The endless explanations of Arab wedding customs that I had to offer my American feminist friends, however, would have led one to think that it was utterly barbaric.

In the aftermath of the events of September 11 and with the recent conflict in Afghanistan, the same stilted media coverage would make anyone think that *every* Middle Eastern woman saw the world from between the peepholes of her burqa's face netting. These traditions are usually used as examples that create a picture of the Arab world as a *1,001 Nights*-like land of wicked and despotic sultans and silenced and imprisoned harem girls—women who need the West to enlighten, educate and save them (But Scheherazade, a Muslim Arab woman and the heroine of *1,001 Nights,* saved herself and her countrywomen, so it doesn't make sense to me *why* Arab culture is attacked as anti-woman, as if no other culture has gender-oppressive traditions of which to be ashamed).

These naming and wedding traditions, and others like them, made me second-guess my professed need to find a feminism that suited me. After all, on one level I liked these traditions—they were deeply embedded in my culture and in myself as a person. When I got married, my husband's eldest uncle asked for my hand from my eldest uncle. Did that mean that I wasn't a feminist? Some of my friends, upon hearing this, wrinkled their noses in disgust and shook their heads sadly at me as if to say, "Poor thing! She's just condemned herself to a lifetime of constant pregnancies, Little League games and soap operas." My God, I thought, was I being kicked out of the club before I had even officially joined?

This experience—feeling emotionally torn between my culture and what white Western feminism told me I had to be—relates almost inversely to another conflict that obstructed the recognition of my feminist identity: America's exoticism of Arab women. Although we were considered veiled and meek, we were simultaneously and ironically considered sultry, sexual and "different." People, especially white feminists, were often intrigued by my "exoticness" and asked me silly questions, like whether Arab women knew how to belly-dance or whether I knew of any women who lived in harems. I was also frequently mistaken as a Muslim, because many people couldn't conceive of an Arab Christian (although Arab Christians and Muslims have long allied themselves against the pervasive stereotypes that threaten to categorize us both). They wanted to know if I had ever ridden a camel and if I would have an arranged marriage and would my husband be taking other wives as well? If this was how little people in general, and feminists in particular, knew of my culture, what was the hope that I would be seriously received as a feminist?

Some Muslim women see no contradiction between feminism and Islam. In her book *Palestinian Women: Patriarchy and Resistance in the West Bank,* Cheryl Rubenberg studies Palestinian women who live in the camps and villages of the West Bank and highlights the phenomenon of the Muslim Sisters *(Ikhwat al-musilmat).* Sometimes called "Islamist feminists," the Muslim Sisters believe that Islam gives women full rights but that the religion has been corrupted by men to suit their patriarchal agenda. One Muslim Sister whom Rubenberg interviewed said that their mission is to bring people back to the true Islam, which historically allowed women the right to be educated, to work, to participate in public life and to own property. According to the Sisters, however, Islam has been perverted by men's patriarchal ambitions in the centuries since the Prophet Muhammad's death. Because of anti-Muslim sentiments (which are inextricably linked to anti-Arab sentiments) and the general misconceptions of Islam in the West (that all Muslim men are terrorists with long beards and all Muslim women are battered and wear veils), it would be difficult for a Western, non-Muslim person to understand the desire of Arab Muslim women to retain both their religion and their sense of feminism.

Another conflict that threatened my development of a feminist voice was my split vision—my ability to thrive in American culture but to also appreciate Arab culture. Further, it was my frustration with white Western feminists who took up issues like keeping one's name after marriage but who sniffed at Arab women, who had always kept their names[1] and whose biggest problem was how to afford bread for dinner? I was living in America, land of the free and home of the brave, while cousins in the West Bank were throwing stones at Israeli tanks and working extra jobs to help my aunts and uncles pay the bills. While I was hopping in my car to work every day, perhaps stopping at a Starbucks for my morning coffee, they were walking to the taxi stop to see if a car was available and willing to drive them around the road-blocks that the Israelis had set up—all just to get to class on time for a final exam. Even worse, it was U.S. money and foreign aid to Israel that kept Palestinians locked in a seemingly hopeless situation that robbed them of their futures.

I think that I had a guilt complex as a result of this split vision: I loathed having to write papers on the "Angel of the House" theory and the imagery of women trapped behind wallpaper, while Arab women were dealing with issues of physical survival.[2] Although I admired the work of white feminists and respected the ways in which they surpassed their own obstacles, those were not my obstacles. I could not focus on the complexities of white Western feminist theory when I knew that Arab women faced very different issues.

And I returned once again to my initial question: Where did I fit in all this?

A few years ago, through a strange set of coincidences, I found an answer. I had started reading the work of Black feminists, such as bell hooks, who took on Betty Friedan full force. She challenged the relevance of Friedan's ideas about housewives to Black women, who have always had to work. Her work led me to Gloria Anzaldúa, who led me to Barbara Smith, and the list grew. I was heartened by the fact that Black women and other women of color had the courage to carve a feminism of their own out of the monolithic block that was generally accepted as "feminism."

About this time I caught up with a friend of mine, an assertive and lively Arab woman from San Francisco, who was visiting when I lived in Philadelphia. I was twenty-four. It was a gloriously sunny day in the city, and we decided to go out. We sat in a coffee shop on Philadelphia's hip South Street section and talked about the way that we both felt locked out of feminism and the lack of relevance that feminism seemed to have for our lives. We also talked about the way that analyses of Arab women's issues seemed to be largely conducted by white Western women.

"But it's white Western feminism that doesn't relate to my life," I interjected.

"True," she agreed. "There *is* actually a group of Arab women who deal with gender issues—their association is called AWSA, the Arab Women's Solidarity Association."

"Arab feminists?" I asked, unbelieving.

"Yeah. I think that you can call them feminists." She gave me the Web site information, and I checked it out immediately upon my return home. I found out that AWSA is a network for Arab women, meant to provide support and to serve as the basis for the Arab women's movement. It was founded by Nawal el-Saadawi, an Egyptian doctor and leading feminist. That sunny Philadelphia afternoon initiated my awareness of AWSA members, who were scholars, artists, writers and everyday women who felt that gender issues in the Arab world and among Arabs in other countries should be discussed and diagnosed by a circle that included Arab women themselves.

Another life-changing event occurred around this time: I met the man I eventually married. As an Arab woman, romance had never been easy because of the strong cultural taboo on dating. I often watched movies and television shows in which girlfriends chatted with each other (usually while doing each other's hair at slumber parties) about the good looks of a new boyfriend, the disappointment of a blind date, the elation over a romantic dinner or the pain of a breakup. I could never chat so easily about romance because it was a distant, remote experience, one that I knew only vicariously through television, films and books. Furthermore, it was difficult to meet American men who were not entranced by my "exoticness" (probably the most ridiculous comment I've ever heard) and the aspects of my culture that they didn't understand (such as not showing someone the bottom of my shoes or genuinely enjoying time with my family, etc.). I also met some Arab men who, ironically, thought I was too "Americanized": my unaccented, perfect English littered with slang; my tendency to wear boots and blue jeans; and my refusal to spend more than three minutes on my hair and makeup testified to that, I suppose, not to mention my vocalized interest in pursuing my career and my (equally vocalized) lack of desire to have children for a long time.

But meeting my future husband was an eye-opening experience. I felt that I finally had met someone who could understand and even relate to my split vision. Not only was he kind and caring, but he respected my intellect, my career goals and my opinions. In other words, he allowed me to be myself—and comfortably so. When, over dinner, I mentioned to him the topic of feminism—a word I had uttered to few men, save my father—he said that I didn't strike him as a feminist. I asked why not, and he offered me an interesting response: "Well, I guess I'm thinking of 'feminists' as what I see here in the States. And they seem largely self-involved. But you care about all kinds of issues, not just the ones that affect you. And I think that you consider the concept of family to be above that of the individual."

I pointed out that women have traditionally been reared to ignore and neglect themselves for the sakes of others (children, husbands, in-laws, etc.). This included Arab women. Women in general had also never had the opportunity to focus on their own development and their own goals. But I also realized that he was thinking of traditional, American, white feminism when he said that, and I explained that I felt that there might be another kind of feminism out there, one that appealed more to women like me, who wanted to be feminists and spouses and mothers.

I could see that he was intrigued by what I was saying, and he admitted that this conversation had redefined feminism for him. "Besides," he asked casually, "Why does there have to be a choice between feminism and family? I think a woman can have both."

He was right.

I knew at that point that with the recent riveting conglomeration of coincidental events in my life—my interest in Black feminism, AWSA and the discovery of a possible Arab feminism, and meeting my future husband—that something exciting was happening. My feminist self—my own version of feminism—was emerging.

It required no great sacrifice of my Arab heritage, no shame at my close ties to my family and no compromise of my own needs. It involved two of the most important men in my life—my father and my husband—unlike the ways in which I saw American feminism making a conscious split from male influence (I should also mention here that although my father and husband are the two best men that I personally know, they are not rare examples of Arab men—their mentalities are not unusual in the Arab world, despite what CNN says). There was no need to define independence as living in isolation from my family and making decisions without their support and advice. There was no imperative to shake my head at the thought of having my own family and being a mother. I could be a feminist in a way that suited *my* life, not in a feminism that would mold me to its ideal shape. After all, wasn't feminism supposed to be about making my own choices?

So here I am—an Arab-American feminist. I am happily married. I work. I write. I plan to have children in a few years. I read the newspaper every day. I call my congressperson about U.S. foreign policy issues that negatively affect Arab women. I follow the news in Palestine and Israel religiously, on both American and Arab news channels (thanks to satellite technology). I cringe first and take action second whenever I come across hackneyed "exotic" portrayals of Arab women. I eagerly read the ever-growing body of work being produced about Arab women. This lifestyle is what feminism means to me now, although I once thought that I would never use this word to describe myself.

Most important, once I realized my own version of feminism, I found myself better able to understand white Western feminism and the many outer storms and internal divisions it has had to weather. Now that I have my own foundation, I see the need for a cross-cultural feminist dialogue, especially after the September 11 attacks on the United States, which have led to an overthrow of the Taliban and an intensified interest on the part of Americans to understand Islam in general. As that interest expands to include the issues of Muslim women and Arab women, it should be clarified that any resulting dialogues must be inclusive of Arab voices in order to be successful. I applaud American feminism for attempting to bridge an intimidatingly wide gap, but that bridge must be rooted in firm ground at *both* ends of the divide. It should no longer be possible to write about Arab women with any aura of expertise or authority without *first* knowing what Arab women need and want.

Falling off the Tightrope onto a Bed of Feathers

Darice Jones

I lived my life for a long time on a tightrope, trying to find my middle ground, to please my audience of parents, friends, teachers and bosses, trying to look good doing it and come out on the other side unscathed. In my little block of Oakland, California, it was not OK to be all that I was. There was too much contradiction involved. I am African and American, Christian-raised but Tao-embracing, invested in the plight of black men but my life partners are to be women, raised working class but with a middle-class education, peace-bound but activism-prone, and a feminist whose politics are centered around all life—not just the lives of women. Part of learning feminism for me has been about learning that you can't be what people want you to be—and learning how to do better than just survive when you fall.

I didn't grow up with "feminism" as an important word. In fact, I didn't come to hear a working definition of it until a college professor created one for me. She said feminism is simply the idea that women should be free to define themselves. A feminist is someone who espouses that belief. I would add that feminism is also about putting that belief into action and working on your own internalized sexism. A feminist is not just someone who envisions a different world but someone who creates a life that will change it.

I can see feminism at work in every area of my life, as I went from a teething ring to an eyebrow ring. In the late seventies, my early years, I watched my mother and her mother stomping out a ground for me to walk on. Full-time working mothers with full-time investments in their communities and churches is the only image I ever had of the women closest to me. So media images of "stay-at-home" moms never penetrated my psyche. They were as fictional to me as Saturday-morning cartoons. Most of the images I saw in magazines, on television and in movies were of white middle-class women, but working-class African-American women were my reality; mothers, aunts, cousins, teachers, even my Girl Scout instructors were black women on a mission to make good in the world.

As early as I can remember, I knew the bar was high. I was expected to conquer any challenge presented to me at school, to excel in extracurricular sports and music, and to be a young leader in our church. These expectations were implicit in the way our family operated. My mother taught me and my four sisters to read as soon as we could speak, and she made us teach each other. That passing down of learning, child to child, laid the groundwork for our deep, close relationships as sisters.

The relationship between my parents was filled with examples of the feminist ideal in action. While we all lived together, until I was twelve, I saw my parents as two equal superpowers, one never bowing to the other. They seemed to have a respect for each other stronger than romance or love. My father, who passed away a couple of years ago, was a big man, intimidating to many because of his size but a man of heart to those who knew him best. My mother is a tall woman, and people responded not to her size but to her presence, her voice, the way she takes over a room just by walking in. So while movies, TV shows and commercials portrayed women as weak and emotional and men as strong and stoic, the Jones's residence was a home in which a couple's home was their castle and the king was more likely to cry than the queen.

When my parents separated, the two equal pillars that had held up my world into adolescence were shaken. When the dust settled, my mother was left holding up the earth, on her own. After working any-where between ten- and sixteen-hour overnight shifts as a nurse, our mother would come straight home and drive us to swim, tennis, crafts or drama lessons. My father lived in the same city and was involved in our lives, and although he never worked an overnight shift, every single ride to every single lesson, my entire life, was given to me by my mother. She made it clear to us that learning was essential to liv-ing. Maybe the even greater message was that a woman's choices, actions and goals were not necessarily dependent on the support of a man. With my mother at the helm of our family, I just assumed that they weren't.

Although my home was a haven for a girl with ambitions and dreams like mine, our Pentecostal church was the first place I encountered a challenge to my right to fully explore my potential. I was thirteen. It was the first place where I saw people close to me reinforce those media images of women "in their places" that I had so easily dismissed in early childhood. The more deeply involved I became in the church, the less sure I became about my right to a full, free, explosive, untamed life. Even though I had been raised in the Pentecostal (Christian) church all my life, it had been peripheral for me at best. With hormones raging, acne taking over, body blossoming and grown men looking, I needed something to define me other than those things. I chose the church. That choice would later determine my responses to my African ancestry, education, friendship, relationships, sexual violence and sexual identity. And if feminism had a face, she would have frowned; if eyes, she would have cried; if hands, she would have slapped that thirteen-year-old me before I ever internalized the church's position on women.

The story of Adam and Eve reveals the church's view on women. The woman in the story is created specifically to meet the man's needs. He is made from earth; she is made from him. She manipulates him and her trickery is his downfall. She is smart enough to fool the man but too dim to realize the scope of her actions. She is disloyal to her partner and conspires with the creature who has the most to offer. All of the suffering she endures, she brings upon herself, including the pain of childbirth and the death of one of her sons. In short, women are inferior, manipulative cheats whose main purpose in life is to bear children and please men. This was not considered an insult to women in my church but a fact of life.

My parents' reaction to my newfound faith only reinforced that I had made a good choice. I remember the day my father, who was not a religious man, got all dressed up to see me sing the lead in our choir. Similarly, my mother, who never blinked an eye when I brought home the expected A on my report card, seemed to take a sense of pride in my loyalty to the church. So while United States politics around women in the 1980s was generally a time for marked advance, I was headed back in time to a destination that was literally biblical. Despite the fact that I had recognized the import of Geraldine Ferraro being chosen as the nation's first female vice presidential candidate, of Whoopi Goldberg's Academy Award for *The Color Purple* and even the rise of several popular television shows with female leads, my teenage heart was numb to every image but one. The image imbedded in my head through no less than three church services a week: Jesus Christ hanging on a cross, giving his life for sins I had committed. For this I had to pay with my soul, and the men who led my church would show me the way.

The lessons came in many ways. All of our ministers were men. They sat in a raised pulpit above and away from the congregation. They were in charge of all the messages to the congregation. Admonishments to women to stay in their places as outlined in the Bible were commonplace: Women, obey your husbands; and single women, obey your preachers. Never wear pants because the Bible says a woman should not dress like a man. Choose a profession becoming a Christian; my broadcast focus was out because I'd have to wear makeup. Always forgive—even cheating, lying, abusive partners. And for God's sake, young women, get married and be fruitful—the younger the better. Don't be gay, period; it is an abomination in the eyes of God.

With admonitions flowing, rushing over the pews like water over a fall, teachings about our African ancestry were notably missing. I was grown before I heard of the Diaspora. I was grown before the feeling was real to me that there must be more to god than rules that, if broken, led to eternal punishment. The feeling that sometimes whatever Spirits moved people to sing and rock and love and look inside must have a woman's face. Some of the god in me must look like me and move like me and soul like me. But Pentecost had no time, room or interest in telling a little curious girl with an open heart that she was a daughter of the Goddess Osun. Osun is a representation of a creative force in the universe that is not male, coming directly from our African sisters and brothers but not found at all in our teachings— not even as an alternative "god view" to be dismissed. When I started studying African religions on my own, in college, I realized that I was both shocked and comforted by representations of spirit that put forth a need for a balance between female and male energy in life; it felt closer to right than the male-dominant philosophies that permeated Christianity.

What you don't know can hurt you deeply. This sin of omission and ignorance committed by the church kept me as far away from my sisters and brothers in Africa as the miles between us. The internalized racism presented to African Americans as part of the United States's ongoing system of oppression of thought, history and culture against us—beginning with the Atlantic slave trade and continuing today with the prison industrial complex—was so deeply ingrained that children even used the words "black" and "African" as insults to each other. No one was rushing to offer other images of Africa besides those found in the *National Geographic* books that lined the shelves in both the school and public libraries. Exacerbating the ignorance about our history was the apathy that pervaded it. Our only passion was God. As a result, we weren't even Christians of action like Martin Luther King Jr. and his cohorts; we were Christians of criticism and isolation and passivity.

The constant image of one god with a male face only perpetuated the sexism that was so accepted that I never even heard it called by its name. I took in silent messages as I watched the twentysomething couples struggle with the church's heavy-handed tenets and old-world views of male and female roles. The women were always encouraged to acquiesce in any disagreements, while the men were encouraged to show strength by keeping their families in line. Men whose wives seemed to conform were openly rewarded with higher posts; men whose wives were less obedient were slower to rise up the church hierarchy. Divorce was one of the greatest indications of spiritual weakness, so the few married women whose husbands were not in church were encouraged to wait them out, let God handle it and at all costs, stay.

But my greatest lesson about the value of women in the church's eyes was a personal one. One of those pulpit kings took off his crown and robe and stepped down from his dais just long enough to rape me.

God had allowed my teenage body to blossom too soon. When I confided in my trusted women in the church, they told me my salvation depended on me forgiving him. Years later when I told our pastor, he told me that that preacher had much more to protect and much more to lose if the news became public. He was a man with a family. I was just a girl. I was a girl too afraid to tell my parents. I was a girl too warped by the fear of losing what felt like the only real relationship in my life—that with Jesus—to leave the church right away. So I paid with my soul, and feminism prayed for eyes to cry for little old me. What she got was an eleven-year struggle from that dusty road of Bible stories, church sermons and women who walked behind to a place where I would rather walk alone with eyes open to the world than in a shadow just to feel like I had some company.

The journey was by no means smooth. Although 1980s politics had failed to touch me, the politics of the 1990s held me in a suffocating embrace. It was in this last decade of the century that all my cultural, religious and political contradictions came to a head. The world was battling over a woman's right to choose, and I was confronted with my own obligation to do so. It wasn't a choice about my body but my mind, and everyone seemed to want a piece. To practice our religion, one had to filter every thought, every move or emotion through the Bible. It was a constant checking and rechecking against biblical tenets and the church's interpretation of those doctrines. The older I became, the more I came to question the teachings. The more I questioned, the more I was reprimanded for being weak in spirit. Mention of other belief systems brought reproach, and instead of exploring questions fully, I was encouraged to put my faith in god and wait for answers from him. It was a way to keep people in line and quiet. The discussion was to be confined to prayers between you and god, preventing you from having discussions with each other.

This narrow view of my spiritual possibilities and total lack of acknowledgment of our forefather's and foremother's beliefs eventually put me on a path away from Christianity. As I started college in 1992, the church was still teaching that pride was a person's downfall, but African-American pride was calling my name. The more time I spent with my young sisters and brothers seeking knowledge about our spiritual possibilities, the more I realized how stifling the church was for a woman with questions. It disturbed and at the same time invigorated me to learn that ours was one of the only religions on earth that lacked powerful images of women as gods.

It is no surprise that the Christian United States continues to show open contempt for its female population through its dissemination of wealth that keeps working-class women and their children last. African-American women and their children are barely in the running. By 1990 a woman's right to choose was being openly attacked by terrorist murderers, while woman battering and rape laws laid down sentences that belittled the crimes. As a rape victim—who could have easily become a teen pregnancy statistic as a result—I found the politics of the time grating on my spirit.

If that wasn't bad enough, there were weekly news reports of women, mostly African-American women, cheating the welfare system. These images were constant and so incessant that they became normalized as a representation of the average low-income African-American mother. Single African-American women were commonly represented as teen mothers, who either abandoned their babies or smoked crack until the babies were born with a multitude of birth defects. Similar news stories about white women were more forgiving and left the audience with questions rather than judgments: What is our country saying when a young woman has to deceive the government about how many kids she has just to get enough support to take care of one child? Where have we gone wrong when a young woman is so afraid that she leaves her newborn to be found by a stranger? When the subject of the same stories were African American, reporters spun them in a way that inevitably left the audience outraged, no questions asked. The shoddy journalism supporting a racism that lived so deep in the average American consciousness that it went unspoken was painful. It was like being slapped across the face with the hatred our high-school history classes tried to convince us died after the civil rights struggles of the 1960s. It was a different kind of hurt than the every day encounters with people who showed contempt for my brown skin, because it was being mass marketed as the truth. I felt as if they were daring viewers to even think about questioning it.

The control over these racist messages about women was totalitarian. Goliath stood firm. Another blow to my spirit was the fact that representations of women that I knew, the woman that I was becoming were lacking. Who would write their stories, who would tell their tales, who would produce news reports asking questions about their plight? I wavered on the tightrope between religion and spiritual freedom, finally choosing to follow my spirit. My spirit motivated me to choose a journalism major in college, and I began to ask questions for African-American women at work.

Angela Davis, 1960s activist and professor at the University of California in Santa Cruz, came to speak at a rally on campus. I was expecting for her to light a fire under all of us, encouraging us to take our fight for a more egalitarian society to the streets! What she said, with a mellow vibe and tone that can only be attributed to older, wiser, black women who've been down roads and seen things we never will, was that our activism was not to mirror the activism of old. This generation faces the challenge of defining activism in a United States that no longer responds to sit-ins and marches. She suggested that our strength would come from building coalitions with other people of color and like-minded folks.

But first I had to build coalitions with the different parts of myself. The sexism within the African Student Alliance on my campus (which mirrored the kind of sexism I'd witnessed in my church and my local African-American community) was pushing out the feminist me. At the same time, I found feminist groups so desperate to hang on to some credibility in the mainstream, pushing against my focus on African heritage and pushing to keep the door closed to the closet behind which I hid my love for women. It seemed less and less likely that I would find a place in the world to fully be myself. I worried that the definition of feminism that my college professor had so eloquently laid out would never become a reality for me.

Of course, it was my mother who set me straight. She told me to stop worrying about what people said and to do what I was here to do. She told me I was an artist, and she said it with pride in her voice. With that, I began to put pen to paper, paint to canvas, voice to air and break down all the systems of thinking and accepted ways of being that excluded some part of myself. I found that while what my mother thought of me was paramount to my spiritual survival, what the world thought no longer mattered. Though I didn't share her religious fervor any longer, I still respected her more than any other person.

I didn't know any other women who'd worked a graveyard shift in various hospitals for more than twenty years to feed, clothe and care for five hungry girls. She'd worked overnight so she'd be home when we got out of school. I had never encountered any other women who would share her meager supply of groceries with the single mother across the street or spend the small amount of free time afforded a woman with five daughters sitting with the elderly folks in our church and taking their blood pressures. She was even willing to challenge our church on some of its interpretations of the Bible and didn't force us to follow those interpretations, as most parents in the church did. When my father moved out, she continued to maintain the household without blinking an eye (at least I never saw her blink). Somehow she created time to go back to college and attain various certificates to further her nursing career. More deep and motivating than any books on feminist theory, I'd spent my entire life face to face with a feminist powerhouse who offered neither explanation nor apology. She taught me an abiding love for self and for humanity—and she taught by example. So I went to work.

I created a cable-access show called *Point of View* to discuss politics. A local show, it aired in four nearby Bay Area cities. For every negative representation I saw of people of color, I wrote a show that allowed us to shine. For every report I read that asked no questions about the plights of African-American women, I created a show and asked the questions myself. The walls between me and effecting change in the politics of oppression, racism and sexism that pervade the United States were starting to crumble. I wrote, produced, sang, painted and created ways to say, "We are here. We are diverse. We are good." I knew I was on the right path when a man approached me in the BART train station and told me he'd taped and shown my Black History show to a group of students at a seminar he gave in Sacramento.

The momentum created by following my mother's lead and becoming a woman of action gave me the strength to slowly open the doors to my closet. My passivity in loving created such a stark contrast to my passion in every other area, I could no longer ignore it. Spoken word provided a platform for me to be honest about falling in love again and again with women. My love of women was the one area in my life where fear of judgment, reprisal and loss still ruled me. Not only had I been raised in a religion that preached that same sex love was abominable, but I had grown up in a community with strictly defined male and female roles, and in a country that openly and lawfully discriminates against same-sex couples. Even feminists seemed obsessed with not being characterized as lesbians. What would it mean about my overall identity if I acknowledged this truth about my makeup? What doors would close? What would my mother think?

I found that just as my questions about our religion had not gone away, and just as my need to seek out my heritage had not been assuaged, in the same way the need to tell the stories of African-American women had risen to the top, so would my orientation reverberate through my spirit and force its way into my voice, my paintings, my writing and my reality. As the 1990s ended and the twenty-first century began, I reached a kind of wholeness. I sat with the woman who had given me all the tools and examples I needed to be strictly myself. I drank coffee and ate eggs and looked into the eyes of the woman who made feminism real for me when I didn't even have words to describe it. I told her that I was in love, that it was not a fad, that I planned to spend my life and raise children with another woman. She didn't accept it. Because of her I knew she didn't have to. I was free to define myself.

How Sexual Harassment Slaughtered, Then Saved Me

Kiini Ibura Salaam

The New Orleans streets of my adolescence were a bizarre training ground where predatory men taught me that—in public—no part of me was safe from comment. At ages twelve and thirteen I was trained to keep my guard up by voices shouting lascivious phrases at me. Clothes were inconsequential, yet I inferred that the miniskirts and tight jeans of my preteen years would worsen the verbal attacks. Repeated lewdness can do that to you. The constancy of male aggression hammered in the suggestion that something bad could happen to me.

Indoctrination

Catcalling men are often a monumental challenge for adult women to navigate; for an adolescent, catcallers can be down right terrifying. After a time the simple act of walking past a group of men unnerved me. The abrupt break in conversation as their eyes crawled over me announced that my body had their attention for a few seconds. These were not casual appraisals, nor were they a simple appreciation of the female form. They were loud (silent) proclamations that informed me of the entertainment and sexual titillation I provided them, just by walking by. By the time my breasts and hips grew in, tense interactions with men on the street became normal. Not easy to deal with, not acceptable, not invisible, but expected.

I was never taught techniques to protect myself from the whispering lips of adult men. In the absence of safety, I developed tactics to handle the pressure.

1. If there is a group of men ahead, cross the street.
2. If there are groups of men on both sides of the street, choose the older ones. They might find you too young and let you slip by without comment.
3. Do not make eye contact.
4. Do not make any verbal or physical motion that can be perceived as an invitation for conversation.
5. If someone speaks to you politely, speak back while staring straight ahead.
6. Keep moving.

Sometimes my tactics could not buy me escape. If I was stopped by a red light or waiting at a bus stop, I was easy prey for the next level of intrusion. Under the pretense of polite interaction between strangers, men often launched into proprietary interrogations. "What's your name?" "How old are you?" "Where do you live?" "Do you have a boyfriend?" These inquires paved the way for forced conversations. To my ears the questions were staccato demands that chafed my self-control and independence. The men delivered these queries as if my participation in the conversation and the choice of whether or not I would be carted off was completely up to them. If I resisted the interaction, I was seen as abnormally hostile or angry without reason. I would answer their questions in a terse sullen manner, looking around for a possible exit. I hated my compliance. I wanted to destroy the assumption that their interest in me eclipsed my own disinterest. I wanted to smash the expectation that I would supply details about my personal life. I wanted to obliterate my own paralysis, my own inability to comfortably remove myself from their proximity.

Without knowledge of feminist doctrines and theories, I knew there was something wrong with catcalling. I don't remember the word "feminist" being used in my house, yet my parents injected the same power, pride and self-governance into my and my sisters' upbringing as they did in my brothers'. When my mother would go away on her Black women's retreats, my sisters, brothers and I shared equal household duties. Decorating the walls of my childhood home were prints proclaiming "If it's not appropriate for women, it's not appropriate at all" and "Women Hold Up Half the Sky," which was a print of the cover art from my father's book of the same title. My home environment convinced me that feminism is the natural result when women are taught their worth.

As an adolescent, no one taught me that catcalling was anti-woman, yet I instinctively felt that it squelched my autonomy and personal power. I quickly discovered the only pass card I had to convince men to leave me alone was being possessed by another man. Hostility or disinterest on my part only resulted in surreal arguments about my right to say "no." I could fabricate names and phone numbers or I could make up boyfriends or husbands, but I couldn't simply say "no" without a fight. Having to lie to protect my legitimate disinterest was ridiculous to me. The men could continue with their pathologies, but the woman I wanted to be wouldn't bow to their demand. Some mornings I woke up adamant. I'd swear to myself, If a man hits on me today, I will not lie. My disinterest is worth something and they are going to respect me. On one of those days a young man approached my friend. She smiled and demurred and told him she was married. He turned to me and said, "What about you?"

"What about me?" I asked.

"You married too?"

"No."

"You got a boyfriend?"

"No."

"Well, give me your phone number," he said.

This is the approach of men on the street. They cast a wide net, fishing for a response. Who the woman is, is irrelevant. Catcallers see the street as a grocery store where they can shop for entertainment, titillation and interaction, but this is my life. I have to deal with every joke, invitation and comment thrown my way. Multiple catcalls become a deluge of harassment that quickly overwhelms.

"You don't even like me," I told him, "You like my friend."

"That don't mean nothing," he said to me, "Stop being so cold. Give me your number."

I refused. With each rejection he grew more belligerent, pulling out the anger that keeps women in line. I feared the verbal attacks that might follow my refusal to give away access to myself. I feared the male anger that was always seething under the surface of men's solicitous remarks.

"See," the young man said, "that's what's wrong with Black people today. Black women don't have time for the Black man."

I grabbed my friend's hand and walked away, once again angry at the male intrusion into my life. I was upset that I couldn't stand on a corner without getting into a fight about sex and race. The men of my youth habitually positioned female disinterest as a hostile act of emasculation or genocide, while their harassment was defended as healthy male behavior. I will always remember the drunk vagrant, who—when my sister refused him—said, "You must like white men." What warped psychology would jump to such a conclusion? When my sister's choice not to date an alcoholic is considered a rejection of Black men as a whole, the relationship between men and women can only be seen as fractured.

By the time I reached college, I was fraught with anger and questions. I wondered who set up this predator and prey relationship. I wanted to know how I could walk by and not be judged by men. The questions clouded my mind. Do men gain power from making me feel unsafe? Do they get off on treating me like a pet or a toy, a nonhuman entity to play with just because I happen to pass by? Is it fun?

Does it ever work? Do they ever wonder what catcalling feels like to me? Do they ever get bored with acting out the same old tired roles? What are men asserting about themselves by catcalling? And how can I opt out?

The Slaughter

During my junior year of college I went to the Dominican Republic to study Spanish. A few weeks after my arrival, I went to an outdoor concert with some friends. When we arrived, a man grabbed me and started dancing a merengué with me. His laughter told me he just wanted to have fun. Giggling, I joined in. It was exactly how I imagined a street party should be. Loud music, laughing crowds, strangers dancing together. My friends and I moved on into thicker crowds. As we paused momentarily, trying to determine how to get closer to the stage, a hand reached out and squeezed my vagina. My head snapped in the direction of the hand, but I was surrounded by a crowd of blank faces. I couldn't tell who had molested me.

I might have written it off as the type of assault you can expect in a rowdy street crowd. But it happened to me again at an upscale dance club in Santiago. My friends and I were squeezing past a row of men on our way to the bathroom, when another hand reached out and touched my vagina. When I made it to the bathroom, I told my friend about the abuse, she said, "Yeah, he did it to me too."

After a few months hanging out in the clubs, I realized these sexual intrusions were partly tied to race. My two white women friends were always the first asked to dance, then the Chicana woman, followed by Black friends with perms. Eventually I identified two types of men who would dance with me: the pity partners and the molesters. The pity partners saw that I had barely danced all night and, out of the kindness in their hearts, took me out on the dance floor. Invariably these men would comment, "Oh, you dance so well!" but at the end of the song, they would walk me back to my seat and never return for another dance. The molesters were men who used the closeness of the merengué as an excuse to press their bodies against mine. I would push them away, keeping my arm locked, struggling to hold them at a distance for the duration of the song. If they were too insistent, I would have to leave the dance floor before the song was over.

Interviews with my girlfriends revealed that the level of abuse I— the only Black woman with natural hair—was suffering was unique. Each of them had had one or two experiences that bothered them, yet all levels of harassment happened to me. The boys on the corner saying "Comb your ugly hair!" The guy reaching out of a passing bus to touch my hair. The man who stopped by the side of the road to pee and decided to turn around and display his genitals to me and my friends. The ancient tradition of throwing berries at a woman when she passes, to show that you think she is beautiful. Just as skin color is an easily identifiable marker for unequal treatment, my natural hair singled me out for sexist disrespect.

My fashion sense died in the Dominican Republic. I began to experiment with using my wardrobe to make me invisible. Baggy T-shirts and oversized pants became the order of the day. Although I understood that clothing does not cause sexual abuse, I hoped bigger clothing could stop it. I needed to believe I had some control over my own safety. But when a man reached out and casually squeezed my breast through a big, shapeless T-shirt, I learned that these acts were beyond my control. My hand shot out in retaliation, but I hit only air. The man walked on, as if molesting a woman while passing her in the street was an everyday occurrence.

When I relayed this story to my host mother, she said, "He must have thought you were Haitian." My host mother's dismissive remark revealed the Dominican belief that nationality (Haitianness) was a legitimate explanation for abuse. Haitian women were the only other adult women I saw with natural hair during my entire nine months in the Dominican Republic (I was in the city of Santiago in 1992, apparently in later years study-abroad students made links with Black women's groups in the capital who identified as Black and had natural hair). I had unknowingly installed myself into a country whose hatred for all things African was infamous. My body learned of this hatred as my boundaries were crossed again and again and again.

My last clash with a Dominican man happened at three o'clock in the morning. My friend and I made the questionable choice of walking down a deserted side street on our way home from a club. We heard footsteps behind us and immediately stepped to the side. A man walked by, rubbing his hand along my friend's arm as he passed. We had become so accustomed to Dominican men taking liberties with our bodies that we were not alarmed by this. Anger flared, we talked about how fucked up the men were, but we didn't think for one moment we were in any danger. We were wrong.

After the man reached the corner—in hindsight I realize he was probably checking to see if there would be any witnesses—he made an about-face and confronted us with a gun. "Don't scream," he demanded. Everything else he said was a blur. My Spanish comprehension evaporated as my mind scrambled to make sense of the assault. He continued mumbling as my friend and I backed away. "Leave us alone," I repeated in a flat voice over and over again. We backed into a corrugated metal fence. The man pulled the shoulder of my top down to my elbow, exposing my breast. My gaze fell to his pelvis. I noticed his fly was open and his penis was dangling. Although my spirit was battered by the myriad of molestations I had suffered during my time in the Dominican Republic, I was not so defeated as to not fight back. I kicked, pushed, did what I could to let him know he wouldn't violate me while I was alive. We struggled until the man stopped fighting. He stared into my eyes, then turned and walked in the other direction. My friend pulled me toward home and we ran.

My host family was not helpful. "If he didn't shoot, he wasn't going to hurt you," they said. "He must not have had bullets in the gun." I wondered if that was true. I wondered how many women he had raped with a bulletless gun.

When I got back to the United States, my teachers noticed I was quiet and withdrawn. My mother's friend said I looked shorter. I slept more and smiled less. When I faced emotional challenges—the same challenges I had previously surfed gracefully—I found myself breaking down into tears. I returned home hysterically afraid of walking too close to men on the street. What I needed then was a feminism that could cover me with a protective cloak. I needed a feminsm that could return my body to me. I needed a feminism that would nestle in the hearts and minds of men. Any political movement is only as advanced as the individuals it represents. Ultimately, the successes of feminism can only be measured by individual women's quality of life. My quality of life on the street was low, and I needed a practical application of feminism so the streets would be, once again, safe for me.

Salvation

In the years after my nine-month stay in the Dominican Republic, I climbed out of my pit of fear and entered into an angry stalemate with men on the street. I viewed the sexual abuse in the Dominican Republic as a more extreme expression of the verbal harassment I had become accustomed to on U.S. streets. The molestation was certainly more painful than catcalls, but the verbal and physical violations in the Dominican Republic and the United States both hinged on men's relationship to women as objects for gratification.

After I left college and grew into womanhood, my old avoidance tactics became too cowardly for me to stomach. Rather than lying about my phone number or my relationship status, I learned to say "I'm not interested." As a grown woman, I understood what I did not know as a teen: I am not bound to respond to men's overtures. Accusations of meanness left me unmoved, I refused to engage in any unsolicited conversation. Freed of my adolescent compulsion to be kind to strangers, I enforced my own agenda with a stubborn willfulness. Rather than cross the street in avoidance, I would plow straight through groups of men, offering a loud "Good morning" or "Good evening" as I walked past. The men were often shocked into silence. By the time they got their game together, I had already passed them by. Despite my new protective tactics, the old rages still owned me. My behavior still consisted of premeditated defensive acts aimed at dismantling male aggression, and random men still had the power to ruin my day.

Four years after my return from the Dominican Republic, miniskirts were no longer part of my wardrobe and most of my warm weather tops were T-shirts rather than tank tops. With a suitcase full of modest clothing, I traveled to the city of Salvador in Brazil's northeastern state of Bahia. From the moment I arrived in Bahia, I was immersed in a culture that exuberantly embraces skin exposure. Rather than cover up their bodies in an attempt to avoid harassment, Brazilian women display an over-the-top sexiness. Many Brazilian girls and women dressed modestly, but I was amazed to see little girls trained in sexy dress from girlhood. In Bahia fatty flesh was displayed as proudly and blatantly as well-muscled limbs, and even pregnant women sported string bikinis.

After days of fruit and heat, I fell in step with the trend. Especially on beach days, I would wear thigh-bearing shorts and skirts and little triangular halter tops. On one such day I walked past a group of men, my bare legs uncovered, my braless breasts jiggling. Without being consciously aware of it, I was on the alert, waiting for some comment to trail after me as I passed. But I heard nothing; not one word, not even a whisper. Their silence rocked my world. In the quiet of the moment I caught myself thinking, "If I am dressed like this, how can they let me slip by without comment?" Through that renegade thought, I was shocked to discover some small dark corner of my heart where I was holding onto self-blame. My indoctrination of woman as victim had been more complete than I had imagined.

The Dogon, the ancient West African astronomists, philosophers and mystics, believe there are multiple levels of knowledge. For a concept to be fully integrated in the human psyche, it has to be learned, the Dogon say, from the front, from the side and from the back. From the front I understood that I was not responsible for men's decision to harass me. It was an intellectual knowing that had no practical proof. From the side I had gathered quantifiable experiences in the Dominican Republic that destroyed any argument that clothing caused sexual harassment. Now, here I arrived to the back, to the heart of the matter. On the most profound level of knowing, I learned I could be a woman—covered or uncovered—and move through the world without censure. I felt the burden of being a desirable thing slipping from my fingers. The blame of causing chaos on the street and the shame of creating deviant behavior in men disappeared.

The slaughter I had unknowingly walked into in the Dominican Republic was being soothed by an equally unexpected gift. These Brazilian men—with their sexist presumption that I should walk around exposed—helped to free me of the expectation of abuse. The false responsibility I had been nursing for men's behavior began to wash away. Even in the following days when a large group of boys yelled, "Hey, look, a girl all alone" during a street festival; even as the low whispers of *gostoso* (sexy, literally, "tasty") fluttered by my ears as I wandered the streets of Bahia—I recognized street harassment as men's drama, not mine. I acknowledged it as something I am forced to navigate but never again would I take the accountability, pain and anger home with me.

By the time my cousin came to visit months later, I had totally embraced the Brazilian style of dress. "You look cute," she told me, her eyes taking in my bare skin with surprise. "I could never dress like that." I told her about the men in the calm neighborhood of Santo Antonio, where I lived. Though I had heard tales of extreme harassment in neighborhoods further from the center of the city, I raved about the freedom I experienced on the streets near my home. In response, she grunted noncommittally, a sound that told me she believed my words, but the reality of it just could not sink into her body. Later at the house she went through my clothes. Looking at the pieces of cloth held together with strings, she said, "I would love to be able to wear this." "Put it on, wear it, nobody's gonna bother you," I said. She thought about it for a second and shook her head, "No, that's alright." She put on a T-shirt instead.

Wandering through my Brazilian neighborhood that afternoon, we entered into a passionate conversation about something—family, art, love—and we strolled past a group of men. Though we were entrenched in a conversation, my cousin stopped abruptly and said "They didn't say anything!" I could tell by the wonder and incredulity in her voice that she, too, had never imagined she could walk past a group of men and not be harassed. Her surprise at being granted freedom was a moment of painful validation. Her expectation of abuse was so immediate, so adamant, that it substantiated my historic anger about catcallers. Her reaction showed me that my fixation on the issue was neither exaggerated nor unwarranted. At the same time it was heartbreaking because it meant the force I had to muster up just to walk down the street is required not just of me as an individual but of a whole society of women. Suddenly I imagined legions of women futilely employing defensive motions to navigate the sexually hostile environment of their city's streets. The next day my cousin wore that halter top.

Reconciliation

Just as there are women who travel to the Dominican Republic unscathed, there are women who travel to Brazil and suffer extreme violations. There is no Shangri-la, no magic safe space to heal women's wounds of harassment. As feminists, we need to approach catcalling from the front, from the side and from the back. It's not enough to condemn men's behavior—we must also heal our past hurts, remove our assumptions and create positive forms of interactions. As women, it is essential that we share our harassment stories with our children (male and female), our sisters, our brothers, our parents and our lovers. Our brothers are potential catcallers, our husbands may have molested girls as teenage boys, our daughters may need a context for the aggression they are forced to thwart in their public lives. Our stories are healing, they tell us that we are not alone. Our experiences are instructive, they point to options for managing the fear and diverting the aggression.

Today I can identify exactly what catcalling is and how it functions in women's lives. At its most basic level catcalling is sexual harassment. Verbal assaults, invitations and compliments are opportunities for men to demonstrate who is predator and who is prey. One catcall yanks a woman out of the category of human being and places her firmly in the position of sexual object. While men readily admit to the assertive flirtatiousness of catcalling, they fail to acknowledge the veiled aggression that often accompanies the act. Depending on a woman's response, catcalls can go from solicitous to angry. There is often a violent edge lurking under the surface causing women to question their safety. When a man screams (or whispers) something inappropriate to a woman, the harassment inserts itself into her consciousness whether she interacts with the catcaller or not. With intrusive overtures catcallers assume the right to engage a woman in a sexual fashion without her permission. This presumptuous crossing of intimate and sexual boundaries is a painful disempowering force. Relentless catcalls destroy women's power to define their own parameters for public interaction. Rather than face the world on their terms, many women walk the streets burdened by anxiety, discomfort and fearfulness.

The reality of the situation is dire, yet since my return from Brazil, I have ceased to think of men as the enemy and myself as the victim. I prefer to think of the catcallers as individuals who choose to yell and rub their groins and aggressively pursue conversations with me. Male expectations and verbal aggression still anger me, but my mental stress is significantly diminished. Rather than try to block their ignorance, I float beyond it. I know now without a doubt that male aggression is not caused by me.

I am aware that men don't consider the cumulative effect of unwelcome sexual comments. Instead, they focus on their individual moment of interaction, insisting that they were just being men. I take a similar attittude when dealing with them now. My response to cat-calls are based on my feelings and the man's attitude. If a man asks me my name, I might say "no," refusing to enter the game. If he seems rational, I might reason with him. "Look," I may say, "You had your choice of whether or not you wanted to talk to me. Shouldn't I have a choice of whether or not I want to give you my number?" If I have the time, and they seem gentle enough, I might enter into a philosophical conversation. When I once refused to give a man my number, he asked, "Why you being so mean?" I said, "You don't want me to give you my number just to be nice, do you? Don't you want me to actually like you?" He thought about it, and said, "Yeah, I guess so." I guess men get caught up in the game, too.

Just as often as women get caught up deflecting the attack, men get caught up pursuing the goal. An ideal interaction with a catcaller snaps him out of his gender-based assessment of me as an object and informs him that I am a human being. Sometimes with a few words, a man can be reminded that I am not that different from him. I too would like to choose who I interact with, sit in silence if I feel like it and make friends based on my interest not because of the force of their aggression. Should a feminist force rise to transform the streets into a safety zone, that force would need to reeducate men. It would need to teach them that every women is not a flirtation waiting to be fulfilled, a conversation waiting for an introduction, nor do we exist to respond to every invitation or overture. Women are individuals with desires, preferences, prejudices and pet peeves. And we want as much control over our own interactions as men demand for themselves.

Living Outside the Box

Pandora L. Leong

Humor can be very revealing. The joke about me at the office first arose during a discussion of the department's anniversary display. "Perhaps we should have something interactive. The rooms are actually pretty nice; we could set up a simulated cell," someone suggested. The commissioner turned to me. "You could stand around inside in a jumpsuit—you could easily pass as one of the kids." A director added, "And then there wouldn't be confidentiality issues!" Everyone laughed. I felt uncomfortable even as I laughed at the prospect of being displayed in a cage. They didn't really see me that way, did they? The actual kids were protected from this exhibition because "we" were the central office for the Department of Juvenile Justice.

This joke turned passing on its head. The typical child in the system is fifteen, black or Latino and male. New York City is one of three jurisdictions in the nation where a sixteen-year-old is considered an adult in the criminal justice system. The Department of Juvenile Justice detains youth who have been arrested or who face a court order, hardly an advantageous identity to borrow. And at some level, I am as "other" as the kids. While I can also pass for middle class, as a "model minority" and in the role of a heterosexual thanks to the preconceptions of society, none of these categories accurately describe me. All too often I find myself in a box inside someone's head, despite both the facts and my desires.

My experience and my feminism have been influenced by the ways race, class and gender intersect. Over the years I have tried to remain mindful of how I pass and how I challenge assumptions. I have consciously chosen not to pass out of solidarity and out of my own anger. Our "colorblind society" not only devalues our differences but also denies our experiences, thereby eliminating the potential for empowerment—and revolution. Passing is dangerous because inherent in denying our identities, we allow presumptions to stand uncontested.

On the flip side of passing, anyone with darker skin endures the constant suspicions of society, manifested in everyone from nervous store clerks to hostile police officers. I grew accustomed to fitting that profile long before I encountered the Department of Juvenile Justice. Less laughter usually accompanies experiences with "security" personnel. Both cops and those who function like cops act to protect the powers of the state, in the most immediate sense, against the marginalized: they exist to watch people who look like me.

Near my university campus in Oregon, for example, open season was declared once the sun set. "Hey! Where do you think you're going?" a voice yelled through the darkness. Walking while brown in middle-class neighborhoods can be the pedestrian equivalent to driving while black. Uniforms boasting the crest of the college emerged. As they approached, they demanded, "What are you doing here?" These confrontations usually occurred when I was on my way to fencing class, when I dressed in baggy track pants and an old T-shirt with a bandana tying back my hair. To eyes unaccustomed to brown skin, my attire transformed me into a Latino adolescent at dusk. These officers presumed that those of us who don't *look* like the Cleavers didn't belong—whether that meant at the campus, in the state or on the planet was unclear.

"Despite the abruptness of your tone, I was merely headed to the gym. Done with the inquisition?" I replied. Whether it was the pitch of my voice clarifying what the sports bra obscured or the unexpected manner of speech verifying my association with the university, my mouth got me out of trouble. Even in the face of my anger, this encounter ended with an apology and a statement of concern about "keeping the streets safe." "From people who look like me" hung in the air. Just what kind of society were they trying to secure?

In that confrontation I escaped by passing for middle class. My unexpected words collapsed the expectations of those assigned to protect me about who they were supposed to protect but reinforced other stereotypes about education. Racial categories shape these assumptions. Proper English sounds "white" while Spanish accents and Black English are often dismissed as uneducated. I was just misidentified, but the kids locked up in New York fit the demographics. A mere 10 percent of detained youth in New York read at the seventh-grade level or above, despite an average age of fifteen.

Only those with access to resources—that is, education—enjoy the latitude to cop an attitude.

Although in some ways I had been passing for middle class my entire life, the reality was very different from the image I invoked. Growing up in Alaska, a sense of geographic isolation shaped my relationship with the world. The climate teaches a certain level of self-reliance, while endorsing a macho attitude about enduring pain and ridiculous extremes. "The Last Frontier" does not tolerate weakness, nor does it forgive those who don't survive. The gold miners and fur trappers have given way to loggers, fishermen and, of course, the oil industry, but conservative values continue to dominate the political landscape. Not an easy place to grow up on the margins. At six years old my life got even more complicated when my father was seriously injured at work. My mother had been at home since my older brother was born; she began a yearlong job search. While she looked, food stamps kept rice on the table.

By watching my parents, I knew you could work hard and still not attain the American dream. The myth of the universal middle class in the States suppresses discussion about individual economic circumstances and prevents a widespread critique of the social factors that perpetuate inequality. The polite silence about poverty instills a sense of shame. I do not apologize for growing up poor, and I refuse to pretend that I grew up middle class. Class consciousness wasn't something I learned about at the small, liberal arts college where everyone called themselves middle class so that they could pretend life was fair.

When I got my first full-time job at fourteen, I made the same hourly rate as my mother. The truth may make people uncomfortable—that truth makes me uncomfortable—but it doesn't begin to compete with living that reality.

In New York City uncomfortable truths are everywhere. One evening at the end of my first month in the city, I was riding home on the subway when a man walked through the car trying to sell batteries. His exacting neatness only emphasized the shabbiness of his clothes. His backpack filled with boxes of double A's grew more onerous as the hours he walked through the trains passed. "One dahl-la, one dahl-la, one dahl-la," he chanted to the indifferent passengers. I am typically indifferent as well, but on that evening I heard my father's accent in his voice. Given this man's tones, our fathers may have been born in neighboring villages. Here he was selling batteries to irritable New York commuters while I was college-educated, completing a fellowship and enjoying health care.

Contrasting his life and mine only begins to explore the gross disparities in our society. With a degree, a legitimate job and the ability to get sick without worrying about the cost, my life is a relative cakewalk when considered in the context of most lives in New York. Critics of affirmative action rally around equal opportunity as an acceptable goal, ignoring the fact that no opportunities are equal if one of us doesn't have enough to eat. I am appalled at the gulf that separates the vast majority from the privileged few. The prospects for that man industriously selling batteries in the subway can't compare with those born with trust funds or whose fathers were presidents. You can't pull yourself up by your bootstraps when you don't have shoes.

The random chance of my advantages haunts me in a world where so many others suffer. Though we live in vastly different circumstances now, that man in the subway and I still seem to have much in common on the surface. Our fathers may have worked on adjacent farms. We were also similarly attired in men's dress shirts and slacks. And this society often considers us indistinguishable. Many of us have lived at the margins of society, and in some eyes we will always belong there, no matter what we attain.

As a child of ethnically Asian parents, I am considered part of the "model minority." Expectations characterize us as studious and polite. These days we are often depicted as hard-working immigrants building a better life, but that has not always been the case. During World War II internment camps were set up for 120,000 Japanese Americans, even as many of their sons, brothers and fathers fought for the Allies. The Chinese Exclusion Acts continued to block immigration until 1943, lumping us with pirates and prostitutes; for the following two decades, an annual limit of 105 people who were at least half Chinese continued. Regardless of whether the boxes commend us or condemn us, Wen Ho Lee's 278 day solitary confinement illustrates that people often expect that our skin determines our loyalties and our character. As long as our Asian ancestors are visible in our faces, we remain perpetually foreign.

Inquiries about my country of origin usually greet me. Compliments on my English have become routine. Upon introduction, people speak slowly and loudly with sincere hopes to facilitate comprehension. This caused such frustration when I started university that I began asking for verbal SAT scores when someone introduced themselves in a patronizing manner. I collected the scores for about a quarter of my dorm the first month. These days, being classified as East Asian doesn't result in hostility as much as an assumption of otherness. For the most part, brown skin and almond eyes translate to a lack of English skill, a talent for math, a quiet demeanor and, most profoundly, the expectation of another culture so close at hand that it has stained my skin.

I once hoped that these presumptions were limited to the States. However, an early morning in Dover, England, revealed the folly of my optimism. As I waited to return to London, a woman struck up a conversation.

"Where are you from?"

"The States."

"No, where are you *really* from?"

"Alaska."

"No, *where* are you *really* from?"

Four A.M. was too early for this exchange. "I was born in the United States."

"Where were your *parents* born?"

She really wanted to know in what box I belonged. I've always thought that "Why are you brown?" would be a more honest question. My mother had to pass a naturalization exam to become a citizen, requiring that she learn far more about the United States than any citizen by birth will ever be obliged to know. I am not "American" in the colloquial sense, but not because I can't remember in what year the Constitution was written. My identification as "American" is inconceivable because I clearly do not look like the dominant blond, blue-eyed notion of an "American." The term itself presumes such exclusivity that it disregards all of Central and South America as well as Canada, and Mexico.

These issues may seem trivial but their constant abrasion leaves wounds raw. When people look at me, they cannot see my leftist feminist views or my childhood in Alaska. They do not see years of activism for reproductive rights, queer rights or domestic violence. Progressive politics have left no marks on my skin. People see my complexion and, if they pay attention, almond eyes. The assumptions revolve around Western markers for an Eastern ethnicity, but they fail to factor in individual circumstances or experiences. About the only thing I share with the Mongol hoards is an assertive attitude. I do not read Chinese or know anything about acupuncture. I don't enjoy any special aptitude for science, and I am hardly inscrutable. Demure isn't in my vocabulary. And I don't play the violin.

Gender adds another lovely layer of expectations to explode. In addition to dispensing with "quiet" and "shy," I cheerfully refute "submissive" and "sexually available." The cultural mystique of the Asian female assigns her the personality—and autonomy—of an inflatable doll. Two hundred years brought us from *Madame Butterfly* to *Miss Saigon*; stories of "Oriental" women sacrificing themselves for the selfishness of Western men still saturate the image of Asian females in the States. Just as the victors write the history, those in power establish the stereotypes. The distortion they establish suits their interests, one that serves them and enjoys it. The back pages of the *Village Voice*, a bastion of liberal leanings, are filled with "exotic Oriental teens" drawn from the primeval fantasies that can only have social resonance among those ignorant of our actual cultures. The presence of "hot Asian babe" in the national lexicon results in the unwanted advances of men who do not seem to understand that this is not Thailand and I am not a whore.

I embraced feminism because it fought the attitude that women were born to please men. Asian women also fight a racial characterization that further entrenches these archaic assumptions about sex. Stories of Asian mail-order brides whose husbands are enchanted by their willingness to cook and clean and service them in every other way leave me wondering where these women's real options are. I am infuriated by the delusions that allow many men in this country to think that an educated intelligent individual with citizenship and economic options would freely choose such a situation. I rarely clean my own bathroom—why the hell would I want to clean anyone else's?

As an Asian woman today, I find myself in the same struggle that Mary Wollstonecraft wrote about in the late 1700s. However, my experience suggests that within the subculture of Asian women, I am also fighting a cultural consciousness that favors a duty to society over the spirit of independence. Individualism may have been a Western male value, but at least it was a Western value. White feminists only had to democratize it; as an Asian feminist, I must introduce it. Asian society places a premium on social order and the advancement of the community; you are taught to sublimate individual desires for the good of the whole. In the Asian worldview I experienced growing up, not only does the individual depend on society, but women—as the weaker sex—depend on men. The depiction of women as needy servants of men enraged me, especially when used to buttress traditional roles and to fortify the heterosexual compact.

Being an Asian dyke is no easy feat. People look at me and see my skin, sometimes before they see my sex. While I only pass for white on the phone, I only pass for male in person. The local barber cuts my hair. I wear suits from the boys' department. Comfort instigated these habits, but people read them as gender signifiers, so I am routinely addressed as "sir" in public buildings. I am mistaken for male far more readily than I am recognized as queer. As an Asian female, my desires are dismissed, trivialized and denied more than white women because I am fighting the fronts of both culture and gender.

The ability to pass as straight has protected many queers from boorish commentary as well as brutal attack, but it also deprives us of clear identification and of dignity as human beings who deserve full civil and social rights, regardless of who we find desirable. If queers remain in the closet, we deny our number and prevalence, reduce our visibility and thereby undermine our existence. To be honest, when I first met another queer Asian woman, the "gaydar" was in the shop. We are simply not visible in society, sometimes not even to each other.

Passing is a double-edged sword. It may allow you to evade harassment, but it also binds you to the expectations entrenched in society. By being out, I challenge cultural assumptions about dykes, just as I confront the white face of feminism by embracing the mantle of feminism. I refuse to pass, thereby challenging expectations that would negate my sense of self. Regardless of whether they were assigned or accidentally acquired, expectations create a comfort zone, a place where we won't be challenged to think. The trick is creating your own definitions, or at least exercising some influence over which category you evoke—as every gangsta rapper and queer pride organizer knows. To define myself is to become visible and redefine the box—or throw it away altogether.

Creating our own definitions can take a lifetime. I became a feminist because of how others see me. I became an activist because I wanted to change how I was treated as a result of those gazes. Feminists come in every flavor; we are not just vanilla anymore, if we ever were. From women who reclaim "cunt" onstage to lesbian separatists living in rural communes, the tent holds scores of perspectives. I began describing myself as a feminist because it gave voice to my anger at the treatment of women in society. Simultaneously feminism speaks of my potential as a creative force, beyond biology. I reveled in a feminism that included the rage of Catherine MacKinnon as well as the joy of Susie Bright.

But as I made my way between goddess worshippers and corporate climbers, I realized no one looked like me. This is hardly a new experience. In fact, my comfort with not fitting in allowed me to feel completely at ease accepting the label "feminist" and all the controversy that comes with it. Being different does not scare me, because I have no choice. At least when I invoked feminism, my political positions were at the fore rather than obscured within the boxes in which people thought my body belonged. Feminism tempered the power of society to label me, or at least interjected my own terms into the debate. And yet, though I still care passionately about feminist issues, they often do not go far enough.

During the 2000 Puerto Rican Day Parade in New York, a number of women were stripped and assaulted. When women clutching their torn clothes approached police, they were told they "needed to calm down" before going to the station to file a report. After public uproar the police blamed their inaction on the city's mood in light of recent police shootings of unarmed black men. The official gaze managed to oppress brown men while simultaneously disregarding women. Tapes of some of the attacks were aired in a belated attempt to identify the assailants. Although I was outraged as a woman, I also wondered whether the police really needed another excuse to harass men of color.

Women object to strange hands on their bodies for the same reason that teenagers become insolent when cops imagine they are criminal simply because of their skin color. The police, however, have the license of law enforcement and all too often punish enmity with violence or arrest. The constant suspicion of cops and the leering attention of the male gaze disregard our experience, reducing us to presumptions and stereotypes whether we are labeled prey or predator. The basic profile of those in power looks the same as it did twenty-five years ago, despite a few token appointments. Is it surprising that we are still trapped in the same boxes?

I chose not to attend the march NOW New York organized in response to the Puerto Rican Day assaults. I agreed that the attacks were atrocious and appalling but NOW's message failed to address racial profiling, oversimplifying the situation. A simple "take back the day" march ignores the racial lines in the sand. The feminism that only sees through the lens of gender does not free those of us with brown skin or those of us who are poor. In my personal experience the hostility of security personnel is far more familiar than catcalls on the street. I recognize the rage of kids in detention because I have felt the very same indignation at the unfairness in both situations. Not only do we need role models, we also need recognition of our similarities as well as our unique challenges. We must expand feminism to consider all people's facets if we hope to move beyond being perceived as a white movement.

I am not society's fear but I am not yet a friend. The anger born of pain and the awareness of the history that flowed before me still motivate me. The bonds of passing and the entrenchment of expectations shape our shared landscape regardless of gender, color and class. I constantly struggle with what people are conditioned to see. The weight of brown skin, female features and memories of poverty intensify my fight. Feminism has historically empowered women to create their own definitions of femininity and what it means to be a woman. But what does feminism offer a woman in South Asia who considers becoming a mail-order bride her best option? Does feminism undermine or reinforce the depiction of men of color as dangerous predators? How does feminism address the availability of meaningful opportunities across classes, the social safety net or the fact that most of those detained or incarcerated are brown, male and poor? For feminism to speak to people of color, it must not only acknowledge the various manifestations of oppression but also draw attention to their interconnectedness.

I have chosen not to pass. To achieve any meaningful change, the way we look at each other and at the world must be transformed. I demand the right to live as a leftist feminist dyke who grew up poor but knows that she enjoys much greater fortunes than most of the people who share her ancestry. No box sufficiently contains any individual, but some of us—whether poor, brown, queer, female or all of the above—endure more corrosive distortion within our society.

My parents are Chinese but I do not exactly look it. I grew up poor but do not sound it. I am female but far removed from the cultural constructs of femininity. I am not what you see. The question remains: Can you learn to see me?

Thanks to Fran for your much appreicated encouragement and support, Steph and Nick for your patience and friendship, & my parents for the strength to be myself -/Doh jeh ngoh fu mo/!

The Black Beauty Myth

Sirena J. Riley

For those of you well versed in the study of body image, I don't need to tell you that negative body image is an all too common phenomenon. The issue of young women's and girls' dissatisfaction with their bodies in the United States has slowly garnered national attention and has made its way into the public discourse. Unfortunately, the most visible discussions surrounding body image have focused on white women. As a result, we presume that women of color don't have any issues when it comes to weight and move on. As a black woman, I would love to believe that as a whole we are completely secure with our bodies. But that would completely miss the racism, sexism and classism that affect the specific ways in which black women's beauty ideals and experiences of body dissatisfaction are often different from those of white women.

To our credit, black women have often been praised for our positive relationships with our bodies. As a teenager, I remember watching a newsmagazine piece on a survey comparing black and white women's body satisfaction. When asked to describe the "perfect woman," white women said she'd be about five foot ten, less than 120 pounds, blond and so on. Black women described this ideal woman as intelligent, independent and self-confident, never mentioning her looks. After the survey results were revealed to the group of both black and white twentysomethings, the white women stood, embarrassed and humiliated that they could be so petty and shallow. They told stories of starving themselves before dates and even before sex. The black women were aghast! What the hell were these white women talking about?!

I was so proud. I went around telling everyone about the survey results. I couldn't believe it. Black women being praised on national television! There they were telling the whole country that their black men loved the "extra meat on their bones." Unfortunately, my pride also had a twinge of envy. In my own experience, I couldn't quite identify with either the black women or the white women.

In my black middle-class suburban family, we were definitely expected to be smart. My family didn't work so hard so that we could be cute and dumb. I'd expressed interest in medical school and I got nothing but support in my academics. Raised by a single mother, independence was basically in my blood. But in a neighborhood of successful, often bourgeois black families, it was obvious that the "perfect woman" was smart, pretty and certainly not overweight. As a child, no one loved the "extra meat" on my bones. I was eight years old when I first started exercising to Jane Fonda and the cadre of other leotard-clad fitness gurus. I knew how to grapevine and box step as well as I knew my multiplication tables. I now have a sister around that age, and when I look at her and realize how young that is, it breaks my heart that I was so concerned about weight back then.

Still, I consider myself lucky. I had an even temper. That made me no fun to tease, since I wouldn't give the perpetrator any satisfaction by reacting. Plus, I had good friends who would be there to have my back. But despite this support, I was a very self-conscious middle-school girl. And that's where I gained the most weight, sixty pounds in the course of three years. Because hindsight is twenty-twenty, it is easy to understand why I put on so much weight then. My mom got married when I was ten years old. The next year she had my first little sister, and then another sister was added when I turned fourteen. I love them, but that's a lot of stress for a little kid. My single-parent, only-child home had turned into a pseudo-nuclear family almost overnight. My grades started slipping and the scale started climbing.

Enter my first year of high school. Being an overweight teenager, I don't need to describe the hell that was gym class. To my relief, I only had to take one year of gym and then never had to do it again. Plus, in high school I had options. In addition to regular gym, there was an aerobic dance class and something called "physical training." Now, considering that Jane Fonda and I were well acquainted, I wanted to take the aerobics class. But when I went to register, the class was full. I guess I wasn't the only one who'd had it with the kickball scene. I was left with either regular gym or this physical training class. I decided that I'd played my last game of flag football and opted for the latter.

Physical training turned out to be running and lifting weights.

And when I say weights, I mean *real* weights. None of those wimpy three-pound dumbbells. We were lifting heavy weights and learning professional weight-lifting moves. Well, it worked. By sophomore year I'd lost over forty pounds. The thing is, I didn't even know it. Remember, I had only enrolled in the class to get out of regular gym. I'd thought it might have been nice to lose some weight, but that wasn't what I was concentrating on. After all, I'd been doing exercise videos since I was a kid and I'd only managed to gain weight.

How did I not notice that I'd lost weight? Well, I was completely out of touch with my body. I didn't want to live there. I don't even think I really considered it a part of *me*. No one ever said anything good about it, so I just pretended it didn't exist. I basically swept my body under the rug. All I was wearing back then were big baggy jeans and sweatshirts, so most of my clothes still fit despite the weight loss. People had been asking me for several months if I'd lost weight before I noticed. They were also asking me how I did it, as if I knew. While back-to-school shopping before my sophomore year, I decided to just see if I could fit into size 10 jeans. Not only did those fit me, I could even squeeze into a size 8.

Ironically, it wasn't being overweight that really screwed up my body image and self-esteem, it was *losing* weight. All of a sudden I was pretty. No one had ever really told me that I was pretty before. So if I was pretty now, then I must have been ugly then. My perception of myself before my weight loss was forever warped. I ripped up pictures of myself from middle school. I never wanted to be fat again! Boys had never really been interested in me before, but now guys were coming out of the woodwork. Family I hadn't seen in years just couldn't believe it was *me*. Some even told me that they always knew I'd grow out of my "baby fat" to become a beautiful woman. At fifteen, this was my introduction to womanhood. I had dates now. I could go shopping and actually fit into cool clothes. I was planning for college and looking forward to my new life as a pretty, smart, successful, independent black superwoman.

For a few years I actually did eat and exercise at what I'd consider a comfortable rate. But after that year of intense exercising, it was impossible to completely maintain my significant weight loss. I just didn't have the time, since it wasn't built into my schedule anymore. I settled in at around a size 12, although at the time I still wanted to be a "perfect" size 8. This actually was the most confusing time for me. I kept telling everyone that I still wanted to lose twenty pounds. Even my family was divided on this one. My grandmother told me that I was fine the way I was now, that I shouldn't gain any weight, but I didn't need to lose any more. She didn't want me to be fat but thought it was good that I was curvy. Meanwhile, my grandfather told me that if I lost twenty more pounds, he'd give me one thousand dollars to go shopping for new clothes. And my mom thought that my skirts were too short and my tops too low cut, even though as a child she prompted me to lose weight by saying that if I stayed fat, I wouldn't be able to wear pretty clothes when I grew up. What the hell did these people want from me?

I wasn't overeating and my self-esteem had improved but for all of the wrong reasons. I thought I was happier because I was thinner. In reality, I still hadn't made peace with myself or my body. Over the years I gained the weight back, but not before dabbling in some well-known eating disorders. I had a stint with bulimia during my second semester of my first year away at college. But I never got to the clinical stage. I pretty much only did it when something bad happened, not on a daily basis. I didn't binge on huge amounts of food. I'd eat two bowls of Lucky Charms and the next thing you know, I'd be sticking the spoon down my throat. This was not at all like the bulimics I saw on those after-school specials. They were eating sheets of cake, loaves of bread, sticks of butter, anything and everything they could get their hands on. That wasn't me.

Then I started compulsively exercising. I mean I couldn't think straight if I hadn't been to the gym that morning. And even after I went to the gym, all I could think about was how great it was going to be to work out tomorrow. I was also planning my whole day around my food. It wasn't necessarily that I was dieting, but I was always aware of when I was going to eat, how much and how long it would be until I ate again. I was completely obsessed.

Around my junior year in college, I finally realized that something was wrong. I just couldn't take it anymore, so I started seeing a counselor on campus. At first I didn't tell her about my encounters with bulimia, but any trained therapist could see right through me. One day she asked me point blank if I'd ever had an eating disorder, so I told her everything. I realized then that what I had been doing was considered disordered eating. I also realized that inherently I knew it wasn't right, since this was the first time I had breathed a word about it to anyone. I had never even tried to articulate it. I decided not to exercise or worry about what I ate until I got through therapy.

Throughout my course of therapy, I was in three body image and eating disorder therapy groups with other young women on my campus. I was always the only black woman. The memory of that television news survey I had seen as a teen comparing body image issues for black and white women stayed with me over the years. Looking at the other women in my therapy groups, I had to wonder if I was an anomaly. I had read one or two stories in black women's magazines about black women with eating disorders, but it was still treated like a phenomenon that was only newsworthy because of its rarity.

As a women's studies major in college, body image was something we discussed almost ad nauseam. It was really cathartic because we embraced the personal as political and felt safe telling our stories to our sister feminists. Whenever body image was researched and discussed as a project, however, black women were barely a footnote. Again, many white feminists had failed to step out of their reality and see beyond their own experiences to understand the different ways in which women of color experience sexism and the unattainable beauty ideals that society sets for women.

Discussions of body image that bother to include black women recognize that there are different cultural aesthetics for black and white women. Black women scholars and activists have attacked the dominance of whiteness in the media and illuminated black women's tumultuous history with hair and skin color. The ascension of black folks into the middle class has positioned them in a unique and often difficult position, trying to hold onto cultural ties while also trying to be a part of what the white bourgeois has created as the American Dream. This not only permeates into capitalist material goals, but body image as well, creating a distinctive increase in black women's body dissatisfaction.

White women may dominate pop culture images of women, but black women aren't completely absent. While self-deprecating racism is still a factor in the way black women view themselves, white women give themselves too much credit when they assume that black women still want to look like them. Unfortunately, black women have their own beauty ideals to perpetually fall short of. The representation of black women in Hollywood is sparse, but among the most famous loom such beauties as Halle Berry, Jada Pinkett Smith, Nia Long, Iman and Angela Bassett. In the music scene there are the young women of Destiny's Child, Lauryn Hill and Janet Jackson. Then, of course, there is model Naomi Campbell and everyone's favorite cover girl, Tyra Banks. Granted, these women don't necessarily represent the waif look or heroin chic that plagues the pages of predominately white fashion and entertainment magazines, but come on. They are still a hard act to follow.

In addition to the pressure of unrealistic body images in the media, another force on women's body image can be men's perspectives. In this category black men's affinity for big butts always comes up. Now, I'm not saying that this is a completely false idea—just about every black guy I know has a thing for the ass. I've heard both black guys and white guys say, "Damn, she's got a big ass"—the former with gleeful anticipation and the latter with loathsome disgust. Of course, dwelling on what men find attractive begs the question, why the hell do we care so much what they think anyway, especially when not all women are romantically involved with men?

Indeed, many songs have been written paying homage, however objectifying, to the black behind. "Baby Got Back," "Da Butt" and "Rumpshaker" are by now old standards. There's a whole new crop of ass songs like "Shake Ya Ass," "Wobble Wobble" and everyone's favorite, "The Thong Song." But did anyone actually notice what the girls in the accompanying videos look like? Most of those women are models, dancers and aspiring actresses whose full-time job it is to make sure they look unattainably beautiful. So what if they're slightly curvier?

Now that rap music is all over MTV, the rock videos of the eighties and early nineties featuring white women in leather and lace have been replaced with black and Latino models in haute couture and designer thongs. Rappers of the "ghetto-fabulous" genre are selling platinum several times over. Everyday, their videos are requested on MTV's teen-driven Total Request Live (TRL) by mostly white, suburban kids—the largest group of consumers of hip-hop culture. It is the latest mainstream forum for objectifying women of color, because almost all of the ghetto-fabulous black male rappers have the obligatory video girls parading around everywhere from luxury liner cruise ships to mansions in the Hamptons. If this doesn't speak to the distinctive race/class twist that these images add to the body image discussion, I don't know what does.

The old mantra "You can never be too rich, or too thin" may have been associated with the excessive eighties, but some of that ideal still holds true today. Obesity is associated with poverty and in our society, poverty is not pretty. Being ghetto-fabulous is all about going from rags to riches. It includes having the money, house(s), car(s), clothes and throngs of high-maintenance women at your disposal. An ironic twist to the American Dream, considering many of these rappers claim to have attained their wealth not with a Puritan work ethic but through illegal activity.

Overweight women of color aren't included in these videos because they aren't seen as ghetto-fabulous, just ghetto (Not that I'm waiting for the day when *all* women can wash rappers' cars in cutoffs with twelve of their girlfriends, but you get the picture). Talented comedienne Mo'nique, star of UPN's *The Parkers,* is representative of this idea. She is a full-figured woman whose character, Nikki, has a crush on a black, upwardly mobile college professor who lives in her apartment building. Through his eyes she's seen as uncouth and out of control. For the audience her sexual advances are funny because she's loud, overweight and can't take a hint. He squirms away from her at every turn and into the arms of some slim model-type.

The professor in *The Parkers* views Nikki the same way that many middle-class people view overweight people, greedy and out of control. Instead, we get to see it through a black lens—ghetto women with no class, talking loud, wearing bright colors and tight clothes. I'm sure in true sitcom fashion, the professor and Nikki will eventually get together, but well after we've had our fun at Nikki's expense.

For the past few years a popular black R&B radio station in Washington, D.C., has a contest where they give away free plastic surgery every summer. You know, to get ready for thong season. Needless to say, the average contestant is a woman. At first it was just breast implants and reductions, but now they've expanded to liposuction and even pectoral implants for the men. That hasn't had much impact on the demographics of the participants. Despite the expanded offerings, the contestant pool remains overwhelmingly female. In order to win the "prize" you have to send in a letter, basically pouring out all of your insecurities to get the DJs to see why you need the surgery more than the other contestants do. Sick, isn't it? Anyone who thinks that black women are oblivious to body insecurities needs to listen to some of these letters, which by the way pour in by the thousands. The one thing they have in common is that all the women really want to "feel better about themselves." Even in this black middle-class metropolis, somewhere these women got the idea that plastic surgery is the way to go. Clearly, it is not just white America telling them this.

Sexism has played a starring role in every facet of popular culture, with men by and large determining what shows up on TV and in the movies, and the fact is that they've fallen for it, too. I have male friends and relatives who buy into these unrealistic beauty ideals and feel no shame in letting me know where they think I stack up, so to speak. Just yesterday, for example, my grandfather decided to make it his business to know how much weight I had gained in the past few months. Now I'm old enough and secure enough to know that his and other men's comments have nothing to do with me, with who I am. But growing up, these comments shaped the way I saw myself.

I've consciously decided to treat my body better by not being obsessed with diet and exercise and not comparing myself to anyone (including my former self). When I'm eating well and exercising regularly, I'm usually in the size 12 to 14 range. This is OK with me, but I know for a fact that this is another place where many white women and I don't connect. As much as we get praised for loving our full bodies, many young white women would rather be dead than wear a size 14. They nod their heads and say how great it is that we black women can embrace our curves, but they don't want to look like us. They don't adopt our presumably more generous beauty ideals. White women have even told me how lucky black women are that our men love and accept our bodies the way they are. I've never heard a white woman say that she's going to take her cue from black women and gain a few pounds, however. In a way it is patronizing, because they're basically saying, "It's OK for you to be fat, but not me. You're black. You're different."

In this society we have completely demonized fat. How many times have you had to tell a friend of yours that she isn't fat? How many times has she had to tell you the same thing? Obviously, when people have unrealistic perceptions of themselves it should not go unnoticed, but in this act, while we are reassuring our friends, we put down every woman who is overweight. The demonization of fat and the ease of associating black women with fat exposes yet another opportunity for racism.

If we really want to start talking more honestly about all women's relationships with our bodies, we need to start asking the right questions. Just because women of color aren't expressing their body dissatisfaction in the same way as heterosexual, middle-class white women, it doesn't mean that everything is hunky-dory and we should just move on. If we are so sure that images of rail-thin fashion models, actresses and video chicks have contributed to white girls' poor body image, why aren't we addressing the half-naked black female bodies that have replaced the half-naked white female bodies on MTV? Even though young black women slip through the cracks from time to time, I still believe that feminism is about understanding the intersections of all forms of oppression. It only works when we all speak up and make sure that our voices are heard. I don't plan to wait any longer to include young women of color in a larger discussion of body image.

Nasaan ka anak ko?
A Queer Filipina-American Feminist's Tale of Abortion and Self-Recovery

Patricia Justine Tumang

Jamila May Joseph is the name of my biracial daughter who was never born. She has dark brown crescent half-moons for eyes and a fiery tongue like her mother. Like her black Kenyan father, her skin is the color of midnight sky. She crawls toward me on the knotted rug and smiles briefly, exposing two white knobs for teeth. Her spirit talks to me in waking dreams. I see her grow up. She learns how to walk and utters her first words. Whispering "Mama" into my ears, she rejoices in love, forgiving me again and again. Sometimes I stop seeing her, a blank space of clarity replacing memories unmade. I look in the corners and underneath the pillows. I call her name but only hear the faint gurgling of wind. I remember then that she is dead, a bloody mass of tissue flushed down the toilet. The abortion was an act of desperation. The malicious guilt never brings her back. *Nasaan ka anak ko?* Where are you, my daughter?

The name Jamila means "beautiful" in Arabic. During my senior year of college I studied abroad in Kenya for five months. While learning about Islam, Swahili civilization and Kenyan culture, I became

370

pregnant. George, my lover, was a Methodist black Kenyan—a rarity for the predominantly Muslim population on the Kenyan coast. I met him at a small guesthouse in Lamu where he worked as a houseboy.

When I returned to New York City after the program ended, I was nearly two months pregnant and had no financial means to support a child. My first intention was to keep it, so I told my middle-class Filipino mother about the pregnancy and she threatened to withdraw her financial support. I was in a bind—emotionally, spiritually and financially. I was in a spiritual turmoil, not because of my parent's Catholic beliefs, but rather because I felt connected to the baby's spirit. However, I could not envision myself giving up the middle-class privileges I grew up with to become a single mother and work two jobs while finishing school.

My mother and I fought about it constantly. She wanted me to finish my education without the burden and the responsibilities of raising a child at my age. I couldn't believe that my devoutly Catholic, Filipino mother was urging me to have an abortion. Several months after it was done, my mother revealed to me that she was pro-choice. She equated the idea of pro-choice with pro-abortion, but I understood what she was saying. I was not in a position to have the baby.

My mother never spoke to me about sexuality when I was a little girl, let alone the topic of abortion, and it was assumed I was heterosexual. When at twenty-one I came out to her as bisexual, she immediately dismissed me. "What do you mean," she asked, "that you are bisexual and that you are attracted to women? That's not natural!" Because she perceived heterosexuality as inherent to my sexuality, she

371

never lost hope that someday I would meet the perfect man and reproduce for our namesake. But a poor black man from Kenya was not what she had in mind.

When I got my first period at the age of eleven, no one talked to me about my body and its development. Instead, my family made jokes about the female children and their impending womanhood. When my younger cousins and I had our first periods, we became the center of jokes at family reunions. Tita Leti, my father's cousin, embarrassed us during Christmas time by giving us gift-wrapped boxes of little girls' underwear. Decorated with kittens or puppies on pink or yellow cotton, my cousin Vinci and I dreaded the thought of wearing them. Periods, we reasoned, were a sign that we were women. Tita Leti joked with our parents, "Now you have to watch out and make sure they close their legs like good girls!" We cringed at their laughter, yet it was only in these jokes that sexuality, always in heterosexual terms, was ever hinted at.

I learned about sexual development from school textbooks and discussed it with my high-school female friends, all of whom were Filipino and straight. We talked the topic of heterosexual sex to death, and had unprotected sex with men. Many of my friends became pregnant and had abortions, though they didn't speak about it. They were perfect Asian girls, they couldn't. They acted calm, collected and recovered. Until I experienced it myself, I didn't realize how much the silence burned my insides and that I too was in denial about the trauma.

My own model minority expectations influenced my decision to have an abortion. I wasn't sure I could cope with my family and society's prejudices against my half-black child. To me, being the model minority daughter meant assimilating, speaking perfect English, adhering to a middle-class lifestyle and establishing a successful career after college. Not being heterosexual, having a biracial baby and being a single mother were not a part of these expectations. Having internalized my parents' expectations and the United States's views on what a model minority is, I felt even more pressure to have an abortion. Not having any financial help from my mother pushed me to my final decision. I took the RU-486 pill and hoped the worst would be over.

For the next couple of weeks I endured a living nightmare. The first dosage of Mifeprex, a medication that blocks a hormone needed for a pregnancy to continue, was given to me in pill form at the clinic. When I got home, I inserted four tablets of Misoprostol vaginally. These two medications combined to terminate the pregnancy nonsurgically. Heavy bleeding for up to two weeks was expected.

I didn't realize the horrible truth of that statement until I lay awake at night in fits of unbearable pain, bleeding through sanitary napkins by the hour. When I was in the bathroom one night, clumps of bloody tissue and fetal remains fell into the toilet. I was overcome with tremors, my body shaking with a burst of heat resembling fever. My cheeks flushed as sweat bled into my hairline. Dragging my feet on the cold alabaster floor, I went back to bed and hid under the covers. Eyes open and bloodshot, knees to my chest, I felt tears sting my swollen cheeks. After hours of pure exhaustion, I finally fell asleep.

Returning to the clinic several days later for a scheduled follow-up, I learned that the gestational sac was still intact. The doctor gave me another dose of Mifeprex and Misoprostol. That night, I stared in horror as a clump of tissue the size of a baseball escaped from my body. I held the bloody mass in my hand, feeling the watery red liquid drip from my fingers. The tissue was soft and pliable. Poking at the flesh, I imagined the life that it embodied. The sac looked like a bleeding pig's heart. For several months after, I couldn't look at the sight of blood without vomiting.

As I was going through this experience, I remembered the subtitled Asian movies from my childhood that featured abortion scenes. In these films the Asian female characters drank exotic herbal concoctions to terminate their pregnancies, then jumped up and down on the stairs. Scenes showed their mothers holding their hands while their fetuses became detached. In one film, a woman in desperation took a hanger and mutilated her body, plunging rusty wires into her uterus. "Did that really happen?" I now wondered. Where were those young Asian women bleeding to death? Were they real? Were they alive? How did they heal from such a trauma? Watching these images, I wondered if I could heal from my experience. Was I alone?

Deciding to have an abortion was the hardest decision I have ever made. I made it alone. Without my mother's support and in George's absence, I felt I couldn't have a child. George was very supportive despite his pro-life Christian views. Communicating over sporadic e-mail messages and long-distance telephone calls, he said he valued my safety and understood the reality of our situation. For a moment, however, I imagined what it would be like if I could marry my poor Kenyan lover and bring him to the United States to be a family. The "American Dream." George would work at a deli or be the black security guard on campus while I finished college and attained a bachelor's degree in Cultural Studies with a path in Race, Ethnicity and Post-colonialism. I would engage him in a postmodern discourse on the white supremacist patriarchy of America and the productions of multiculturalism in the media and art, while he brought home his minimum-wage salary. Our daughter would live in a world that would exoticize and tokenize her for her kinky hair, brown skin, Asian eyes and multilingual tongue. What does it mean that I had the capability of giving birth to new possibilities but chose to bleed her away?

I thought of my mother. A young, vibrant and hopeful Filipina immigrant who came to America many years ago, determined to make a decent living in the land of "equal opportunity." She was twenty-two years old when she gave birth to me. I was twenty-two and bleeding away. Feeling utterly dehumanized, my body an unrecognizable, grotesque monster spitting out blood, I wondered about the possibility of spiritual rebirth from experiences of trauma and dehumanization. I thought of loss and survival and what this means for many of us raised in immigrant families from "developing" countries. I thought of my parents' transition from being working-class to middle-class and remembered clearly the losses we paid for assimilating into a racist culture. Society gave us capital for becoming model minorities yet systematically berated us because of our differences. We lost our mother tongue and shed our rich cultural histories as we ate hamburgers and spoke English like "true Americans."

During this time I longed to read writings by women of color for inspiration. I scanned the libraries and searched on-line for feminist narratives written by women of color on abortion and found none. Most of what I did find documented the political history of abortion, as it impacts the lives of white women. A friend suggested I read Alice Walker's *In Search Of Our Mother's Gardens*. Choking on tears, I read about Walker's abortion in the mid-1960s when she returned to the United States from a trip to Africa. She had been a senior in college and discovered that she was pregnant, alone and penniless. Thinking of Walker's time, when safe and legal abortions were a privilege, I counted my blessings and buried my pain into the depths of me, far from eyes that see, to a solitary place where whispers mingle and collide in silence.

In the culture of silence that was pervasive in my Filipino household, children—particularly little girls—were not allowed to speak unless spoken to. I learned at an early age the art of keeping silent. I knew to keep quiet when my father's expression became stern and a hardened thin line formed on his forehead like a frowning wrinkle. All the pains, the joys and the heartaches of my life festered inside me, creating gaping wounds between the silences. My tongue was a well, containing words fit to burst and flood the Pacific Ocean. Yet only English came out. In short. And polite. Sentences. At home and abroad we sang in English, raged in English, loved and dreamed in English.

As a child I found unexplainable joy in singing Tagalog songs that I had learned by listening to my parents' Filipino audio tapes given to us by visiting relatives. They were played only on special occasions. Although I couldn't understand a word, I sang unabashedly. The act of singing Tagalog was dangerous and daring. Rooted in a desperate aching to speak a language other than English, I felt like a mischievous child stealing a cookie from the forbidden cookie jar, and I slowly savored every bite. In this hunger I realized the power of voice even while I couldn't speak. At a later age I realized writing was another way to emerge from the silence into a place of healing.

I looked to writing as a means for what black feminist writer bell hooks has termed "self-recovery." I wrote for survival about the physical and emotional abuse I experienced as a child in a sexist household. And later, I wrote to recover from my traumatic abortion. I found strength in the words of Alice Walker, Cherríe Moraga, Nellie Wong, Audre Lorde, Lois-Ann Yamanaka, Gloria Anzaldúa, Maxine Hong Kingston, Angela Davis and Mitsuye Yamada. I read until my vision was a blur. The battles and writings of these women inspired me to heal. I too wanted to break the silence.

When considering abortion options, my friends in New York encouraged me to take RU-486. They told me it would be easier, a quieter trauma. Finding information on the pill wasn't difficult. It was introduced to the American market in September 2000 but had been available in Europe for many years. I conducted research on-line and realized I had to make a quick decision. It was only prescribed to women fewer than seven weeks pregnant and I was a budding eight weeks then. RU-486 appealed to me because it had an efficiency rate of 99 percent and was non-surgical. I contacted a small primary health-care clinic in Brooklyn that offered the pill for women pregnant up to nine weeks. It was the same price as a surgical abortion and was advertised as "less traumatic." According to my research, RU-486 was given commendable reviews by women who had tried it.

If I had known how traumatic my experience with the pill would be, I would have opted for the surgical method. Not that it would have been less disturbing, but anything would have been better than the three weeks of horrendous bleeding and cramping I endured. My friends' support helped me through the difficult moments, but those who had urged me to take the pill had known nothing about it. Those who had had surgical abortions just thought the pill would be "easier" by comparison. The doctor who had prescribed me the pill told me that although she had never taken it, she had heard that the procedure was only slightly uncomfortable. I had no adequate aftercare or education about the side effects, except what was written in small print on the pamphlets. My doctor had informed me that all the information I needed to know was right there. I felt so terrifyingly alone in the process.

Much of the pro-life debate in the United States has centered on the protection of life. Not just any life, but the lives of white babies. My baby wasn't white. Reproductive rights are not just white women's issues. When I researched abortion costs at various clinics in New York, I found that only a few provide a sliding-scale option. The *Roe v. Wade* decision granted the right to abortion but not the access. The time has more than arrived to discuss the racism, classism, homophobia and heterosexism of some doctors and clinicians regarding abortion and health-care. I align myself with the pro-choice movement, but that does not mean I advocate abortion. Instead, I believe women of all backgrounds should have the right to a clean and safe abortion by a licensed practitioner if that is their choice.

Healing eventually came from actively talking about my abortion with my mother and friends. Whether through speech or writing, it meant consciously remembering the experience. It meant talking about how our bodies have never been our own. For centuries we have been controlled, sterilized and raped by masculine, imperialist and white supremacist forces. The predominantly white and racist feminist movement of the 1970s ignored the relationship between racism, sexism, classism and homophobia. This pervasive feminist thinking has denied the complexities of the oppressions I fight everyday. In the growing emergence of "third wave" feminism, feminism isn't reduced to one English-speaking white face from North America. Asian-American feminists must not remain invisible in the feminist struggle, because we too are angry at the injustices that we face in this country. We yearn for a feminism that addresses our realities as Asian-American women and women of color, one that incorporates race, class, gender and sexuality in its analysis and application. We long for a feminism that addresses the struggle of reproductive rights for women of color in the United States and in the "Third World."

Even for those who can afford to get an abortion, in my experience there has been a serious lack of education about procedures and proper emotional and physical aftercare. While some women have had positive experiences with RU-486, mine was not. Almost a year after the abortion, the pain still visited me from time to time. For so long I tried to deny that I had undergone a shocking experience, and I entered a period of self-punishment. I pretended to be recovered, but the pain pushed itself outward. Regret and guilt caused severe anxiety attacks that left me breathless, convulsing and faint.

When I returned to the clinic after the abortion, I was told I needed therapy for my depression and anxiety. A white female doctor began asking questions about me, my family and my refusal to seek therapy. I suggested that I join a support group for women of color who had abortions and was informed by the doctor that there were none, to her knowledge, in New York City. She asked me why I would feel more comfortable around other women of color and not a white man. I resented her questions, and she pressed on, a few words short of calling me a "separatist." Since my own abortion, I have realized that women of color need access to post-abortion therapy that is affordable and sensitive to different cultures and sexualities.

To heal I had to let go. I didn't let go of the memory but of this imaginary noose that restrained me and kept me from self-love. I hadn't learned as a child to love myself. Rather, I had been taught to be a good Filipina girl and do as I was told. This noose now came in forms of denial, self-punishment and attracting unsupportive people in my life. I also had to take some time away from my mother, to retreat from her anger and hurt to process my own. The first few months after the abortion we didn't speak that often. Eventually I entered therapy, which my mother paid for out of guilt, despite our emotional distance. Talking about my abortion with another woman of color was a relief. I found support and a safe space to open up.

My mother eventually broke down. She called in tears and apologized for not supporting me during my ordeal. I knew in my heart that if I was to forgive myself, I must also forgive her. She too was wounded and realized that she would not have known what to do in my situation. I felt closer to her at that point.

Healing has never been as easy process for me. Something always interrupts it—new relationships, disagreements with family or friends, old issues, work and school. Denial coats the pain and prevents actual healing. When I become scared of my emotions and feel buried, I remember to love myself and know that I am not alone. I struggle with my inner demons constantly. Although I am only in the beginning stages of my healing process, I feel that I have now entered a place of peace. Regret does nothing to change things. Although my decision was difficult, I made the best choice for my circumstances. It is my daughter's spirit that calls me out of grief. In my insistence on remembering her, I have found healing. She comes to me in dreams and comforts me during difficult times, giving me a vision for the future where there is love instead of suffering. Being with her, I find a place where there is healing from dehumanization. I struggle for her vision everyday.

Can I Get a Witness?
Testimony from a Hip Hop Feminist

shani jamila

I used to think I had missed my time. Thought I was meant to have come of age in the sixties when I could've been a Panther freedom fighter, challenging the pigs alongside Assata, Angela and Kathleen. Oh, but I went deeper than that. I saw myself reading my poetry with Sonia, Ntozake, Nikki and June . . . being a peer of Audre, Alice and Paula Giddings . . . kickin' it with revolutionary brothers like Huey, Haki, and Rap . . . all while rocking the shit out of my black beret. When she needed advice, I would've *been* there for Patricia Hill Collins as she bounced her preliminary ideas about *Black Feminist Thought* off me. Now can't you see the beauty in this? I would have been building and bonding with a community of artists and activists that had this whole vibrancy radiating from its core, and so many of my role models would've just been crew.

I know right now some of y'all are probably like, "OK, this child's on crack . . . that decade was not all that!" But don't front. When you heard the stories of your parents, aunts, uncles and family friends—or even if you just watched some TV special talking about the mystique of the sixties—didn't it ever make you wonder what happened with our generation? Who were our revolutionaries? What sparked our passions so high that we were willing to risk our lives to fight for it? Where was our national Black Arts Movement?

It seemed natural that we should have one—after all, we had flavor for days . . . high-tops and Hammer pants, jellies and Jheri Curls bear witness to that! And as an African-American child coming of age in the first generation to endure the United States post-integration, I can *definitely* testify that we had our own struggles: AIDS, apartheid, affirmative action, the prison industrial complex and underdeveloped inner cities are only a few examples. Growing up, these were the things that would run through my mind as I'd cut out collages from *Right On!,* and wonder what happened to us. Seemed like coping with issues like these would've hyped us up enough to create our own culture of resistance. The glossy pages trying to stick to the walls of my room competed futilely with the vibrations emanating from my spastic MTV imitations as Power 99FM's bass blasted. I danced around the images of Public Enemy and Queen Latifah that now decorated my floor, rapping all the lyrics to "Fight the Power" as I mourned our inactivity.

As I got older, I realized what I'd missed in my youth. Largely due to globalization and growing technology, in addition to some banging beats and off-the-chain lyrics, we'd had an *international* Black Arts Movement shaping our generation. As a kid, I didn't recognize hip hop as a vibrant and valuable sociocultural force—I just thought the culture was cool. I loved the music but never conceived of it as a revolutionary outcry. After all, I'd learned in school that activism was a concept confined to the sixties. . . . so even though I felt empowered by the Afrocentric vibes and in-your-face lyrics, it seemed like the culture came a few decades too late for a critical context. In fact, individuals and organizations whose work challenged me to think critically about Black people rarely even entered the public school curriculum. In my high school's halls we were taught a very narrow and revisionist view of world history that boiled down to this: white was right, Africa was an afterthought. In addition to the massive amounts of potentially empowering information that was erased by those messages, a holistic history just was not taught.

Not only were my people not reflected in the syllabi, but I didn't see a proportionate reflection in the faces of my classmates either. As one of only three Black faces in the honors program, all of whom were middle-class females, I often questioned why our representation was so disproportionate. The subtext shouted that the reason wasn't a deficiency in the newly integrated school system but rather the failings of people of color. We were tacitly taught that our token presence proved racism and sexism were over, so the problem must have been our peers' inability to achieve. I knew this wasn't true but as a child I was often frustrated because I didn't know how to prove it, as it was often demanded that I do.

See, my generation came of age with the expectancy that we could live, eat and attend school among whites. Race and gender were no longer inscribed in the law as automatic barriers to achievement, making the injustices we encountered less obvious than those our predecessors had faced. But the issues didn't go away. Instead, we found that an adverse consequence of integration and the "gains" of the sixties was even more heavily convoluted notions of race and gender oppression. Economic class stratification has also continued to evolve as a serious complication.

The paradox of the Black middle class as I experienced it is that we are simultaneously affirmed and erased: tokenized and celebrated as one of the few "achievers" of our race but set apart from other Black folks by our economic success. It is the classic divide-and-conquer technique regularly employed in oppressive structures; in this case saying that Black people are pathological—but you somehow escaped the genetic curse, so you must be "different." These lessons were regularly reinforced with camouflaged compliments such as, "Wow, you're so pretty/smart . . . are *both* of your parents Black?" Other times the insults would blaze brazenly, like the comments made by the white girls in my Girl Scouts carpool when we drove by a group of Black children playing in their yard: "Ooooh, Mom! Look at the little niglets playing on the street!" Their snickers echoed in a familiar way that suggested they'd shared this joke before. As the pain and rage began to well up within me, their dismissive comments also gathered force: "God, like, don't be so sensitive, Shani. We're not talking about *you*. You're different." I waited expectantly for the adult in the car to tell her children they were out of line and to apologize. She said nothing. I began to wonder if I was overreacting. Maybe it wasn't such a big deal. Maybe I *was* different. Maybe I thought too much.

• • •

Over the years I learned how to censor myself and adapt to different surroundings, automatically tailoring my tongue to fit the ear of whatever crew I was with. Depending on the composition of the crowd, the way I'd speak and even the things I'd talk about were subject to change. White people automatically got a very precise speech, because I knew every word out of my mouth was being measured and quantified as an example of the capabilities of the entire Black race. Around Black people I slipped into the vocabulary I felt more comfortable with but remained aware that I was still being judged. This time it was to see how capably I could fall back into "our talk" without sounding like a foreigner, if I could prove my suburban upbringing and elitist education had not robbed me of my authenticity as a Black woman.

Passing this litmus test meant the most to me. Because if the daily trials weren't enough, when the flood of college acceptance and rejection letters began pouring in and I got into schools my white "friends" weren't admitted to, all of a sudden the color they didn't see before came back fierce. My GPA, test scores, extracurricular activities, and recommendations were rendered irrelevant when they viciously told me the only conceivable reason I was getting in over them had to be affirmative action. I realized the racial logic being used against me was something that pervaded all class spheres. Whether you were a beneficiary of affirmative action or you were seen in the imagery of welfare queens (whose depiction as poor Black women defies actual numerical stats), we were all categorized as niggers trying to get over on the system.

While most of my memories from childhood are happy ones, I also remember a constant struggle to find a sense of balance. For every "reward" token status bestowed, it simultaneously increased the isolation I felt. I didn't think there were many people who could understand how and why I was struggling when by societal standards I was succeeding. I worried that I was being ungrateful because I knew so many who had come before me had given their lives in the hopes that one day their children could have the opportunities I'd grown up with. Despite the public accolades I received for my accomplishments, until I went to college I felt shunned by whites and suspected by Blacks. I was looking for a place to belong.

In 1993 I took my first steps on the campus of Spelman College, a Black woman's space in the middle of the largest conglomeration of historically Black colleges and universities in the world. This is not your typical institution. One of only two colleges of its kind surviving in the States—at Spelman Black women walk proud. Our first address from "Sista Prez" Johnnetta B. Cole told us so. As is characteristic of speeches to incoming first-year students, she instructed us to look to our right and look to our left. We dutifully gazed upon each other's brown faces. She spoke: "Other schools will tell you one of these students will not be here in four years when you are graduating. At Spelman we say we will all see to it: your sister *better* be at your side when you *all* graduate in four years!" Loud cheers erupted—we were our sisters' keepers.

At Spelman I learned new ways of learning, thinking and challenging. It was in this place that I was first introduced to a way of teaching that was unapologetically rooted in Black women's perspectives, that addressed the reality of what it means to be at the center of intersecting discriminations like race, class and gender. My formal education about my people began to expand beyond Malcolm and Martin. I learned about activists like Sojourner Truth and Maria W. Stewart, journalists and crusaders like Ida B. Wells, preachers like Jarena Lee, freedom fighters and abolitionists like Harriet Tubman, scholars like Anna Julia Cooper, poets like Frances Ellen Watkins Harper and community leaders like Mary Church Terrell. Here our core courses were entitled "African Diaspora and the World" and "Images of Women in the Media." The required reading on the syllabi included books like Paulo Freire's *Pedagogy of the Oppressed*, Frantz Fanon's *The Wretched of the Earth,* and Patricia Hill Collins's *Black Feminist Thought.* In these books and classes I found the answers to questions I didn't even have the language to ask with the education I'd received in high school.

This is what made attending a historically Black college such a turning point in my life. I don't want to romanticize my collegiate experience to the point where it was like I opened up a book and suddenly became some sort of guru, but what being exposed to this community of scholars and activists did do was give me a framework for my feelings. The value of having my thoughts nurtured, legitimized and placed into a historical context, in addition to the power of being surrounded by sisters and brothers who were walking refutations to the stereotypes I'd grown up with, gave me a space to blossom in ways I couldn't have imagined. I felt validated and affirmed by the idea that

I no longer had to explain why Black folks were different from the purported standard. Instead of being made to justify what mainstream society perceived as deviance, I was supported in the effort to critically challenge how societal norms even came to be. I loved that when we would discuss slavery, an integral part of the conversation was slave revolts—Black resistance had finally entered the curriculum. It was the first time I saw people reflective of myself and my experiences both inside and outside of the classroom. Living and learning like this was revolutionary for me. It changed my life.

Of course, being on an all women's campus, gender was also a regular topic of conversation. I was part of some beautiful dialogues where brothers would share the struggles they endured excelling academically that they didn't face when they'd shine in the more "acceptable" realms of sports or music. Sisters would relate back with testimonies of feeling forced to choose between our Blackness and our womanhood—a choice as impossible, a professor pointed out, as choosing between our left and right sides. In stark contrast to the race debates, however, these moments of raw honesty took place on a slippery slope. Gendered analyses were not granted the same sense of universal urgency attributed to race. Rather, they were received with suspicion. Many people perceived the debate over gender dynamics as a way to pit Black folks against each other. In heated conversations my peers would choose camps, placing race, gender and class in a hierarchy and declaring loyalty to one over the other. Protests would be peppered with frequent warnings that Spelman was notorious for inculcating crazy mentalities in its students. We were told we better watch our backs before we turned into one of those (gasp!) feminists too.

Yup, the dreaded F-word continues to be so weighed down by negative connotations that few people are willing to voluntarily associate with it. Hurled out like an accusation, it is enough to make many sistas start backpedaling faster than the rising stats on violence against women. The reluctance to be identified with something perceived as an internally divisive force inside historically oppressed communities is understandable. Many feminists of color felt it too, which is largely why Black feminist theory and womanism emerged. Unfortunately, much of what Black feminism really stands for has been stereotyped or obscured by school systems that don't devote time to Black women's intellectual traditions. A sad consequence has been that in addition to having something designed to advance our people become a tool of division, millions of people have been kept in the dark (so to speak) from a wealth of really important information and support networks.

Because of all the drama surrounding the word "feminism," there are mad heads who identify with feminist principles but feel conflicted about embracing the term. But let's examine what it really means. At root, Black feminism is a struggle against the pervasive oppression that defines Western culture. Whether taking aim at gender equity, homophobia or images of women, it functions to resist disempowering ideologies and devaluing institutions. It merges theory and action to reaffirm Black women's legitimacy as producers of intellectual work and reject assertions that attack our ability to contribute to these traditions. In stark contrast to the popular misconception that Black feminism is a divisive force that pits sisters against brothers, or even feminists against feminists, I view it as an essential part of a larger struggle for all of our liberation. Our fight for freedom has to be inclusive.

Of course, my understanding of Black feminism is rooted in the theoretical texts written decades before I was first introduced to them in college. Many of these theories remain relevant, at the very least as an essential historical base. However, for any movement to maximize its effectiveness, it has to be applicable to the times. It is incumbent upon us as hip hop feminists not to become complacent in the work that has come before us. We have to write our own stories that address the issues that are specific to our time. For example, some people think it's an oxymoron when I juxtapose a term like feminism alongside a genre of music that has been assailed for its misogyny. It seems obvious to me, however, that just as the shape of what we're fighting has changed, we need to examine how we as a community of activists have changed as well. Hip hop is the dominant influence on our generation.

Since my birth in 1975 four years before the first rap single achieved mainstream success, I have watched the hip hop movement, culture and music evolve. I mark important events in my life by the hip hop songs that were popular at the time, linking my high-school graduation with the Souls of Mischief's album *'93 til Infinity* and my first school dance with the song "It Takes Two" by Rob Bass. My ideas of fashion have often been misled by hip hop artists like Kwamé, whose signature style resulted in the proliferation of polka dots in American schools around 1989. My taste in men has also been molded by hip hop aesthetics. I entered my love life interested in brothers who were rocking gumbies like my first boyfriend. As I got older, I discovered my own poetic voice, and I cannot begin to place a value on the amount of inspiration I got from this musical movement and the culture it birthed. I am a child of the hip hop generation, grounded in the understanding that we enter the world from a hip hop paradigm.

Those of us who embrace feminism can't act like hip hop hasn't been an influence on our lives, or vice versa, simply because claiming them both might seem to pose a contradiction. They are two of the basic things that mold us. However, we must not confuse having love for either one with blind defense. We have to love them enough to critique both of them and challenge them to grow—beyond the materialism and misogyny that has come to characterize too much of hip hop, beyond the extremism that feminism sometimes engages in. As women of the hip hop generation we need a feminist consciousness that allows us to examine how representations and images can be simultaneously empowering and problematic.

We have to engage with the rap lyrics about women and the accompanying images found in video scenes. A friend, Adziko Simba, once told me, "It seems bizarre to me that we African women have reached such an 'enlightened' point that we are defending our right to portray ourselves in ways that contribute to our degradation. . . . Did Sojourner Truth walk all those miles and bear her breast in the name of equality so that her heirs could have the right to jiggle their breasts on BET?" I completely feel her, though I don't think the role of feminism is to construct "proper" femininity, or to place limits on how women are able to define and present themselves. I think doing so is actually antithetical to the movement. Teaching women not to be sensual and erotic beings, or not to show that we are, is diminishing and subverts the locus of our own uniqueness as females. Why shouldn't we be able to celebrate our beauty, sensuality, sexuality, creative ability or our eroticism? They are all unique sites of women's power that we should not be taught to hide, or only display when someone else says it's appropriate. On the flip side we shouldn't support each other to the point of stupidity. We have to demand accountability from each other, no doubt. We need to be cognizant of the power in this music and of how we are representing ourselves on a global scale and on the historical record. These examples demonstrate how wide open the field is for sisters of the hip hop generation to address the constantly shifting space women occupy. But these areas of concern should not be solely relegated to the Black feminist body of work. Hip hop activists, intellectuals and artists all need to take a leading role in confronting the fragmenting issues our generation deals with.

So, yeah, I used to think I had missed my time. I thought the flame lighting the hearts of activists had been snuffed, *Survivor*-style. But liberating my definitions of activism from the constraints and constructs of the sixties opened up my mind to a whole new world of work and progressive thought. Now I draw strength from the knowledge that people have been actively combating sexism, racism and other intersecting discriminations for a long time. Many of those icons I respect are still on the scene actively doing their thing for us. That knowledge is my ammunition as I join with them and my peers to continue fighting those battles and the other fronts unique to our time. We can't get complacent. The most important thing we can do as a generation is to see our new positions as power and weapons to be used strategically in the struggle rather than as spoils of war. Because this shit is far from finished.

Notes

Foreword

1.Originally published in 1981, the third and revised edition of *This Bridge Called My Back: Writings by Radical Women of Color*, edited by Cherríe L. Moraga and Gloria Anzaldúa, was reissued in 2002 by Third Woman Press of Berkeley, California.

Introduction

From the poem "A Litany For Survival" by Audre Lorde. Used with permission of the publisher.

browngirlworld: queergirlofcolor organizing, sistahood, heartbreak

1. Staci Haines, *The Survivor's Guide to Sex: How to Have an Empowered Sex Life after Child Sexual Abuse* (San Francisco: Cleis Press, 1999), p.121.

Organizing 101

Another version of this essay appears in *Fireweed: A Feminist Quarterly of Writing, Politics, Art and Culture* issue #75 May 2002.

Love Feminism but Where's My Hip Hop? Shaping a Black Feminist Identity

1. Coker, Cheo, dream hampton, and Tara Roberts. "A Hip-Hop Nation Divided," *Essence Magazine* August 1994: 62-64, 112-115.

Davis, Eisa. 2000."if we've gotta live underground and everybody's got cancer/will poetry be enuf?: A Letter to Ntozake Shange" In *Step into a World: A Global Anthology of the New Black Literature*, ed. Kevin Powell, 380-384. New York: John Wiley & Sons.

_____. "Sexism and the Art of Feminist Hip-Hop Maintenance." *To Be Real: Telling the Truth and Changing the Face of Feminism*. ed. Rebecca Walker. New York: Anchor, 1995. 127-142.

Morgan, Joan. *When Chickenheads Come Home to Roost: My Life as a Hip-Hop Feminist*. New York: Simon & Schuster, 1999.

Roberts, Tara and Eisa Nefertari Ulen. "Sisters Spin the talk on Hip Hop: Can the Music Be Saved," *MS Magazine* February/March 2000. 70-74.

Ulen, Eisa Nefertari. 2000. "What happened to Your Generation's Promise of 'Love and Revolutiuon'?: A Letter to Angela Davis." In *Step into a World: A Global Anthology of the New Black Literature*. ed. Kevin Powell, 401-403. New York: John Wiley & Sons.

2. Rose, Tricia. *Black Noise: Rap Music and Black Culture in Contemporary America*. Hanover: Wesleyan UP, 1994.

In Praise of Difficult Chicas: Femnism and Femininity

Originally appeared in another form in *Hopscotch* as "Funky Women with Duende; Feminism and Femininity", Volume 2 No. 2. Copyright © 2000 by Duke University Press.

Dutiful *Hijas*: Dependency, Power and Guilt

1. The term *marianismo* refers to Maria, La Virgen Maria (the Virgin Mary).
2. Rosa Maria Gil and Carmen Inoa Vazquez, *The Maria Paradox: How Latinas Can Merge Old World Traditions with New World Self-Esteem* (New York: Perigee Books, 1997), Page 8.
3. De Burgos, Julia, *Roses in the Mirror: Translated Poems of Julia De Burgos*, (San Juan, Puerto Rico: Ediciones Mairena, 1992). hooks, bell, *Black Looks* (Boston, MA: South End Press. 1992). Angela Davis, *Women, Race and Class* (New York: Vintage, 1981), Assata Shakur, Assata (London: Zed Books Ltd, 1987).
4. bell hooks, *Feminist Theory: From Margin to Center*, (Boston, MA: South End Press, 1984), p. 24.
5. Here the term *Americanas* refers to the values of *blanquitas* (white women), who are assumed to divorce themselves from their families.

Femme-Inism: Lessons of My Mother

1. Joan Nestle's words that appear in "Femme-Inism: Lessons Of My Mother" originally appeared in "The Femme Question," *The Persistent Desire: A Femme-Butch Reader* © 1992 Joan Nestle. Reprinted with permission of the author.

Bring Us Back into the Dance: Women of the Wasase

1. Louis Karoniaktajeh Hall, *Rebuilding the Iroquois Confederacy*, (Kahnawake Mohawk Territory: Rotiskenrakete - Kahnawake Men's Society, 1998) p. 12.

It's Not an Oxymoron: The Search for an Arab Feminism

1. In Arabic culture women traditionally keep their family names when they marry. Their children assume the names of their fathers, but women are considered to be members of their original families always. This is unlike the Western tradition of marriage, in which a woman is symbolically "given away" by her father to her husband's family.
2. The "Angel in the House" is a theory put forth by Virginia Woolf in her essay *A Room of One's Own*. She says that the Angel in the House is the epitome of Victorian womanhood, whose image haunts Woolf as a writer and attempts to stop her creativity. The Angel represents an era in which "feminine" women were uneducated and uncritical of their own oppression. The "wallpaper" allusion refers to Charlotte Perkins Gilman's story *The Yellow Wallpaper*, in which a woman goes mad when her husband restricts her ability to write.

Cheryl Rubenberg's poem is from "It's Not An Oxymoron: The Search For An Arab Feminism" is from *Palestinian Women: Gender and Patriarchy in the West Bank*, by Cheryl A. Rubenberg. Copyright © 2001 by Lynne Rienner Publishers, Inc. Reprinted with permission of the publisher.

About the Contributors

Ijeoma A. was born and raised in West Africa. In 1995 she made her first trip to the United States to attend college in Ohio. As a student, she became acquainted with a multitude of new cultures that allowed her to appreciate her own. Her writing career debuted in 1998 when she became a columnist for one of the popular student publications. In that column she shared her natal culture, placing it alongside American culture so that readers could see America through her African eyes. Since graduation, she has worked in Washington, D.C.

Born in Guyana, South America, **Paula Austin** came up in the subways of New York City and now lives in Durham, North Carolina, with her two cats. For the past ten years she has been a literacy teacher, trainer and advocate and a pupil of the late Brazilian historian, philosopher and education activist Paulo Freire. Currently, she is the director of the North Carolina Lambda Youth Network, which provides leadership and organizing skills to lesbian, gay, bisexual and transgender (LGBT) young people. She is a writer, a self-identified femme, a justice worker, a friend, a lover, a sister, an aunt and a daughter. She is practicing yoga, going to therapy and keeping her house clean. She has been published in *The Persistent Desire: A Femme-Butch Reader* (edited by Joan Nestle, Alyson Publications, 1992), and *Jane Sexes it Up: True Confessions of Feminist Desire* (edited by Merri Lisa Johnson, Four Walls Eight Windows, 2002). She is sometimes pursuing a master's in the history of education at North Carolina Central University in Durham.

Born to migrant farm workers in Northern California, **Cecilia Ballí** was meant to be a *Tejana* and was raised just so, on the U.S.-Mexico border city of Brownsville, Texas. She began writing as a high-school senior for her home-town paper, the *Brownsville Herald*. Graduating from Stanford University with

397

double majors in Spanish and American studies, she now leads a double life as a cultural anthropology graduate student at Rice University in Houston and as the first Latina writer for *Texas Monthly*. She has also written for the *San Antonio Express-News* and contributed to *Latina* magazine. Cecilia is currently writing an essay about the border for a forthcoming book by Cinco Puntos Press of El Paso. Her biggest accomplishment, however, is being born to her mother Antonia—always the most meaningful reason for her work.

Siobhan Brooks was a union organizer at the Lusty Lady Theater in San Francisco. She is in the documentary *Live Nude Girls Unite!* and is now doing graduate work in sociology at New School University in New York City. Her research is on race, gender and labor relations within the sex industry. Her writings have appeared in *Feminism and Anti-Racism: International Struggles* (edited by France Winddance Twine and Kathleen Blee, NYU Press, 2001) and *Sex and Single Girls* (edited by Lee Damsky, Seal Press, 2000). Siobhan interviewed Angela Davis for the *UC Hastings Law Journal* (winter 1999). In addition to being a writer, she is also a freelance model and is on the cover of the new anthology *On Our Backs: The Best Erotic Fiction* (edited by Lindsay McClune, Alyson Books, 2001).

Susan Muaddi Darraj is a freelance writer based in Baltimore, Maryland. She earned her M.A. in English literature at Rutgers University and is continuing her studies at the Johns Hopkins University. Her essays, fiction and reviews have appeared in *The Monthly Review, Mizna, Sojourner, Baltimore Magazine, Pages Magazine, New York Stories, Baltimore City Paper*, the *Philadelphia Inquirer* and elsewhere.

Erica González Martínez lives in El Barrio, New York City, and has written for the *Village Voice, Hispanic* magazine and other publications. She looks forward to continued spiritual growth, running her own full-time business, writing more about the truth and bearing witness to the fortification of the East Harlem community and Puerto Rico's independence. She is humbled by the blessings of divine power, and grateful for the support of her ancestors, family, friends and compañero.

Kristina Gray dreams of the day when little black girls want to be rock stars when they grow up. Her writing has appeared in *Ms.* magazine as well as in her own zine *Namaste,* a cut-and-paste affair dedicated to identity politics and obscure pop culture references. She was born and raised in the Washington, D.C., area and received her B.A. in communication from Goucher College in 2001. She hopes to find a real job soon so she can pay back her student loan.

Kahente Horn-Miller is a member of the Bear clan of the Kanienkehaka Nation at Kahnawake. A mother of two, she is currently completing her M.A. in anthropology at Concordia University in Montreal, Canada. Kahente has used her education as a vehicle for gaining understanding about her culture. This process became especially relevant to her after she had her first child. She believes "our survival as a vibrant and living people depends on young women like myself taking the time to listen, learn and pass on what we know to our future generations. In my research and writing, I present the little-explored perspective of Kanienkehaka traditional women. I hope that my contribution in this anthology will give you a glimpse into our world and one ancient, yet new, solution."

Rebecca Hurdis is a graduate student in the Comparative Ethnic Studies Ph.D. program at the University of California, Berkeley. Her work emphasizes the intersectionality of race, gender and the history of women of color feminism in the United States. Born in Korea and adopted at the age of six months, her formative years were spent in New England. She is also interested in interrogating the social, political and personal complexities of transnational and transracial adoption. She has resided in Northern California for the past six years.

Kiini Ibura Salaam is a writer, painter and traveler from New Orleans. Her short stories have been published in the *African American Review, Dark Matter: A Century of Speculative Fiction from the African Diaspora* (edited by Sheree R. Thomas, Warner Books, 2000), and the collaborative novel *When Butterflies Kiss* (Silver Lion Press, 2001). Her essays have been included in *Men We Cherish: African-American Women Praise the Men in Their Lives* (edited by Brooke M. Stephens, Anchor Books, 1997) and *Father Songs: Testimonies by African-American Sons and Daughters* (edited by Gloria Wade-Gayles, Beacon Press, 1997). She has also written for *Essence* and *Ms.* magazine. Kiini is currently crafting *Bloodlines*, her first novel. She is the author of the *KIS.list*, an e-report on life as a writer. Her work can be found at www.kiiniibura.com.

Soyon Im is a writer and web developer. From 1998 to 2000 she was *Seattle Weekly*'s controversial sex columnist, Cherry Wong.

shani jamila is a teacher, traveler, hip hoppian and cultural worker. She is a proud graduate of Spelman College and holds a master's in African Diaspora cultural studies from UCLA. shani has visited or lived in more than twenty countries, including a year spent in Gabon, Central Africa, where she taught more than three hundred students and co-sponsored an intercontinental book drive to found a school library. She is also the recipient of a Fulbright

Fellowship that allowed her to spend a year studying women's activism in Jamaica and Trinidad. Her work on hip hop feminism has been profiled internationally via colloquia, radio, television and extensive newspaper coverage. In addition, she is a poet who has performed in North and South America, Africa and countries throughout the Caribbean. Artist, academic and activist, shani's drive is to reach and reflect her people.

Darice Jones is a queer artist of African descent. She resides in Oakland, California, where she grew up. Jones works in many mediums, including writing, spoken-word performance, painting and photography. She uses her art as a vehicle to tell her own story and to expose underrepresented voices to the light. She recently traveled to New Delhi, India, and performed spoken word to open her paper on a panel of women discussing harm reduction. She is currently writing a mystery novel and collaborating on an autobiographical essay/poetry book with her older sister. Other projects include two queer-centered screenplays, one focused on the concept of karma, as well as a one-woman show slated to perform around the Bay Area.

The former managing editor of *Urban Latino* magazine, **Juleyka Lantigua** helped launch a monthly newspaper and a quarterly magazine while on a Fulbright Scholarship in Spain. She is a nationally syndicated columnist with *The Progressive* magazine's Media Project. In 2001 she published her first book, *Memories of an Immigration*, a collection of essays by Dominican immigrant children (Ediciones Alcance). Also that year, she guest edited the summer edition and an abridged Spanish edition of Harvard University's *Nieman Reports*. Juleyka serves on the faculty of the Frederick Douglass Creative Arts Center and lives in Brooklyn, New York.

Pandora L. Leong grew up in Anchorage, Alaska, as the child of first-generation immigrants, where she began to take part in feminist activism. Race and class joined her other interests during her studies in politics and history at university. Leong currently works for a human rights nongovernmental organization and continues to aspire to create a pro-choice, queer-friendly world free of violence and misogyny and the tyranny of chocolate on dessert menus.

Adriana López is the editor of *Críticas: An English Speaker's Guide to The Latest Spanish Language Titles*, published by *Publishers Weekly, Library Journal* and the *School Library Journal*. Formerly, she was the arts and culture editor at Soloella.com and the editor of *Latin Scene* and *Latin Teen* magazines. Her features, essays and arts reviews have appeared in *Hopscotch: A Cultural*

Review, Lit, El Diario la Prensa, Frontera, Urban Latino, Rhythm and Black Book, among other publications. Through the Progressive Media Project her op-eds concerning U.S. and Latin American relations have been published in newspapers throughout the country. She is currently finishing her master's in journalism at Columbia University and is a member of WILL (Women in Literature and Letters), a collective of women of color writers.

Stella Luna is a proud Chicana and community activist and first and foremost the mother of a wonderful little boy. She holds a bachelor's degree in Chicano/a studies from Arizona State University. Her degree follows the recognition of being named 2001-2002 Deans Council Scholar for the Arizona State Chicano/a Studies Department. She is also recognized in the HIV-AIDS community as a grassroots organizer and public speaker on behalf of HIV-AIDS infected women. Her short-term goals include securing a prominent position in the service sector of HIV education, advocacy and intervention, concentrating on minority women and children. Long-term goals include completing her master's in public health, starting her own nonprofit organization, watching her son grow up and living, living, living.

Bhavana Mody was born in Nashville, Tennessee, and grew up in the town of Glasgow, Kentucky. She attended the College of Wooster in Ohio, where she studied cultural anthropology. Mody now resides in San Francisco, where she develops and coordinates a leadership program for urban high-school students. In her spare time she enjoys exploring the city and ocean, practicing yoga, cooking and biking.

Leah Lakshmi Piepzna-Samarasinha is the proud granddaughter of mixed femme slut girls who were raising hell against colonialism and genocide in 1930s Sri Lanka. A Toronto-based spoken-word diva and intermittent crisis counselor, she has performed her work at Desh Pardesh, the Desi-Q L/B/G/T South Asian Queer Conference (San Francisco, 2000), Artwallah, rebel girl and many other Toronto spoken word venues. Her writing has been published in the anthologies *Femme, A Girl's Guide to Taking over the World*, reprinted in *My Dangerous Desires: A Queer Girl Dreaming Her Way Home* (Amber Hollibaugh's collected essays) and is forthcoming in *Dangerous Families: Queers Surviving Sexual Abuse, Bent on Literature, Brazen: Transgressing Femme Identity*, and *Planting a Tree: mixed queers speak*. She is currently completing her first collection of spoken word and biomythography, *consensual genocide*. She sets mics on fire wherever she goes.

Gwendolyn D. Pough is currently an assistant professor of women's studies at the University of Minnesota, Twin Cities Campus. She completed her B.A. in English at William Paterson University in New Jersey, her M.A. in English at Northeastern University in Boston, and her Ph.D. in English at Miami University of Ohio. She is currently working on a book-length project that explores black womanhood, hip hop culture and the public sphere.

Lourdes-marie Prophete is a graduate of East Flatbush, Brooklyn, and Bryn Mawr College, in Pennsylvania. Existing in sites of fringe and tech e-space, she makes film/video and Web spaces with a community focus. Her work combines anthropology with media and has helped enfranchise the thoughts and ideas of communities from New York to New Delhi. She is excited to have this opportunity to share her thoughts in print.

Sirena J. Riley is a graduate of the Women's Studies program at the University of Maryland-College Park. She has been a campus organizer at the Feminist Majority Foundation and currently codirects the Campus Leadership Program. When not traveling across the country working for women's equality, Sirena is a jazz singer who doesn't want to sing jazz, exactly. A huge Prince fan who owns twenty-six of his CDs, she has been inconsolable since she found out that he decided to become a Jehovah's Witness.

Almas Sayeed is a senior at the University of Kansas majoring in philosophy, international studies and women's studies. Her academic interests include women's relationship to nationalism, revolution and the state. She recently returned from Birzeit University, in the West Bank, Palestine, where she studied Arabic and the Palestinian-Israeli conflict. After graduation, Almas hopes to pursue a graduate degree (or get a job!) in a field related to international women's development. She is forever indebted to family, good friends and housemates who have served as patient sounding boards, phenomenal editors and invaluable advice givers.

Tanmeet Sethi resides in Seattle, where she divides her time between writing, activism and a career as a family physician. She is the cofounder of CHAYA, an organization created to empower South Asian women in crisis around domestic violence, and remains an active board member. Her main interests in medicine are serving marginalized communities, integrative medicine and maternal-child health. Her work has been anthologized in *The Unsavvy Traveler* (Seal Press, 2001).

Taigi Smith is an essayist and television producer who grew up in San Francisco but now makes her home in Brooklyn, New York. She immortalizes her memories through words, and writes to breathe life into stories that beg to be told. She is a storyteller and a traveler, a woman who is obsessed with making her life experiences a tangible part of American history. Her essays have appeared in *Listen Up: Voices of the Next Feminist Generation* (edited by Barbara Findlen, Seal Press, 2001), *Testimony: Young African-Americans on Self-Discovery and Black Identity* (edited by Natasha Tarpley, Beacon Press, 1995) and *Step into a World: A Global Anthology of the New Black Literature* (edited by Kevin Powell, Wiley, 2000) as well as in such periodicals as the *San Francisco Chronicle* and *New York Newsday*.

Born and raised in California, **Patricia Justine Tumang** left the West Coast in 1998 to pursue her college education in New York City. She received a B.A. in cultural studies with a path in Race, Ethnicity and Postcolonialism from Eugene Lang College in 2001. Her commitment to antiracist feminism from a queer Filipina-American perspective permeates her life and writing. This is her first published essay.

I wish to thank the Fall 2001 "Memoirs of Race" class at Eugene Lang College for their sthoughtful insights on this essay; Professor Gary Lemons for his tenacity, guidance and infectious spirit; George and Jamila in Kenya for all the love and humility; Debrah for her courage and strength; Ray and Preston, for all the pampering; Tenea, for resisting the demise of the spirit; and to my mom and loved ones for their love and support. Lastly, to my daughter Jamila whose spirit roams the earth and mountains of by being, nakupenda.

Cristina Tzintzún currently lives in Columbus, Ohio, where she avoids attending college by any means necessary, after going for three days that reminded her why she hates school. In her spare time she enjoys reading, *riding her bike*, making yummy vegan food and hiding from vicious yuppie neighbors when she goes swimming at the quarry.

Lisa Weiner-Mahfuz is a community activist who has spent the past ten years doing antioppression organizing and training in various movements for social justice. Originally from the New England area, she now lives in Washington, D.C., with her partner of three years.

Selected Titles from Seal Press

Listen Up: Voices from the Next Feminist Generation edited by Barbara Findlen. $16.95, 1-58005-054-9. This newly revised edition with eight new essays features the voices of today's young feminists. Topics include racism, sexuality, identity, AIDS, revolution, abortion and much more.

Body Outlaws: Young Women Write About Body Image and Identity edited by Ophira Edut, foreword by Rebecca Walker. $14.95, 1-58005-043-3. Filled with honesty and humor, this groundbreaking anthology offers stories by women who have chosen to ignore, subvert or redefine the dominant beauty standard in order to feel at home in their bodies.

Sex and Single Girls: Straight and Queer Women on Sexuality edited by Lee Damsky. $16.95, 1-58005-038-7. In this potent and entertaining collection of personal essays, women lay bare pleasure, fear, desire, risk—all that comes with exploring their sexuality. Contributors write their own rules and tell their own stories with empowering and often humorous results.

Cunt: A Declaration of Independence by Inga Muscio. $14.95, 1-58005-015-8. An ancient title of respect for women, "cunt" long ago veered off the path of honor and now careens toward the heart of every woman as an expletive. Muscio traces this winding road, giving women both the motivation and the tools to claim "cunt" as a positive and powerful force in the lives of all women.

Shameless: Women's Intimate Erotica edited by Hanne Blank. $14.95, 1-58005-060-3. Diverse and delicious memoir-style erotica by today's hottest fiction writers.

Young Wives' Tales: New Adventures in Love and Partnership edited by Jill Corral and Lisa Miya-Jervis, foreword by bell hooks. $16.95, 1-58005-050-6. Wife. The term inspires ambivalence in many young women, for a multitude of good reasons. So what's a young, independent girl in love to do? In a bold and provocative anthology, 20 and 30somethings attempt to answer that question, addressing who the wedding is really for, how to maintain one's individuality and the diversity of queer unions.

Breeder: Real-Life Stories from the New Generation of Mothers edited by Ariel Gore and Bee Lavender, foreword by Dan Savage. $16.00, 1-58005-051-4. From the editors of *Hip Mama*, this hilarious and heartrending compilation creates a space where Gen-X moms can dish, cry, scream and laugh. With its strength, humor and wisdom, *Breeder* will speak to every young mother, and anyone who wants a peek into the mind and spirit behind those bleary eyes.

Seal Press publishes many books of fiction and nonfiction by women writers. Please visit our Web site at **www.sealpress.com.**